THE GANGS OF
BIRMINGHAM

THE GANGS OF BIRMINGHAM

From the Sloggers to the
Peaky Blinders

Philip Gooderson

MILO BOOKS

Published in June 2010 by Milo Books

ISBN 978 1 903854 88 4

Printed and bound in the UK by
CPI Mackays, Chatham ME5 8TD

MILO BOOKS LTD
The Old Weighbridge
Station Road
Wrea Green
Lancs PR4 2PH
United Kingdom
www.milobooks.com

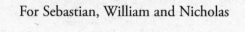

For Sebastian, William and Nicholas

Also from Milo Books

THE GANGS OF LIVERPOOL
by Michael Macilwee

TEARAWAYS: MORE GANGS OF LIVERPOOL
by Michael Macilwee

THE GANGS OF MANCHESTER
by Andrew Davies

CRIME CITY: MANCHESTER'S VICTORIAN UNDERWORLD
by Joseph O'Neill

My son, bad men may tempt you and say,
'Come with us; let us lie in wait for someone's blood;
Let us waylay an innocent man who has done us no harm.'

Proverbs, 1 vv 10-11

It seems that, in addition to the more ordinary forms of street violence, a delightful pastime prevails in Birmingham called 'slogging.' This amusement is of the most exciting description, and any number of people may enjoy it at no greater cost than the chance of a broken head. The parties engaged form themselves into opposing bands, who chase each other about and 'throw large stones at each other as fast as they can.' They give variety to their proceedings by throwing stones at inoffensive passers-by, often women and children, whom they also assault and rob. The police, it is added, are on these occasions not to be seen.

Manchester Guardian, 17 June 1874

Philip Gooderson, M.A., Ph.D., is a former schoolteacher with a special interest in the history of Victorian street gangs. He is the author of two previous books.

Contents

GANGS OF BIRMINGHAM

Slogging Gangs 1870–1900

Key to Slogging Gangs:

1 Cheapside
2 Gun Quarter
  (Loveday, Price, Weaman St)
3 Livery St. (Hall St.)
4 Bishop Ryder's
  (Sheep, Old Cross St.)
5 Bordesley
6 Lozells (Clifford St.)
7 Suffolk St.
8 Park St.
9 Milk & Barn St.
10 Allison St.
11 Hope St.
12 Spring Hill
13 Ten Arches & Wainwright St.
14 Nechells
15 Parade
16 Farm St.
17 Highgate St.
18 Great Barr St.
19 Nova Scotia St.
20 Whitehouse St.
21 Charles Henry St.
22 Adderley St. (Peaky Blinders)
23 Cliveland St.
24 Barford St.
25 Adams St.
26 Moorsom St.
27 Bow St.
28 Garrison Lane

— Major Roads
-- Railways
River
Canals

Map labels

NECHELLS
SALTLEY
BORDESLEY GREEN
SMALL HEATH
SPARKBROOK
BORDESLEY
DUDDESTON
BLOOMSBURY
ASTON CROSS
ROCKY LANE
GREAT LISTER ST.
GARRISON LANE RD.
COVENTRY ROAD
CAMP HILL
HIGHGATE
ST. BARTHOLOMEWS
DERITEND
ST. MARYS
GOSTA GREEN
BISHOP RYDER'S DISTRICT
ASTON
ASTON ROAD
THE OLD PECK
NEWTOWN ROW
GUN QUARTER
Snow Hill Station
Moor Street Station
Canal Basin
DIGBETH
MARKETS
ST. MARTINS
New Street Station
Town Hall
BALSALL HEATH
PERSHORE RD.
BRISTOL ST.
ST. THOMAS'
BATH ROW
LEE BANK RD.
ISLINGTON
LADYWOOD
BROAD ST.
SANDPITS
Canal Basin
ST. PAULS
LIVERY ST.
JEWELLERY QUARTER
ALL SAINTS
PARADE
ICKNIELD ST.
BROOKFIELDS
HOCKLEY
ST. GEORGES
FARM STREET
SOHO HILL
LOZELLS
SPRING HILL
SMETHWICK
Winson Green Prison and Asylum
Rotton Park Reservoir
EDGBASTON
HIGHGATE ST.
RIVER REA
SPARKBROOK
CURZON ST.

SCALE
0   ¼   ½ Mile
0   500m   1 Kilometre

Introduction

SOMETHING NEW AND sinister happened to English urban society in the three decades between 1870 and 1900. It caught the authorities unawares, and for many years they had little effective response. While the wider Victorian public basked in the glories of empire, the great cities of the Industrial Revolution became breeding grounds for violent young gangs of a kind never seen before. They emerged from overcrowded slums and tenements, where life was held cheap, many died in infancy and only the Poor Law provided a safety net against poverty and old age. Violence was part of day-to-day existence and came from all directions. One way to cope was to band together, perhaps first with brothers and sisters, then later with fellow workers and neighbourhood friends. Those youngsters who had survived childhood – no mean feat in itself – sought to find comradeship, protection and, above all, excitement in the few hours not taken up by earning a living.

The dangers of not having physical protection in such a dog-eat-dog environment were evident in the treatment of those on their own: they were often victimized, ill-treated and even assaulted. Parents were preoccupied with work, babies or drink. Alcohol dulled the pains of ordinary existence and provided temporary escape or pleasure, but it also fuelled the violence, of which the worst was in the home. Youngsters erupted onto the streets, where they found the police an unfriendly but irregular presence. Close behind them were magistrates with powers to birch the small and fine or imprison those in their teens and older. The gang offered some protection against such forces, because usually it was only the daredevils and the foolhardy who were caught.

In Manchester, these gang members became known as scuttlers, perhaps from the sound their clogs made as they 'scuttered' or ran across the cobbles. In Liverpool they were called cornermen, for their habit of congregating on street corners. London would produce the hooligans, named after a particularly troublesome Irish family. And in Birmingham they were called first sloggers – a 'slog' was a fight – and later peaky blinders, for the fringe of hair or cap peak they typically wore over one eye. Their existence had been largely forgotten until recently, when our contemporary concern with the rise of juvenile, as opposed to criminal, gangs, first in the USA and then in Britain and elsewhere, opened our eyes to hidden elements in our Victorian past. Youth is now a precious commodity that we are anxious to put to good use. Youth in 1870 was abundant and was swamping Victorian cities in a surge of humanity, caused by the high birth rate and by the demands of the industrial economy for cheap labour. These urban children had to learn quickly to survive.

Yet by 1870, the struggle for survival was not so extreme in British cities. The cost of living was heading downwards, and, at that point in time, work of all types was plentiful. Even children and young people could earn a wage which not only might be essential to the family income, but, perhaps for the first time in the history of industrial Britain, could provide a little left over for personal leisure. This fuelled a craze for street gambling, while spare coppers were also spent on extra food and drink and on entertainments such as the concert hall or the circus. Leisure time had become recently available through factory and workshop legislation. Saturday afternoon was emerging as the new time off from work – as well as Sunday – replacing what in Birmingham had traditionally been a free day on Monday.

The nineteenth century city demanded extreme demonstrations of toughness from its young people and women as well as its men. This was often individually tested in fights in the yard or street. However, as class-stratified Victorian society settled down after mid-century, there was a tide of movements for social bonding. For the working classes, this took the form of friendly societies, co-operatives and trade unions, following in the wake of the middle classes, who had established clubs of all kinds. This mood may be said to have affected the young people on the streets, although some have argued that they were ganging together in primitive forms of reaction against attempts to compel them into full-time education, following the Education Act of 1870. The evidence for this is unclear and it seems more likely that the development of board schools, in which Birmingham led the way, actually encouraged a new sense of identity amongst the town's youth, adding to loyalties already felt towards trade or craft and providing new grounds for competition.

Also evident is that with the growth and spread of the industrial town

came the development of distinct areas generating their own loyalties. Even separate streets had their own identity. This encouraged local bonding in terms of difference from and even hostility towards other streets and neighbourhoods. In some places, especially in the USA, this local identity had an ethnic basis which would continue to develop with successive waves of immigration. This was true at first in many British industrial towns, especially in the aftermath of the first period of mass immigration, notably of the Irish in the 1840s and 1850s. The extent to which such ethnic differences remained important into the 1870s and beyond is a matter for debate. They seem to have made an important contribution to the first wave of slogging in gangs. From the 1870s, the consensus regarding Birmingham is that ethnic differences became increasingly unimportant and that, on the whole, the town's working class had developed a remarkable degree of homogeneity by 1900. The findings here tend to confirm this view.

All of the material that follows was filtered by higher class institutions, notably the newspapers and the law courts, and so we need to be mindful of the element of fear generated by young working people 'on the loose' in the streets. There is no doubt that by playing up the role of 'gangs', local newspapers, hungry for sensational news, hoped to gain a larger circulation and even the police hoped to achieve greater recognition, perhaps in the form of increased numbers or pay or both. Such considerations should not blind us to the reality of street gangs, even if often they were gaggles or crowds rather than blood-brotherhoods. In some ways the gang was a new Victorian problem which grew to monstrous proportions as the word became over-used. A reaction set in and the phenomenon suddenly seemed to shrink. At the same time the growth of alternative forms of leisure, especially sport, distracted many young people, apart from the most hardened *habitués* of street life. Such new forms of diversion and entertainment showed up the street for what it was – only a marginal improvement on the home or the school playground. Yet the street was always there and remained valuable as territory and space, and would never lose its special appeal, in spite of changes in fashions of leisure.

The Victorian city was a vibrant place. Birmingham, which became a borough in 1838 and a city in 1889, had a special reputation for vitality.[1]

---

1 Extension of boundaries in 1891 and 1909, finally including Aston, Handsworth and other areas by 1911, raised the population to 840,202 and the city to the rank of England's second after London.

The town was not just bustling, it was buzzing with activity. De Tocqueville, visiting from France in 1835, was struck by a kind of work frenzy: 'they work as if they must get rich in the evening and die the next day'. He considered the Brummy 'intelligent in the American way' and 'busy people' with 'faces brown with smoke' from workshop or forge. He found it a noisy place, too, as 'one hears nothing but the sound of hammers and the whistle of steam escaping from boilers'. It was also a down-to-earth place in which you would be more likely to find ostentation than old-fashioned snobbery because so many of its families (even in the twentieth century) had recent and close connections with industry. 'A cold-blooded lot' was the view on Birmingham people of an Independent Labour Party man giving advice to the local Social Democratic Federation about the likelihood of generating enthusiasm for socialism in a Birmingham audience in 1894.

Early Victorian Birmingham had that American-style, democratic feel, with such a number of small masters and so many skilled men. In 1841, only eleven per cent of adult males were classified as unskilled, far fewer than in other big towns. This social structure had enabled the cooperation between the middle and working classes as in Thomas Attwood's Political Union which had pushed so hard for the reform of Parliament in the early 1830s. The Radical Richard Cobden told his friend John Bright that Birmingham had a 'healthier' social and political climate than Manchester in that 'the industry of the hardware district is carried on by small manufacturers employing a few men and boys each', in contrast with Manchester's ruling capitalist oligarchy lording it over large numbers of mill-workers. When Bright lost his seat for Manchester in 1857, he moved to Birmingham, from where he led the campaign for further parliamentary reform, and remained its much-revered MP for over thirty years.

However, the difference between Manchester and Birmingham seemed to be less clear-cut by 1870. Some craft-based local industries faced a rocky future. The town's factories were getting larger. The day of the small manufacturer seemed numbered. Political leadership was being seized by a new group, who were not only middle class and Nonconformist, but also rich and exclusive. They focused their attention on amenities, such as cheap gas and water, for all. However, the town's problems could also be identified as those of the poorer classes, in terms of health and education and demands for higher wages and shorter hours. These people in all big towns were slow to find their own class voice, but in Birmingham, as in

Manchester and Liverpool, their children took less time to make their presence felt. This was not in the form of political demands, but in outbursts of raw and often violent exuberance. The loudest but least articulate disturbance of the elite's tranquillity came from the town's youth.

CHAPTER 1

Midland Metropolis

THE EIGHTEENTH CENTURY philosopher Edmund Burke famously described Birmingham as 'the great toy-shop of Europe'. Toys have since changed their meaning, but in Burke's time they meant small metal items, intricate pieces of craftsmanship from key-locks to bracelets. In fact Birmingham made anything that could be fashioned from metal and much else besides, and its preeminent role in this regard expanded in the nineteenth century. Indeed the town and surrounding area made much of what we associate with Victorian Britain. Chance Brothers supplied all the glass for the Crystal Palace, the home of the Great Exhibition in 1851, and then more when the palace was moved to Penge, totalling nearly two million square feet of glass. It was also the home of the steam engine: James Watt and Company, of Soho, displayed a giant, 700-horsepower engine at that same exhibition. Local manufacturing expert W.C. Aitken noted how Birmingham provided for people from cradle to grave. 'It hangs the bells round the coral on which we cut our milk-teeth, it furnishes us with the mystic circle of the wedding-ring, and when we have "shuffled off this mortal coil" it will decorate our last cradle of elm or mahogany,' he wrote. By 'our last cradle' he meant the coffin, or rather the breast, foot and handle plates and other adornments, made of tinned iron, silvered or gilded for the well-to-do and called 'lace', which went with it. The town's manufacturers were pioneers in providing for the needs and fancies of the modern consumer society.

Common goods too came from the town. Nails were a traditional Black Country and Birmingham product, while screws were made on a massive scale by Nettlefold and Chamberlain. Pins were mostly made in Birmingham: 500 million tons a week by the end of the century. Needles were made in nearby Redditch, and the steel wire for them came from Birmingham. If clothes were made in Leeds, buttons came from

Birmingham, and soon overtook buckles as clothing fashions changed. While some large factories had sprung up by 1865, the typical manufacturers, as in the jewellery and gun trades, were small masters and outworkers. Spare limbs were available for the disabled and even the artificial replacement, if you lost an eye, was likely to have been made in the town, the most popular colour being grey. They were not always used for their intended purpose; in one case, a woman pawned her partner's son's glass eye for a shilling to buy a drink.

The penny post was the work of Rowland Hill, son of a Birmingham schoolmaster; before 1840, it had cost ninepence to send a letter from Birmingham to London. The subsequent surge in letter-writing was carried out with the help of Birmingham steel pens, which like postage had tumbled in price. Amongst the biggest producers were Josiah Mason and Joseph Gillott, both Birmingham heroes. In pen-making as in button-making, women provided most of the labour. Mass education after 1870, championed by the Birmingham-based National Education League, helped writing to reach the bottom of the social ladder, and the postcard soon became a common form of communication.

The small scale of many such businesses explained why Matthew Boulton attracted so much attention when he set up a large factory to produce buckles, toys and trinkets. It was built in 1762 at Soho, near the Hockley Brook, from where it obtained power for its watermills. The skills of the craftsmen gathered together in four squares of workshops and warehouses, supported by Boulton's capital and marketing, enabled Soho to compete with the fine ornaments and clever mechanical devices made in France and other parts of continental Europe. By the late 1770s, Boulton and James Watt were building and improving steam engines and Boulton opened the Soho Foundry. Later their partner William Murdock pioneered gas lighting. All three were buried in Handsworth Church.

By the end of the nineteenth century, the factory had become the typical unit of production, accompanied by the rise of engineering with its demand for small, standardized parts. Machine tools were replacing skilled artisans, and traditional hardware (iron) production was in decline. Gas and oil engines, and later electric motors, were all products of this rapid technological change. Many traditional crafts were overtaken by factory production. One example was that of the spur rowel maker, providing for horseriders in a tradition that went back to the Middle Ages. There had not been many of these specialist craftsmen even in the middle of the nineteenth century, but by the end of Victoria's reign there was only one left, off Newtown Row. The rest of the production had been mechanised.

This gathering of labour into workshops and factories had led to some level of worker organisation and to occasional conflict with owners and managers. Although in Birmingham strikes were reputed to be infrequent and mainly non-violent, violence had been traditionally rife within Birmingham places of work. Slogging, defined by the *Birmingham Daily Gazette* in 1873 as 'mercilessly stoning passers-by', may have emerged more strongly as the violence within trades became less important. The occupations of the 'sloggers' reflected the changing nature of Birmingham's industrial society. In the 1870s, iron and brass workers dominated, with a handful from the other trades. By the 1880s and 90s, brass and iron still held the field, but there was an increase in those described in press reports simply as boatmen, labourers or hawkers, with a few from new trades such as cycle-making. The town was less dominated by the small craftsman or skilled worker, yet the huge variety of skills and products remained a prominent feature of its industry.

Patterns of leisure were important for the growth of slogging: the weekday dinner hour and the habit of going out on Sunday afternoons were particularly important. Saint Monday, a weekly holiday, was the name for Birmingham's traditional way of starting the week and was a custom still widely followed in the 1840s. To keep Monday free often involved working until late on Saturday. However, Saturday half-holidays were introduced in the early 1850s by the largest factories and the spread of the steam engine, which worked as easily on Mondays as any other day. This led to the grudging acceptance of the five-and-a-half day week, with Saturday afternoons free instead. Slogging in gangs would sometimes take place on Mondays, but was far more common on Sundays, the Sabbath for the respectable and the day for shopping, rest or recreation for the remainder.

CRIME WAS the constant companion of established trades and industries in this workshop culture, drawing on the huge pool of local skill and ingenuity. Famous both for metal skills and for its printing tradition – it was the home of Baskerville print – Birmingham naturally became the home of forgers, especially of paper money. During the Napoleonic Wars, when the Royal Mint allowed Bank of England notes to become legal tender, the town was described as 'the fountain-head' for forged banknotes of low denomination: one, two and five pounds. A witness at the trial of thirteen forgers and coiners at Lancaster Assizes in 1809 said scathingly that such notes could be bought in the West Midlands town 'wholesale, enough to load a jack-ass'. From Birmingham, the notes passed easily to north-west England, Wales and Scotland. However in London proximity to the Bank of England greatly increased the likelihood of false notes being detected, not least by the bad colour of the paper they were printed on and also from the fact that they often bore the signatures of Clerks of the Bank of England who were long since dead.

Birmingham's most famous forging gang was led by William Booth. He was a farmer with two hundred acres of land, but farmwork became merely a cover for his other operations. At Perry Barr, five miles from the town, he occupied an isolated farmhouse surrounded by heathland and woods and there forged notes imitating those of the Bank of England and local banks. He was also his own engraver, and used his family, servants and certain skilled accomplices to help him. Unfortunately for Booth, one of his servants was arrested in Walsall in 1812 trying to pass off a forged £2 note. Booth received a warning that his enterprise had been rumbled, but he carried on. When he was told that the 'runners' or police were on their way, he refused to believe it. However, just in case, he and his wife arranged for various incriminating blanks and plates to be hidden or buried away from the house.

Perhaps he continued to think that the constables would never come, for when they did so he was caught 'red-handed' printing notes. The authorities had made their preparations well and brought a *posse* of ten special constables and seven mounted dragoons to break into Booth's little fortress. Although the ground floor was impregnable, and Booth had barred the windows and lined them with wrought iron, the assistant keeper at Birmingham prison, named Chillingworth, managed to climb a ladder up the side of the house and break enough glass in an upstairs window to witness Booth taking paper the size of banknotes from a rolling-press to burn in the fire. Then he climbed up further to the small garret window and managed to break it. He forced his body through into the low garret or attic, and the constables followed him. From there they made their way down to the parlour, where they found Booth in a dirty flannel jacket, with his hands covered in printing ink.

He offered no resistance and the head constable handcuffed him. In the chamber or bedroom were found materials for making paper, impressing water-marks and copper-plate printing. When the constables broke down the wall above the huge chimney of the main fireplace they found many burnt papers, some of which were usable as evidence. Later an employee, John Ingley, told them the whereabouts of other hiding places.

Eight members of the gang, excluding John and Richard Ingley, who turned King's evidence, were put on trial at Stafford Assizes in August 1812. Booth faced a range of charges, including forging Bank of England notes, making Bank note paper and forging the King's stamp on Hull Bank notes, as well as coining counterfeit silver dollars. The judge, Sir Simon Le Blanc, told the jury to regard any acts of the employees where they were following Booth's instructions as if they were acts he had performed himself. John Ingley had been brought up from infancy with Booth and the evidence he gave against his former playmate and master was reported as affecting Booth more than 'any other circumstances of the trial'.

By contrast a servant, Elizabeth Chidlow, loyally refused to testify against him and was, in the words of one newspaper, 'to use a sporting and gaol phrase, "bottom"'. She had no defence counsel, nor even any help from Booth's barrister, even though the master-forger was supposed to have the reputation of being generous to his neighbours and servants. No doubt her hopes had been raised by the judge's instructions about the limited culpability of Booth's servants and household. So when she was sentenced to fourteen years' transportation, 'she burst into a violent paroxysm of rage and grief and imprecated curses on the head of Booth and her accusers'. Others got lesser sentences: George Scott had been acquitted of forgery, but was transported for seven years for coining dollars, as was John Yates the elder. Yates' two sons and William Barrowes were acquitted. The Ingleys were exempt from prosecution and Mrs Mary Booth was discharged.

Booth himself was sentenced to death. The popular fascination of broadsheet writers with his life story was increased by the fact that four years earlier he had been acquitted of the murder of his elder brother, John, whose death was thought at the time to have been the result of a kick in the head from a horse. After his second trial, Booth became even more of a local celebrity, for the manner of his death. The hangman's noose broke at the first attempt, and he fell down the ten-foot drop. Many people thought he had been killed as he hit the ground. However he was not dead and obligingly climbed back up to the scaffold for a second stepping-off. It took fifteen minutes to get the noose fixed, for him to say his final prayers again and for everything to be ready, but this time when he let go his handkerchief as a signal, the wooden trap-door, or 'drop', did not respond and had to be forced open, before he finally was hanged. He was only thirty-three but was said to have left as much as £6,000 to his widow and their two girls. Certainly large amounts of gold and good notes as well as false money were found near his house. Booth's grave at Handsworth became a tourist attraction and he was reburied under a gravel path to stop people trampling over others in their search for his grave. Booth Street in Handsworth was named after him.

Booth's execution did not provide the intended deterrent. All kinds of forged paper, from railway tickets to marriage certificates, circulated in Victorian Birmingham. The town's engraving and printing traditions meant that the forgery of banknotes continued to be a fine art. James, or John, Griffiths, alias Wilson, was the most skilled Birmingham forger of the Victorian period. Printing banknotes was his speciality and he formed part of a firm or gang that stretched to London and back. A forty-one-year-old copper-plate printer by trade, he disguised his work by making his neighbours in Dudley Road, Winson Green, think that he was just a small farmer with some land at Smethwick. In August 1862, the Inspector of Bank Notes at the Bank of England noticed a strange thing. A forged £5 note had been presented at the Bank, and, for the first time ever, one had been made on genuine Bank paper. The paper had been made at Messrs Portal's mill at Laverstoke in Hampshire since 1720. It had never been successfully imitated and never been previously stolen. Now a steady trickle of fivers and tenners forged on Laverstoke paper began to find their way to the Bank in Threadneedle Street.

Close inspection of the forged notes showed that the paper had been sized but not glazed, so it must have been stolen during rather than after the production process. Some paper had been lost before, but it was not till that August that a considerable amount of paper had gone missing. It was clearly an inside job and a reward was offered for information.

A City of London detective, Henry Webb, and two Birmingham detectives, William Manton and George Tandy, decided to follow the movements of the man whom the press would call 'the extraordinary character' of Birmingham Heath. Griffiths' movements were watched night and day for three weeks before the officers finally pounced. The three detectives walked into the backyard of No. 2 Brown's Buildings, forced open the kitchen door, rushed up the stairs and found Griffiths in the front room on the first floor. Like Booth half a century before him, he was discovered with his sleeves tucked up and his hands covered with ink. He was 'in the very act of "working off" counterfeit banknotes upon a regular copper-plate printing press'. He seemed frightened by the sudden intrusion, perhaps fearing a rival gang.

'Don't strike me, I shalln't resist,' he cried.

He had a small stove for drying the inked paper and some 'mother' plates for making notes and watermarks, as well as a supply of paper from Laverstoke, including rupee paper used for making the new banknotes for India. Griffiths at once admitted his guilt, but blamed the people he had been dealing with for 'putting a plant' on him. In fact he had been given away by the London receiver of the stolen paper, who had brought it to Birmingham and delivered it to him in a pub called the Robin Hood. The engraver of the plates, from South London, told the police that he had been working for Griffiths for years. So this gang which had never been close-knit unravelled with remarkable speed.

Griffiths took the detectives on a tour of his land in Smethwick and proudly demonstrated his system for finding his hiding places. This involved taking the correct number of paces from the corner of a certain field. In two or three places in the earth bank under a hedge he pulled out packets containing a total of twenty 'supplementary' plates, mainly for numbering and signatures, which he handed to Detective Manton. The Bank Inspector explained in court that the 'mother' plate, such as had been found in the forger's front bedroom, contained only the body of a note, without date, signature or number. The printing was only complete when the plates, hidden in the hedge, containing that additional information were also applied, to print a finished banknote apparently correct in every detail.

Griffiths told the detectives that he had been forging Bank of England notes since 1846. Later he took them to Rotton Park, at Edgbaston, close to the reservoir, where he had hidden more plates, this time for printing false notes of the Macclesfield Bank. He also dug up a bottle wrapped in gutta percha and containing forged notes of the same bank, also carefully wrapped up and ready to be passed. Some notes were already endorsed on the back, as used banknotes were, with names of different people from the Stratford-upon-Avon area. Another important plate was found buried in Aston Manor.

Griffiths was angry in court at having been betrayed by others, for the sake of the Bank's reward, he supposed. At another time he blamed an old woman connected to the 'firm'. Perhaps this was the Mrs Mayner of

'Mayner's Firm' to whom he also referred – either the master criminal whose identity was never disclosed or someone who merely formed another shady link in the criminal chain which passed to and from the paper mill at Laverstoke.

It emerged that an apparently chance meeting between two criminal partners (a man and a woman) and a local mill worker at a pub in Whitchurch, close to the Hampshire paper mill, had led to the corrupting of the worker and later his foreman too. These two stole and supplied the paper, which in small quantities found its way via London to Griffiths at Birmingham. Yet at the four-day trial at the Old Bailey, in January 1863, the main charge was not one of theft from the mill, for which there was only circumstantial evidence. Instead the weight of the law fell on Griffiths, for 'feloniously uttering and forging a five-pound note'. He was considered to be the most dangerous of the four defendants and was the only one to be given penal servitude for 'the rest of his natural life'. Mr Justice Blackburn, in passing sentence, described him as a man of enormous talents, 'the only person possessed of sufficient skill' to execute a forgery of a banknote in such a way as to deceive not only an ordinary person but also 'anyone with a competent knowledge of the matter'.

VICTORIAN RESPECTABILITY also shied at Birmingham's reputation for base coining, which took place on a much bigger scale than forgery, although again in traditional small workshops. This worldwide practice had deep roots in the West Midlands. In 1872, builders discovered the remains of large coiners' furnaces under the false floor of a closet in Winson Hill House, Soho, said to date back over a hundred years. Stories of fictitious gangs of coiners thrilled theatre audiences, yet many local theatregoers lived side by side with real ones for whom they had little sympathy.

Coiners operated in gangs, with roles for each member. Specialists were needed for engraving and rolling, as well as for passing or uttering the coins. The most famous was William Booth, described above. Apart from forging notes, Booth and George Scott had produced an exceptional range of counterfeit coins, including contemporary gold third- and quarter-guineas and silver half-crowns and shillings purporting to be a hundred years old as well as the Spanish silver dollars which were common currency in their day. Later, one of Booth's own copper penny tokens was discovered with his name on one side and a wheatsheaf on the other.

Many tradesmen had provided such tokens in the days when there was a shortage of the Mint's copper, so this was at least one aspect of his operation that was not strictly illegal.

One coining gang soon after Booth's time operated from the premises formerly occupied by a master coiner called Beebee, who had been convicted at Warwick. Although the house had strong defences it was no match for the Birmingham constables and their assistants, no doubt exhilarated by their previous success against Booth's stronghold, when they arrived in June 1813. It took only one of the runners to break an entry. He climbed a ladder and from there 'leaped at the upper window and with his left hand catching hold of an iron bar, with a hammer in his right hand broke the barricades, forced his way into the room and let in the other officers', according to a report in the *Hull Packet*. The constable's force arrested four men and one woman whom they caught trying to destroy paper, blanks and dies in two hot stoves. The gang had a large grindstone ready to deface the die in case of surprise, but their bolts and bars had not given them enough time to do this in the event of such a well prepared attack. They had been selling counterfeit three-shilling pieces at seven shillings a dozen and were thought to have been active for many years. John Henshall, Thomas Hadley and Joseph Leather were found guilty and were sentenced to fourteen years' transportation.

In the early Victorian years, metal-working was transformed by a technological breakthrough. By use of the new electro-battery, base metal could be covered by a thin layer of silver or gold and passed off as precious. Once electro-plating was pioneered by the Elkington brothers of Birmingham for the making of silver plate, its possibilities for transforming base coin to a much higher standard were soon realised. Numerous arrests revealed the popularity of the new process, and the small gangs associated with it proved harder to track down.

Birmingham claimed to have the best dies and the best brass, and to have more plentiful supplies of German silver, an alloy of copper with nickel and zinc, than London, where, it was claimed, coiners were obliged to steal pots from taverns to use the pewter for their fakes. So Birmingham coiners supplied the capital with brass-based half-crowns. In 1851, the *Daily News* warned the public in London that the new electro-plated half-crowns could no longer be detected by their poor milling around the edge or being bent by gadgets called 'coin detectors'. Their only distinguishing features were the peculiarity of their ring or sound and the fact that they were lighter in weight than the genuine coin.

The counterfeits had to be passed as well as made. One passer, utterer or smasher, as such criminals were variously called, had a 'den' in a lodging-house in Thomas Street, a notorious haven for the homeless and criminally inclined. He was said to pass as much as fourteen or fifteen bad shillings on a good day. He made use of any children who took refuge from violent or destitute homes in the same lodging-house. One day, three boys, the eldest being sixteen, went out for him to pass base shillings in different shops in Handsworth. Two had their 'shillings' rejected by a tobacconist and a fruiterer, but the third was served by a baker's son who was less wise to smashers and gave good change for a penny cake bought with a counterfeit shilling. The boys had paid threepence to their boss, identified only as a 'tall fellow with a black beard and moustache', for each of their 'shillings'. When the shopkeepers alerted the police the three children were arrested, along with the mystery man's wife, but the man himself escaped.

Birmingham coining gangs circulated their products as widely as Manchester and Dublin. The best places to pass counterfeit coin were fairs and markets where the passer was not known. Racecourses such as Doncaster, Derby and Ludlow were also popular. In April 1884, a gang of four men were caught at Saltley station about to board a train for Liverpool on their way to the Croxteth Park races. They each carried parcels of base silver from shillings to half-crowns, wrapped in tissue paper to prevent them from being scratched. They were stopped and searched by three policemen. John Kain, an irondresser, became very violent and called out, 'Rowst!' ('Run away') to the others. One did escape but was later recaptured. They were all found guilty at the Warwickshire Assizes. At first major coining offences had been punishable by death, then by transportation and finally from 1868 by periods of penal servitude. The leader of this gang received eighteen months' penal servitude and the other three between nine and fifteen months.

As passers, women were thought to be less detectable than men. However by 1890 this part of the work had been supposedly taken over by a group of criminals different from and inferior to the coiners. The coiner himself would take orders from the passers by going the rounds of the pubs they frequented on a Friday evening and asking how much 'soft' they required that week. On Saturday, the coiner met the passers at a designated pub, collected good money from them in pre-payment for the bad and told them of another pub where they should meet him in half an hour, and then another after that and so on. At one of the pubs somewhere along this chain, a woman would appear unexpectedly with a packet of soft coin, which she would hand to the coiner. He would immediately distribute to the passers before he vanished through the back door. It was reckoned that this was the only moment when the police would be able to catch him, and this was very unlikely unless they had been following closely. Passers were then advised to go out in couples, each passer with a carrier. The carrier should have the supply of base coin in his pocket. The passer should have only one base coin on him or her at any one time so that, if challenged, they could claim ignorance, apologise and proffer good money instead. At the slightest sign of trouble, the carrier would receive a predetermined signal from the passer, such as the movement of his hand to his mouth, and then could walk off quickly. If coiners and passers had kept to these rules they would have been difficult to catch, but they did not. A steady trickle of both appeared before the courts, showing the growing effectiveness of Birmingham's detectives.

Birmingham coining gangs in the age of Victoria enjoyed one last resounding feat of notoriety: the theft and transformation of the first Football Association Cup. The Cup, about eighteen inches high with the figure of a player on top, was made of silver. In 1895 it was won by Aston Villa F.C. for the second time. It was placed in the factory shop window of William Shillcock, a boot and shoe manufacturer with a growing specialist line in football boots and balls, but disappeared that September. The Cup was never found. Its whereabouts remained a mystery until 1958, when a man of eighty-three in a Birmingham Corporation Welfare Hostel decided to tell his story to the *Sunday Pictorial*, before it was too late. Harry Burge, who had spent forty-six years of his life in gaol, confessed that he and two others had stolen the Cup by forcing open the back door of the shop with a jemmy at midnight. The Cup was broken up and melted down in an iron pot. Burge's two companions, he said, had moulds for making counterfeit half-crowns, and they used the silver to make a number of them. Some of the half-crowns were passed ironically in the Salutation public house, kept by the Aston Villa forward Dennis Hodgetts and often used by Villa players. As Peter Morris, historian of the team, remarked in his book *Aston Villa*, 'They might well have had the forged half-crowns passed on to them without realising that they had been made out of the very Cup they had helped to win in the previous April.'

With the growth of police surveillance, coining gangs slowly died out. Meanwhile Birmingham craftsmen, especially the younger ones, aimed for adventure and danger on the streets through slogging rather than the uncertain profit and the strong risk of being caught in coining. Slogging itself had roots in earlier forms of rowdiness, which was abundant in the mid-Victorian period.

CHAPTER 2

A Fighting Tradition

POLITICAL GANGS WERE on the Birmingham streets long before the sloggers made their appearance in the 1870s. Parliamentary reform in 1832 failed to eliminate the widespread problem of electoral bribery, and both Tories and Liberals hired 'roughs' at election times to protect their meetings and to make trouble for their opponents. Rough, or ruffian, was the standard contemporary word for a low-class rowdy and potential villain, of whom there were many on the streets of Victorian cities. Industrial towns such as Birmingham and Nottingham had a ready supply of such men, sometimes known as 'lambs', a sarcastic reference to their unruly behaviour. Their leaders often had colourful nicknames or titles, such as 'Morgan's Cock', who headed some Tory roughs from Coventry at the South Warwickshire election in 1865. Others joined in street disturbances for their own enjoyment or for any perks on offer.

At the time of the 1867 by-election, a gang of about nine men armed with sticks and headed by their captain, a gun finisher called Frank Wilson, went up and down New Street in Birmingham shouting for Mr Sampson S. Lloyd, the Tory candidate, and, according to the police, striking anyone who happened to be in their way. Wilson was distinguishable as a Tory captain by the piece of white ribbon he wore in his buttonhole. His stick, which caused laughter in court at his description – 'only a bit of bamboo cane' – was in fact as thick as a man's wrist, with a large knob at the end. Knocking down ordinary citizens, including an old man of about seventy, and removing another man's watch in the struggle, were additional to the men's political duties. Fighting and stoning the police proved their downfall. One, a pearl-button maker of Allison Street who had previous convictions, was sentenced to two months in prison. In the following year, a rival gang ran around the streets before the General Election shouting, 'Hurrah for the Liberals.' A lamp-maker who had drunk too much whisky followed the others carrying in his arms a large bust of the Liberal hero, John Bright, again standing as a parliamentary candidate for Birmingham. Armed with sticks and demanding money for drink, they rushed into one of the Tory district committee rooms at the Lamp Tavern in Bishop Street. In the scuffle to stop them snatching food set aside for their opponents, one of them robbed the Tory committee chairman of his gold watch. This kind of behaviour only invoked disdain from Birmingham's political leaders, but was a traditional part of the electoral process, itself only known to the town since becoming a parliamentary borough in 1832, and one that hung on in Birmingham long after the introduction of the secret ballot for elections in 1872.

However it was religion and ethnicity, rather than politics, which provoked the most street violence in Birmingham in the late 1860s. Ethnicity was always a potential cause of group hostility in nineteenth-century towns. Birmingham housed a smaller proportion of Irish immigrants than many other Victorian cities, yet they made a big impact on the town. They were famous for being hard-working, especially in the building trade – though were rarely given credit for this – and hard-drinking. This latter trait often led to tavern brawls, with fists abetted by jugs and spittoons, or 'spitting-boxes'. The Irish, on account of their poverty, often got the blame for the spread of fever, notably typhus, which may well have been brought by some migrants at the time of the Famine in the same way that 'famine fever' was taken to Canada. However such fevers were not exclusively caused by the Irish, and in Birmingham smallpox was a much bigger scourge than typhus or cholera.

While there was no Irish ghetto in Birmingham, they predominated in areas like Park Street, the scene of devastation during the so-called Murphy Riots of the 1860s. Park Street continued to be a popular meeting place for anyone who wanted to pick a quarrel with the police. The siting of St Chad's Roman Catholic Cathedral in Bath Street (now Queensway) attracted a number of Irish to the Gun Quarter, but by the 1870s they had also moved across the canal into Cecil, Princip and Hanley streets and were spreading out across Birmingham.

Irish mass brawls, famous for their flamboyance and noise, broke out in a variety of places. A man was killed in a St Patrick's tide row in 1860, said to have started with muck-throwing by a girl and to have ended when a labourer called John Kennedy declared that he would fight 'all the Connaught men in Cheapside'. In view of the large proportion of

Connaught men among the Birmingham Irish, this was an unwise challenge. He attracted a 'great rush of men', who beat him to death. Six were later arrested for his manslaughter, two of whom finally got six months in prison. Another Irish row in Meriden Street, off Digbeth, in July 1862, culminated in two 'sturdy' Irishmen, drunk and belligerent, assaulting two policemen.

Sometimes there was a general gathering from different parts of the town. In November 1870, about twenty Irishmen and women headed for the Lawley Street area of Duddeston and began searching for an unnamed person in the pubs, armed with broken swords, pokers and 'neddies' – leather slings with a lump of lead attached to one end. They found the Plasterers' Arms barred against them, so they knocked down a wall, smashed the panels of the doors and finally forced their way in. Later they marched off again, but five of them were arrested in the evening and received between one and three months for wilful damage and assault.

Whenever a row broke out among the Irish population of the Park Street neighbourhood, which was not uncommon, it aroused all the prejudice of the Anglo-Saxon press. In June 1871, a forty-year-old hawker called Hannah Murphy attacked the house of a Bridget Maley and scratched her face. The *Birmingham Daily Mail* reported that 'bricks flew, women screamed and tore each others' hair and an admiring crowd looked on'. It turned out that Mrs Maley had called Mrs Murphy a 'nasty' name because she refused to thrash her children for fighting, then broke her windows and threw pails of water over her.

The Fenians, strictly called the Irish Republican Brotherhood (IRB), were bent on achieving Irish independence by force and were regarded as the main security threat to Victorian Britain. This was especially true in the aftermath of the American Civil War, when many discharged Irish-Americans were ready to join in another fight. Birmingham featured prominently in Fenian plans in the 1860s when one such veteran of the American conflict, Ricard Burke, alias George Berry, alias Edward C. Winslow of Winslow and Co, arms dealers, visited the town and spent £2,000 buying arms and ammunition from manufacturers, which were then sent to a shipping clerk based in George Street. Burke was also involved in a plan to capture Chester Castle in 1867, with the aim of transporting the large reserve of arms held there via Holyhead to Ireland for use in a general Republican uprising. The plan was discovered and abandoned, and the rising itself proved a failure. However, Burke planned and carried out the rescue of the two leading Fenian officers at Manchester in September 1867, leading to the murder of a police sergeant. Burke escaped arrest, but three others of the rescue party were executed and became known in Republican circles as the Manchester Martyrs. Burke and an associate were later arrested in London, where an abortive rescue plan involving the blowing up of the prison wall at Clerkenwell resulted in twelve deaths and widescale destruction of houses in the area close to the prison. Together with a third man from Liverpool, they were tried on a charge of conspiracy against the Queen, and Burke was sentenced to fifteen years' penal servitude. He was released early from Woking Invalid Prison in 1872, on the grounds of insanity, although in America he later recovered and became an engineer. There would be two further Irish Republican conspiracies in Birmingham in 1883 and 1884, the first of which came close to blowing up a large part of Ladywood.

The Fenian scare of 1867 led to the recruiting of 2,000 special constables in Birmingham, chosen from a far greater number who volunteered for duty. They were eager to take up the staves, blue ribbons and lanterns which were stocked in the police stations, but the scare passed and the specials were disbanded. This excitement, however, paved the way for a far bigger menace to peace than Fenianism, namely the Protestant lecturer, William Murphy. Murphy conducted an anti-Catholic lecturing campaign in the West Midlands, which reached a crescendo in Birmingham in June 1867. His inflammatory language about Roman Catholic practices, especially the secrets of the confessional and of alleged goings-on in convents, incited his Protestant audiences and drove his Catholic opponents, including most of the Birmingham Irish community, to distracted fury and vows of vengeance. The focus in Birmingham was provided by two meetings held by Murphy in a tent erected in Carr's Lane on the Sunday afternoon and evening of 16 June. Inadequate policing and huge crowds of people allowed troublemakers to start throwing stones, and rioting followed. In the Catholic area between Moor Street and Park Street, a series of skirmishes took place between the Irish and the police, who made charges with drawn cutlasses. By eight o'clock, the Mayor was ready to read the Riot Act but it was not thought necessary. Murphy, described as 'the chief exciting cause', slipped away quietly. The Irish managed some retaliation against Protestant landmarks in mainly Catholic areas, such as the Old Meeting House in the Inkleys and Mr Cattell's shop in Snow Hill.

The following day was a Monday, the traditional local day off. Murphy's plan to hold another meeting in the evening kept the tension high. Park and Freeman Streets were once again the focus of disorder, with the police trying to break up the crowds. The press blamed local thugs and the Irish, but this time the Irish community of Park Street felt literally under siege. That evening, a battle royal developed once the Irish labourers had returned home from work. The police not only charged the crowds – again with drawn cutlasses – but were supported by large numbers of 'English' roughs, many with bludgeons. The Irish were reduced to defending their territory by stripping bricks, slates and tiles off their own houses and pelting their attackers. By the end of the evening, their homes in Park Street were in ruins, and the police had arrested many of the defenders. One woman died of injuries received during the riot. It was little wonder that many people in Birmingham nursed a grievance against the police which would take years to be worked off in mob assaults on individual constables and small groups of policemen interfering in popular street activities.

In November, five months later, sectarian violence took a different turn with an attack on the new Anglo-Catholic church of St Alban's in Conybere Street, Highgate. This had been the scene of a number of demonstrations and interruptions of services by Protestant objectors, who considered that the incumbent, Reverend J.S. Pollock, was a Papist because of his High Anglican practices. The climax was the riot which occurred on November 20. At first it was said to resemble a bread riot, as a gang of around two hundred marched from a meeting behind the Town Hall. They first hurled stones through the windows of a confectioner's. Then the damage to shops and property became indiscriminate until the mob reached the church. One reporter concluded that the 'military array' in the street opposite the church showed that 'their organised plan of movement' had been decided upon beforehand and that 'they were under appointed leaders'. There were cries of 'Down with Father Pollock' as they threw stones at the vestry windows and at the stained glass window at the east end of the church. There were also 'Hurrahs for Murphy' from the crowd, and one man got onto the roof and tried to tear off the wooden cross. Only the intervention of the police prevented the mob from breaking down the church door and 'completing the work of destruction'. One estimate was that the crowd numbered between one and two thousand people, most of whom were young and some of whom had marched from Murphy's 'Protestant Camp' in Wrottesley Street. The fact that no arrests were made may suggest that once again the police favoured the Protestants.

The disturbances were clearly linked to the Fenian rescue at Manchester in September and the fate of those under sentence of death there in Strangeways Prison. Birmingham was divided, but once again the majority of youths on the streets favoured a tough line with Catholics and Irish rebels. The night after the attack on St Alban's, a mob of over six hundred, 'chiefly youths of eighteen or twenty', again started off from the Town Hall. By turns they shouted and cheered for 'Garibaldi' (an English-adopted hero for being an enemy of the Pope) and 'Murphy', and shouted and groaned against 'Pollock' and 'the Pope'. One section of the mob headed for St Chad's Cathedral and would have got inside during a service if a man had not managed to close the strong iron gates just in time. They threw stones, but ran out of ammunition and were distracted by a number of young Irishmen running at them down Weaman Street. The Irishmen were following a leader who called out, 'Come on, boys! Here they are!' and they recklessly charged the much bigger Protestant crowd in front of the cathedral. One young Irishwoman resisted half a dozen opponents crying, 'Kick her,' until she was rescued by the police. This time the police took the Catholic side, defended their cathedral and received Irish cheers. Some of the mob headed off to attack the Convent and Oratory in Hunter's Lane and St Peter's Catholic Church in Broad Street. Once again, the *Post* reported that the Murphyite mob was 'under recognised leaders, whose orders … were obeyed with a precision and promptness almost worthy of a volunteer corps'. The leaders were 'a few score men, who walked at the head of the crowd and who acted together, while the number following were comprised of roughs, who acted without concert'. No further damage to Catholic property occurred, partly because the police and the Irish stationed themselves outside the churches, the convent and the cathedral. Officers co-ordinated their efforts by means of the telegraph between police stations.

The following evening, another Protestant march to St Alban's was stopped before arrival in Dymoke Street by twelve officers with drawn sabres. The police charge wounded two rioters and cleared the rest. Later it was necessary for a detachment of police to break up another body of roughs pulling up railings in front of Bretherton's repository in Cheapside and breaking windows and lamps. Five people were taken to the General Hospital.

On the Saturday night, the Irishmen were again out protecting their churches, and police leave had once more been cancelled. This time the trouble spread to Balsall Heath, but there the Worcestershire police were ready with sword bayonets. Ill-feeling between the Irish and English was still running high, with new demands for vengeance against the Government for 'murdering' the Manchester Fenians, articulated by an unknown street orator standing at the gates of St Mary's Church in the heart of the Gun Quarter. Another anti-Government meeting took place around the corner in St Mary's Row. Dr Suckling, a prosperous resident, foolishly ventured out that evening with pipe and slippers to find out the cause of the noise and was promptly attacked by angry Irishmen. As he tried to get back inside his house, he found that his wife had shut the door on him and he received two deep wounds in the head. A similar attack took place at the nearby Rose and Crown public house. After a row between Irish and English, the Irish were turned out, but came back later and started smashing the large windows at the front. The landlord heard the sound of breaking glass and, like the doctor, put his head out to establish the cause, only to find himself struck across the forehead with a hatchet. Ten others had injuries treated at the General Hospital that night.

On the Sunday, the Birmingham police chief prohibited a Catholic funeral procession to St Joseph's Cemetery, Nechells Green, intended as a mark of respect for the three Fenians executed at Manchester the day before. Instead the mourners were allowed to go in groups of three or four. About 2,500 people gathered at the cemetery, some wearing green rosettes and many wearing green ribbons and funeral black crape bands in their hats. After kneeling, with heads uncovered, to hear the litany, they were told by Inspector Kelly not to go away in marching order. A large number of Irishmen did not hear Kelly or did not wish to comply with his instructions, as they formed up, four deep, and marched to Gosta Green, where they were met by more police and asked to disperse and go home. They headed to Old Square for a meeting, but again were forestalled by the police and eventually dispersed. In such ways were the relations between police and Irish in Birmingham gradually normalised, but not without much future non-political violence.

Soon after the riots, a brassfounder of Bow Street received threatening messages. Then, one Monday night, he was nearing home when he was faced by about twenty people armed with sticks, pokers and stones. Realising that he was their intended prey, he ran away, only to be overtaken by half a dozen youths and beaten on the head and hands. The only explanation he could give was that he had been a spectator at the Park Street riots – and perhaps not a passive one, to have been singled out in this way. In Nova Scotia Street, near St Bartholomew's Church, there were weekly confrontations between 'the different parties', and English inhabitants claimed to have received threatening notices 'from their Hibernian neighbours' with the intention of clearing the street of the English, according to reports in the *Post*.

When the Irish accused of rioting on that fateful 17 June went before the courts most were discharged, though three were sentenced to nine months in prison for attacking a policeman. Retribution continued. Two publicans known to be supporters of Murphy, one in Weaman Street and the other in Dale End, were attacked by angry Irishmen. One of them, an ex-pugilist and leader of the Murphyite mob called Roberts, shot dead an Irish attacker called McNally in his pub, and did not even have to face trial at the Warwickshire Spring Assizes, as the judge, Montague Smith, advised the grand jury beforehand that it was likely to prove a case of self-defence.

ETHNICITY SEEMS to have been one of the bases of the slogging gangs of the early 1870s, at least in the Digbeth area, although it receded as the Irish were assimilated. The lingering echoes of Murphy were heard in continued vendettas and street-fights (see Chapter 5). The fighting tendencies of the Irish may well have contributed to some of the territorial battles around the Gun Quarter, in Cheapside and out towards Gosta Green and Duddeston, as well as to the ferocity of Park Street and Allison Street. Yet streets like London Prentice Street and Green's Village, with significant Irish populations, although deprived and violent, made less obvious contributions towards slogging.

Park Street, famous for having to be virtually rebuilt after the devastating anti-Irish riots of 1867, continued to have a rough reputation and was constantly in the spotlight for various 'outrages'. Park Street's deprivation was mirrored in health statistics which showed its death rate to be far higher than any other street in Birmingham, partly because of its many lodging houses. It was a long street with a varied ethnic mix. By 1890, Park Street and Bartholomew Street were associated with the small Italian colony drawn to the city to escape the poverty of their home country. Their women wore elegant peasant dress and some of their men played street pianos. Most of their takings came from poor people like themselves anxious to hear the latest songs of the day, which the musicians could memorise and play or sing after just one visit to a music hall or pantomime.

The Jewish community, with its synagogues, was based in the area north of Holloway Head, and was associated with tailoring. This was a sweated trade where workers of all ages toiled at home or in cramped workshops for long hours and tiny pay, and Jews were blamed as middlemen and sweaters. Prostitutes would say that they would rather ply their own trade than go back to tailoring. In fact Jewish immigrants were as likely to be the victims as the controllers of sweating. However as the community grew it branched out into other trades such as jewellery. Immigration from Eastern Europe increased in the 1880s and 1890s as Jews fled from the Russian pogroms. The baiting of these impoverished immigrants with such intended insults as 'sheeneys' or 'you Polish Jews' became a disreputable pastime, and it was not unknown for gangs to enter this district to cause trouble. In one instance in 1892, a gang battered at the door of the George Inn in Inge Street, a pub frequented by Jewish people. The man who answered the door was hit on the head with a bottle and had to go to hospital. A twenty-year-old brasscaster was arrested. Shortly after, his mates took revenge on David Fiddler, a young Polish-born hawker lodging in the same street, whom they seized and beat up one Sunday morning. Fiddler was at first too frightened to give evidence in court, but did in the end, sending three of his tormentors to prison for two months each. Fiddler was assured by the Bench that 'the law in Birmingham was strong enough to protect foreigners', and that if there was any more such trouble the police should be notified.

The Romany or gipsy community had one encampment in an area of Handsworth close to the outlying Birmingham hamlet of Nineveh. It was liable to flooding as well as to local intolerance. Gipsies were famous as fortune tellers and hawkers. Some were in trouble with the police and there was considerable ill-feeling towards them, reinforced by popular and children's literature. One dark, 'good-looking' young man called Loveridge incurred the anger of the Winson Green residents by paying 'attentions' to a local girl. When he admitted to her that in fact he was already engaged to another, he compounded the insult by refusing to give back her gifts. For this he was waylaid by a mob on his way home from work, and had to take shelter in a house and then escape in disguise, in spite of his injuries. His enemies made two or three visits to the camp to find him and threatened to burn it down when they could not.

Another gipsy camp, on the east side of town, was complained of vitriolically, in 1864, in a letter to the *Post*, for its site 'upon one of the most unhealthy spots in that wretchedly-drained village', meaning Sparkbrook.

Smallpox was feared in this 'wandering tribe'. As Sparkbrook grew, the Romanies sought out other waste ground such as at Cherry Wood Lane and towards Hay Mills. The community could protect itself and was usually too much on the outskirts to be of interest to many sloggers.

BIRMINGHAM AND the Black Country shared a great fighting tradition. Indeed, according to Thomas Harman, compiler of *Showell's Dictionary of Birmingham*, the area had 'a shocking bad name' for it, even if Coventry had a worse name for 'parson-pelting'and 'woman-ducking'. By the 1780s, bareknuckle fights were big business. In one famous encounter, Jemmy Sargent, a professional, took on Isaac Perrins, one of Matthew Boulton's workmen, for 100 guineas a side. To the surprise of the pundits, it was Sargent who knuckled under after being knocked down thirteen times, in as many rounds, by the knock-kneed hammerman from Soho, whose mates, it is said, won £1,500 in bets. Such was the interest in the sport that the famous Birmingham bareknuckle prize-fighter William Futrell published the first boxing newspaper. Futrell himself was undefeated until July 1788, when he met the much younger 'Gentleman' John Jackson and was overcome in a fight, watched by the Prince of Wales, which lasted one hour and seventeen minutes. Jackson later became champion of England.

Women too were famous for their fighting in the Black Country, often stemming from arguments at rough places of work such as ash mounds, brickyards and pit heads. In nail and rivet shops, women and girls worked alongside men as they hammered iron into nails. So the fight between two nail makers, 'Black Hannah' Stevenson, aged forty-three, and Elizabeth Chater, aged twenty-three, both of Dudley, in May 1884, caused no surprise. It took place at the foot of a slag heap near Old Hill and the umpire awarded victory to Mrs Chater, as Black Hannah did not wait for the signal to start before throwing herself at her opponent. The Warwickshire police arrived, and half the spectators flew across the county boundary into the safety of Staffordshire.

Prize-fighting was enormously popular in Birmingham. The coroner at an inquest in 1831 thought that in his time there had been a fourfold increase in the number of assize cases caused by this deadly sport. The pacifist Quaker Joseph Sturge once tried to stop a bout in Edgbaston Fields, but as he waded into the crowd, his coat was ripped and his watch was stolen by pickpockets. Brookfields was another favoured site, on part of the old Birmingham Heath, and to 'make a Brookfields job of' someone passed into the local vernacular to mean a murderous assault, often as a threat against policemen.

One of the best known pugilists of the mid-Victorian period was Bob Brettle. Born at Portobello, Wolverhampton, in 1831, and a glassblower by trade, he had started as a prizefighter at twenty-one, became a champion and left the sport in 1862, taking the licence of the White Lion, Digbeth. He was described at his death in 1872 as a popular referee and stakeholder for all events in the sporting world. He had taught boxing at the White Lion, but later sold up and went to America. He set up a liquor store in Boston, Massachusetts, but violated the liquor laws and was imprisoned. Soon afterwards he returned to Birmingham and opened the White Lion beerhouse in Bell Street. Even this he had to give up, and shortly before his death he was said to have returned to glassblowing for a living. He had been a controversial figure, with enemies as well as admirers. It was remarked ruefully at his death that 'very few pugilists attain any great age' and he died in poverty. The subscription for his widow and children raised £28, of which all but half-a-crown went on funeral expenses, including the costly cortege from Birmingham to the churchyard at Harborne.

Some set-piece fights led to fatalities, such as one near Tamworth in 1881 that ended the career of the lightweight champion, James Highland, of Ward Street, St George's, at the fists of James Carney, of Wheeler Street, Lozells. Highland's ribs were described afterwards as 'like rainbows'. He was put in a cab after the fight and driven back to Birmingham. That evening he drank ten or twelve glasses of whisky 'with a little water' at the White Swan in New Canal Street. He was given a lift home and fell badly as he got out of the cart. At the assizes, the defence argued that he had died from a chill followed by excessive drinking. The jury disagreed and found Carney guilty of manslaughter, but Mr Justice Baggaley restricted his sentence to six months' hard labour. Highland left a wife and child.

Of the new breed of glove-fighters, Alf Greenfield was one of the first, and the most famous. He had worked on the canals and made his boxing debut against Pat Perry at Sutton in 1877. He was an already established figure when, in 1883, he won the British heavyweight championship belt in a fight with Jack Burke at the Free Trade Hall, Manchester. The following year, his silver championship belt was stolen from the sparring saloon at the back of the Swan With Two Necks public house in Livery Street, where he was landlord. Shortly after this, he was arrested for 'fighting without weapons' in New York during an encounter with John L.Sullivan, the famous 'Boston Strong Boy', at Madison Square Garden. The *New York Times* regaled its readers with a description of the two boxers in court, whose appearance created a sensation. Greenfield wore 'a Piccadilly topper, a long green ulster and a big horseshoe pin'. It was feared that the US authorities intended to administer a death-blow to glove-fighting, but the jury found the boxers not guilty of taking part in a prize-fight, a decision which would help to establish boxing as a legitimate sport. In a rematch in Boston, Sullivan won after four rounds and he went on to retain the heavyweight championship. When the great Sullivan came to Birmingham to fight at Bingley Hall a year later, he was greeted at New Street by Greenfield and a huge crowd who made it hard for them to get from the station to a four-wheeler. Transatlantic trips made some British fighters rich and famous and in any event local heroes. Greenfield's complimentary benefit was staged in the Museum Concert Hall in the Bull Ring in 1886, and he kept on his sparring saloon for a time. He moved to the Three Tuns in Digbeth, but the pub was badly damaged by fire in 1891 and within two years had been admitted to Winson Green Asylum, where he died, aged forty-two, in 1895.

From 1882 under English law, bareknuckle contests were regarded as assault causing bodily harm, even when the participants were in consent, and drove a further nail into the coffin of such arranged fights. There were some attempts to get round the law by fighting in small gloves, although these were almost as dangerous as fighting with bare fists and were sometimes stopped by the police. Prize-fights between local men remained popular. One at Northfield in 1877 between two labourers, James Ireland and Charles Norton, was interrupted when they were already stripped to the waist and a number of other pugilists from different parts of the town were holding the rope that formed the ring. The Balsall Heath magistrates said it was the first case of its kind at their court, so the fighters were let off lightly with sureties of £10 each. Even more of a local fight was the one planned between Joseph Turner, aged twenty-four, and Edward Clarke, aged twenty-two, both of St George's Street, Birmingham, at the Boar's Head Inn in Perry Barr. Nearly eight hundred people turned up to watch on a Sunday afternoon in September 1887. The fight was for only a sovereign and was abandoned at the cry of 'police'. The crowd often appeared overnight, as for the contest, also at Perry Barr, in 1884 between two Black Countrymen, called 'Big Ben' and 'Stinger'. Scouts were positioned to watch out for the police, but there was no need and after an hour's fighting on slippery ground, the two hundred spectators dispersed in different directions. Other fights took place on the county boundary at Handsworth and Sutton Coldfield.

Street-fights often resembled prize-fights by involving local loyalties, personal rivalries and heavy drinking. Indeed the press referred to them as 'pugilistic encounters'. One example was when John Haley a slater from Allison Street, took on an opponent in Freeman Street in the early hours of a Monday morning in August 1868, and caused a 'great disturbance'. Another impromptu stand-up fight arose between 'Boxer' Bradley and a labourer called Thomas Holland in Harding Street. A large crowd gathered and stoned the police when they tried to arrest Holland. Usually the fight was stopped by the police, as when Paddy McDonald, a labourer of Lancaster Street, having had too much to drink on Christmas Day 1894, quarrelled with and took on a young man just returned from the army on furlough. The soldier was said to have trained with Anthony Diamond, 'the Birmingham boxing legend', who won a series of Amateur Boxing Association titles in the 1880s and took the licence of the Turk's Head, Duke Street. So the soldier was regarded as more than fair game. McDonald was arrested, having, at twenty-one, had already the same number of commitments to prison for drunkenness as his years of age.

Group fights were also common. Often they seem to have been accidental encounters, as when Isaac Walpole, aged twenty-three, of Nelson Street South, and several others met George Cartland, a brassfounder of Lower Essex Street, near the Markets area, with a number of other young men on a Monday evening in June 1867. Fighting and kicking ensued, and then Walpole pulled a knife which sent Cartland to the Queen's Hospital and the perpetrator to prison for two months with hard labour. Walpole was drunk and his action was regarded as cowardly by the press.

Fights arose between men of the same trade, often from 'trade jealousy'. In October 1875, two file cutters, both of Lichfield Street, decided to settle their dispute in the Old Square. However, twenty-one-year-old Jesse Roslin brought his friends with him and they attacked the other file cutter so savagely that he spent two weeks in hospital and was unable to work for another month after that. The friends escaped, but Roslin faced a £5 fine or two months in prison.

Family 'jars', or fights, sometimes drew in other people. Two brothers were told one Saturday night that their sister's husband had been ill-treating their mother. Taking other youths with them, they chased him through the Holloway Head area and eventually caught up with him in Granville Street where he took refuge in a shop. In the scuffle that followed, he stabbed them. The jury at the sessions accepted his plea that the stabbing was in self-defence, and he was discharged. 'Rows' flared up constantly in the overcrowded areas, sometimes raking up old scores or starting new ones. They could spill easily into 'free fights', like the one involving the hurling of buckets, fenders, fire irons, and snow that took place one wintry Saturday in 1874 in a court in Dale End.

The town's fighting spirit was sometimes vented on strangers on days out in the surrounding countryside. Parties of excursionists got drunk and started fights with locals in holiday places such as Llangollen. Some excursions were annual events. St Chad's Roman Catholic School in the Gun Quarter went on its annual excursion to Shustoke in rural Warwickshire in August 1872. The school took with it a large number of 'friends', said to have amounted in all to about a thousand people, who spent most of their day in or close to the Griffin Inn. In the afternoon, many went rambling through the lanes and the fields of the neighbouring estate, which had belonged to the Dugdale family for over two centuries. The boys soon got into trouble for stealing fruit. One boy was caught by a man engaged especially to protect the orchard belonging to the landlord of the Griffin. The man hit the boy with a stick, but he struggled free. Other boys started raiding fruit trees in the garden of Mr Dugdale's woodman, who came out of his cottage and drove them off. It was not long before they returned to try again, and this time out came the gamekeeper, Thomas Booton, with his gun. He was used to taking potshots at distant poachers, so when the boys started throwing stones, he discharged his gun. Later, at the petty sessions, he would claim that he had fired over the crowd, but when his case came before Warwickshire Assizes, he admitted to having fired into it, but without taking deliberate aim. In the process he shot a sixteen-year-old boy from Water Street, called James Carter, in the arm.

The shooting infuriated the mob, said to have grown to about two hundred men and boys. The gamekeeper was hit by a number of large stones and fled, finally taking refuge in another cottage, but not before being heavily beaten by a couple of men. Another teenager, James Millett, from Hospital Street, was also injured, this time with a scalp wound. He and Carter were taken back to the Griffin and, that evening, were transported to Birmingham General Hospital. Booton, it turned out, was also in a bad way. At eight o'clock that evening he was found in the cottage, conscious but covered in blood. He too was conveyed to the hospital and treated for head wounds. He was kept in for five weeks and was not expected to live, but from his hospital bed he managed to identify one of the men who had attacked him.

As a result, Patrick Cunningham, aged twenty-two, of Steelhouse Lane, was charged with assault and intent to murder the gamekeeper. Cunningham was an ironworker at a carriage works in Saltley. It emerged that he and another man had chased Booton around the Shustoke church wall and into a field beyond. They caught up with him and wrenched the gun out of his hands. The gun went off in the struggle. Terrified, he asked them what they were going to do and if they were going to murder him. Cunningham, in a fury, swung the gun over his shoulder and brought it down with a terrific blow on Booton's head, fracturing his skull.

There was much annoyance among the excursionists at the authorities' apparent disregard for Booton's use of his gun. Two Catholic priests, who had been with the party, initially refused to come forward when the police demanded witnesses. The police issued a warrant for the other man who had attacked the gamekeeper, but they never found him and were told that he had absconded to America. At the second special petty sessions at Coleshill in October, Booton was at last considered well enough to appear, although with his head still in a large bandage. The charge against Cunningham was changed from assault and intent to murder to one of wounding with intent to do grievous bodily harm. The ironworker was eventually acquitted and the gamekeeper, who was the prosecutor in this case, was censured by Mr Justice Bovill for firing into the crowd.

PUBLIC HOUSES were always a major focus for trouble. Beerhouses and pubs were a resort for people of all ages and major providers of the alcohol that fuelled so much of the town's violence. Arguments could soon escalate into rows, not necessarily calmed when women came looking for their men. Fights often started in the pub and then spilled out onto the street. Sometimes the building itself was attacked. A typical case was of boys being refused drink. In May 1871, a young nailcaster appeared in court 'minus his coat'. On the previous Sunday night he and some friends had asked for a drink in the Swan beerhouse in Livery Street. The landlord, who was elderly, bravely replied, 'We don't supply beer to boys.' At this, he was narrowly saved from being roughed up by the intervention of a brewer. So the young 'desperadoes' turned on the brewer, knocked him down and kicked him as he lay on the floor. The nailcaster threw a glass at him, which caused a 'fearful' wound over his eye, and then made off with his billycock hat. For this he received the maximum sentence of two months.

Pub glass went first in any set-to. Worst was when a publican had upset a whole gang of roughs. This happened to John Fulford, of Heath Street South, when forty or fifty came to his house, struck him in the face with a brick, smashed his windows and put out the street lamps. Refusing to serve a man who had already had too much was frequently the trigger for trouble. A young brassfounder dealt a blow with his buckled belt to the landlord of the George and Dragon, Church Street, shortly after Christmas – a big drinking time – in 1876. The landlord struck back with the butt of a revolver and both ended up being taken to hospital while a mob smashed all the pub's windows. The brassfounder was sent down for five years.

Fighting often broke out as young men and women came out of the pubs, especially on Saturday nights. Often it was just widespread 'knocking about', but a fight between two individuals could lead to severe wounding or even death. Such was the case of an apparently chance encounter between two young men in their late teens, both married with one child. It was a Saturday midnight and time for both to leave the Swan Pool tavern in Lichfield Road, next to Aston railway station. The two men, both from Birmingham rather than Aston, came out simultane-ously, though apparently from different parts of the tavern. A third also came out at the same time, and his evidence was confirmed by a policeman standing outside. The third man testified that George Newey, an eigh-teen-year-old toolmaker from John Street West, off Summer Lane, began dancing about in the road and offered to 'run', or fight, anybody.

'I am the leader of the Black Band in Harding Street, Newtown Row,' he boasted, 'and I don't care a b-- who knows it.'

'Greasy Bob' Davis, an oil-refiner from Grosvenor Street, replied, 'You, the captain? A little fellow like you?'

The two men started to struggle in the road, and then Newey took a glistening object from his coat pocket and stabbed Davis with it several times. The witness, Samuel Westwood, ran after him and Newey threat-ened to stab him too. He thought Newey looked 'half-and-half' rather than fully drunk. Davis died from his wounds.

Superintendent Bloxham said that Harding Street, off Summer Lane, was a very low neighbourhood, full of thieves and with many stabbing cases and assaults on the police. The surgeon found stab wounds in Davis' thighs, in one arm and the fatal one in his stomach. At the Warwickshire Spring Assizes of 1868, three weeks later, Newey was undefended, but his sentence was limited to five years' penal servitude on the grounds of provocation. This was long enough for him to reflect on his role as Birmingham's new 'Claude Duval', a notorious highwayman of the days of King Charles II and hero of Victorian penny dreadful stories, to whom Newey was said to liken himself.

CHILDREN LEARNED to fight early. Each trade had its own traditions, usually involving putting the new boys 'through it', almost as a rite of passage and often not just once. Children were made to fight each other to entertain men in many trades. Apprentices of one master might fight those of another in a dinner break.[2] This was easily carried over into working boys attempting fights with schoolboys. It was a regular feature of dinnertime at King Edward's Branch School, in Meriden Street, Digbeth, in 1871, for factory boys to pass the school and throw stones at the school-boys as a challenge to a fight. On another occasion, the aggressiveness of the King Edward's pupils was blamed by their opponents' parents.

One way in which boys could prove themselves worthy of their craft was by fighting boys in other trades. They might be neighbours and have daily opportunities to preserve or change the pecking order. Encounters were not always harmless. One dinnertime clash between boys from Gold's hinge manufactory in Great Lister Street and those from Stephens' glassworks in Dartmouth Street, Duddeston, led to a fatality. Just before 2 p.m., on Wednesday, 30 May 1866, arguing and fighting were seen between a dozen or so boys of the two firms on Heneage Street bridge, where they usually went in their dinner-hour. The key witness was a bystander who saw a boy being hit with a fist, pull his jacket off for a fight and then follow his companions as they ran off, pursued by boys from the glassworks.

The boy was nine-year-old Thomas McGee, an edger at the hinge factory, described as a 'little Irish boy' who lived with his parents. McGee was overtaken by the glass boys, but sat down on a step and put his jacket back on. The witness said he had a knife in his hand. He was heard to use a 'very bad' word in reply to some glass boys, one of whom, a taller and

---

2 Clive Behagg (see bibliography) called this the 'folk violence' of a workshop culture.

stronger boy, identified later as ten-year-old John Davis, gave him a box on the ear. Then McGee 'threw his arm around, having the knife still in his hand and the knife struck (the glass boy) below the left breast'. This fatally wounded Davis who ran down Dartmouth Street, clutching his left side, while McGee shut up his knife, put it in his pocket and ran away to the side of the canal. The bystander gave chase and caught him. McGee cried, 'Master, pitch me into the canal.' Instead he was held until a policeman arrived and he was taken into custody.

At the inquest, the bystander said that 'there was nothing to make me think McGee was lying in wait for any of the glass boys'. Another witness heard Davis scream as he turned into the gateway of his place of work and collapsed. The witness picked him up, tried to close his wound between finger and thumb, carried him to Woodcock Street and then by cab to the General Hospital, but he was dead on arrival. The pocket knife was described as of the sort that might be used for cutting bread and cheese. The coroner's view was that McGee was only just old enough to be considered capable of committing a criminal act and that he had been provoked and had shown no malice. So he was effectively acquitted, pending the confirmation of the magistrates. The stipendiary magistrate, T.C.S. Kynnersley, was less indulgent towards this case 'that would not exclude manslaughter', with the view that 'it was a felony to cause the death of anyone by carelessness'. However he agreed that the death could have been accidental, and McGee was discharged. The *Birmingham Daily Post* thought the knifing was the result of 'practical jokes'.

Where numbers of boys from two big establishments worked side by side, the confrontations were on a bigger scale. Livery Street, on the edge of the St Paul's Ward, was the centre of prize-fighting, so it was not surprising that the boys of two rival and neighbouring firms, Billing's printers and Pemberton's brassfounders, would try out their brawling skills on each other. Friday was wage day and could be a time for trouble. One Friday evening in January 1874, as Billing's lads were leaving work after receiving their wages, they were met at the gate and attacked by twenty to thirty of Pemberton's boys, and a number of them lost some or all of their money. The next day, the lads of both works met after finishing their week's work at dinnertime and a mass fight broke out. The road was completely blocked, as all the other workers and many passers-by gathered to watch. Eventually the police dispersed the boys but made no arrests. However the fighting resumed on the following Wednesday afternoon. Again the Pemberton brass boys took the initiative, but both sides used a variety of stones, sticks and other weapons. On being told what was happening, Mr Billing left his office, rushed among the boys with some of his men and handed a number into police custody.

The next day, seven thirteen-year-old printers from the north side of the town were taken before the stipendiary by their foreman, who told the story. Mr Billing was reluctant to press charges against his own boys, and they were discharged by Stipendiary Kynnersley, who said that he would have liked to have flogged them all and hoped Parliament would give the Bench that power. Whatever the stipendiary decided, it seemed that the brass boys were still on top. In both cases of trade fighting it seems not unreasonable to presume that the outcomes of such large-scale fights would fuel the causes of smaller group confrontations or for a group to pick on an individual found suddenly off guard and on his own.

CHAPTER 3

The Sloggers' Environment

THE 'BRUMMY' working man thought himself the best in the world, and was often arrogant and bullish towards strangers. Town, however, was not always superior to country. At harvest time in August 1872, seven reapers from Worcestershire on their way to a job at Harborne called in at the Gun Barrels Inn on Birmingham's Bristol Road. Soon afterwards, a gang of six Birmingham roughs also entered the house and tried to sell a blunt hook to them. Next they asked the reapers for a drink. Reluctantly the latter handed the hat round and mustered eightpence between them. Instead of spending the money on drink, the roughs pocketed it and began taunting the reapers. After a challenge to a fight, each side chose one of their number to a face-off in a neighbouring field, but when the rough got the worst of it, his mates piled in to help, armed with stones. After a fifteen-minute free-for-all, the roughs ran away.

Pugnacity was prized in an eighteenth century tradition which long resisted the nineteenth century's efforts to tame it. A good brawl was relished and men from different trades might end up fighting each other or even side by side. Every trade in the city had its club, even before the advent of trade unions. 'Club night' was a potentially dangerous time when, after monthly club money had been paid in and business was over, the members would start drinking. Arguments ensued and often turned to fisticuffs. The club night for the bricklayers at the Flying Horse, Hampton Street, in August 1875, proved fatal when, after the end of business, Patrick O'Donoughue of New Summer Street was attacked by two other Irish labourers and later died of his injuries. Afterwards they denied kicking him, and no adult would admit to having seen what had happened, even when the unconscious body of O'Donoughue was picked up from the taproom floor, smothered in sawdust, and later, already dead, carried home. Yet two small boys happened to have been passing the inn at the time and had seen the three men fighting as they looked in through the doorway. They testified to that effect at the assizes, and the jury rejected the defence counsel's attempt to discredit their evidence by arguing that their minds had been too much 'fired by sensational literature'. The judge, Baron Bramwell, did not believe that either and gave the two men ten years' penal servitude for manslaughter.

According to the 1871 census, the largest single trade group was the ironworkers, representing the traditional hardwares of the West Midlands, with the brass workers catching them up and overtaking them by the end of the century. The gunmakers came third. They had benefited from the wars of the 1850s and 1860s and their income reached a peak with the Franco-Prussian War of 1870-1. Next came the jewellers, including goldsmiths, silversmiths and workers in precious and semi-precious stones, whose numbers were also steadily increasing. Last came the glassmakers and buttonmakers. The pecking order of the trades was highly contested, as much among adults as among the young. Gunmakers, ironworkers, and brassfounders all vied for supremacy. The Irish element in the building trades provided them with physical backbone, while the brickmakers institutionalised traditions of violence. Although many jewellers were sensitive artists, some were ready for combat. The pearl-button makers in particular did not want to be ignored and the glassmakers of Duddeston were a fiery set.

One of the most successful of Birmingham's 'metal-bashing' trades in the late nineteenth century was the bedstead industry. Ornamental brass or iron bedsteads were a new Victorian fashion and rapidly became what in the twenty-first century would be called 'must have'. By 1908, local firms made three-quarters of British-made bedsteads and had a thriving export market. Another new brass trade, following the rapid spread of gas lighting, and again with customers all over the world, was gas chandelier production. There were jobs for many lads, and a few women were employed in the lacquering and wrapping up of finished goods. Brass finishers were not long-lived. The acid finishers or dippers were most at risk, especially from respiratory and stomach conditions called 'brassfounders' ague', and they were advised to cover their mouth and nostrils and drink 'copious draughts' of milk to counteract the effects of the acid.

Tin was another major metal industry, with many tinplate workers and whitesmiths. A whitesmith led the Barn Street sloggers. Brass, iron and tin were called the 'metal-bashing' industries because physical strength was as necessary as skill. Among the oldest trades was nailmaking.

Traditional nailers were now mainly found out of town in Bromsgrove or villages such as Kings Norton or Harborne, though the nailmakers who worked at Shaws' factory in Glover Street, Bordesley, were another tough lot and no doubt contributed to the reputation of the local Bordesley gang. The gas workers, although not part of the skilled trades, were also a muscular bunch and two Corporation gasworks were in the heart of slogging areas in Duddeston and Bordesley. By contrast, those bound to sweated trades, such as hook-and-eye carding or tailoring, had little leisure time or physical capacity to be on the streets, let alone money to afford betting, drink or fines.

As slogging gangs developed, they do not seem to have been composed exclusively of one trade, just as men in employment passed easily from brass to iron and back again. By the end of the century, some sloggers who had earlier described themselves in terms of a craft had become simply labourers. Some of these were men made unemployable by drink, violence and criminal records. They were usually too proud to call themselves unemployed.

LIKE TRADES, turf or territory could be an excuse for hostility in the expanding towns of the nineteenth century. Birmingham was developed by the sale of small estates, owned by local landowners, which came to form distinct neighbourhoods or enclaves. At the same time, the better-off moved further out. Many of the elegant houses near the centre became overrun with manufacturing premises and the gardens filled up with living quarters and 'shopping' (workshops). Architecturally there was little difference between the areas, but 'the old hardware village' quickly became a series of hamlets, each with its own identity, although remaining part of a unified whole.

The town's roughest and most chaotic area lay between the main canal wharf and New Street station. Navigation Street was a byword for violence of all types, and its drifting population of drunks and prostitutes a continual source of trouble to the police. Riots could break out at any time, and the more serious led to deaths, including that of a policeman in 1875 (see Chapter 8).

Others areas had more stable populations. Both jewellery and gunmaking involved a number of processes carried out separately by different craftsmen but requiring them to live close enough together to form their own quarter. The Jewellery Quarter expanded in the 1850s and moved outwards from its old base on the Newhall estate into the rapidly-developing Vyse estate, north-west of the town centre. Although fashions changed, it enjoyed steady prosperity right up to the First World War. These jewellers were not such easy victims to the tougher elements in Birmingham society as one might think. The fringes of the quarter, such as Camden Street and the streets between the Parade and Livery Street, called the Newhall estate, had a particularly rough reputation, perhaps protecting the softer core. The Jewellery Quarter in some respects represented the elite of Birmingham's craftsmen and women. It was not for nothing that their trade was among the city's most successful, and that the Icknield Street Board School gained the highest number of King Edward scholarships – passports to secondary education in Birmingham's famous King Edward grammar schools – in the late Victorian period.

The Gun Quarter, where the gunmakers reigned supreme, was due north of the town centre, gathered round St Mary's churchyard and including St Chad's Roman Catholic Cathedral. It was bounded to the north-west by the Birmingham and Fazeley Canal and to the south-west by Snow Hill station and the railway to Wolverhampton and Dudley. The gun trade was dominated by small masters, and was very vulnerable to the ups and downs of the arms trade. The Birmingham Small Arms Company, although founded in Steelhouse Lane in 1861, soon set up new factories outside the town at Small Heath and Adderley Park. Other master gunmakers also moved out of the area to escape the overcrowding, and much of the housing in the quarter deteriorated with the fortunes of its occupants.

It was an area renowned for its toughness. There were as many drunken, violent men in the brothels of Weaman Street, in the Gun Quarter, as in Thomas Street. Lancaster Street was notorious for pickpockets, and it was the stone-throwing of a twelve-year-old from Lench Street in October 1869 that started a campaign by the magistrates and police against the activity. The locals made short shrift of interfering policemen. A crowd of young men, led by a gun finisher and axle-tree filer, 'pitching and tossing' in Weaman Street, retreated into Slaney Street when approached by two constables and there showered stones and half-bricks at them, causing a scene almost as bad as the Murphy Riots. On Boxing Day 1872, a gun finisher assaulted a man in Sand Street and the next night, with his gang, was seen throwing a large stone which struck a constable, leading to a total of four months in prison with hard labour.

John D.Goodman, the doyen of the town's gun manufacturers, wrote of the 'employment of a considerable number of young boys' in the gun trade who could be seen at any time of day, 'one with half-a-dozen stocked guns on his shoulder, conveying them from the stocker to the screwer; another with a tray full of locks for the polisher; a third on his way with a few barrels to the Proof-house, and so on.' In terms of wages, the gunmakers were at the top of the tree in the early 1870s, when slogging became a youth fashion. Youngsters in the gun trade were said to be the ones who most liked a fight.

Not all occupations had single territories. The pearl-button makers were to be found not only in the Jewellery Quarter in Caroline and Northwood Streets, but in many other parts of the town as well, such as off Broad Street and in Moorsom Street, off Newtown Row. They were often prominent in fights. The brassworkers of early and mid-Victorian times were to be found in a great swathe from Ladywood in the south-west, through Broad Street, to Digbeth and Bordesley to the south-east and further north towards Ashted, and Bloomsbury. Brass bedstead-making by the 1880s went on in Digbeth, Highgate and Bordesley, and also in Smethwick. Brass tubing was also moving into large works such as found in Heath Street, Soho, a long street leading towards Smethwick and a regular slogging ground. Iron foundries could be found in most localities, and founders, moulders and strikers made good fighters. Along with the brassworkers, the iron workers were the men most likely to be arrested for slogging.

Pritchett Street, beyond the Fazeley Canal between Newtown Row and Aston Road, in St Stephen's Ward, had more diversified industries, including brass founding, electro-plated cutlery and pearl-button making. There were running feuds between local boys and those of the Gun Quarter. One case caused laughter in the magistrates' court when a young pistol filer from Weaman Street appeared for assaulting a forger savagely with a stick, simply because he lived in Pritchett Street, which the Weaman lad regarded as inferior and so would not 'associate with him', now that he no longer lived in the Gun Quarter. The court laughed again when the pistol filer justified his action by recounting how the forger had run after him with a carving knife the previous week in the Gun Quarter. What outsiders found ridiculous, local people took very seriously.

Livery Street, heading out towards Hockley from the town centre, not only had a reputation for pugilism but also for housing a strong criminal element. A gang of five 'rough-looking fellows', two of whom came from Great Hampton Street, a continuation of Livery Street, were arrested on the pavement for obstruction in May 1864 and were shown to have twenty previous convictions. Neighbouring Church Street was the den of a number of burglars who were caught busily filing skeleton keys that same year. The fact that they formed part of Duddeston's Lawley Street gang of thieves – according to the police – with a third 'branch' in Milk Street, off Digbeth, indicates that Birmingham's criminal fraternity was not as territorial as might be expected. The two leaders of the gang got seven and five years' penal servitude, while a thirteen-year-old boy, employed to squeeze through holes that the others could not, received four months in prison, with one week of each month to be spent in solitary confinement.

Henrietta Street, off Livery Street, at a meeting point between the Jewellery Quarter and St George's Ward, also had a reputation for affrays, such as the one in August 1862 in which a mob of over two hundred people were drawn into stoning two policemen. A resident who provided shelter for the constable was savagely kicked. He explained afterwards to a court that some of the pubs in the area were 'filled with persons of low character the whole of Sunday mornings and that at about noon they were turned into the streets in a frightful state of intoxication.' The result, he said, was that there was not much else but quarrelling and fighting for the rest of the day. The street was a meeting place for a gang of youths who came from a variety of places round about and from a variety of trades, including iron and brass, and incorporating a couple of Irishmen, some of whom lived close by. The residents' main cause for concern was that they were noisy, violent and blocking the way. An especially aggressive display on the warm Whit Monday of 1870, when everyone was out of doors, led to a clash with the police, an attempted rescue and a total of eight fines and prison sentences.

The Thomas Street area to the south-east of the Gun Quarter, in Market Hall Ward, was not so important for slogging but was regarded as particularly rough and criminal. Its 'low' lodging-houses were notorious as criminal dens, especially for coiners, bag-snatchers and prostitutes. In the late 1850s, the police were in hot pursuit of what they called 'the Thomas Street gang of thorough thieves'. When policemen raided the lodging house of Ann Eaves at 21 Thomas Street in January 1863, they found stolen goods scattered through every room. Of the boy thieves, some were in bed; others were up and smoking stolen cigars. Middle class improvers identified lodging houses for the poor with disease and 'moral deprivation', meaning crime and prostitution. In two such houses in the

Thomas Street area, the landlady kept the door at the foot of the stairs locked with a chain and padlock by day to prevent burglary, and by night to keep the lodgers in and to ensure that they did not 'decamp' with 'whatever furniture or moveables they could carry with them'.

The Inkleys, Old and New, and Green's Village, off Hill Street, near the markets and New Street railway station, were also usually associated with poverty and crime more than slogging (the Inkleys would later be rebuilt as Hinckley Street). Their lodgings were cheap enough to make Green's Village a refuge for the Irish after the Famine. These streets had narrowly survived the demolition work for the station in 1854. The police and magistrates were delighted when, in September 1859, the last of the five members of 'Dillon's Inkleys gang' was caught after robbing a warehouse office. All five ended up serving terms of transportation or penal servitude. Another gang preyed on travellers coming from the station. One innkeeper tried to prevent this by personally meeting his guests off the train, only to find that the gang came to insult and threaten his wife and servants while he was out. On Saturday nights these areas were as threatening to well-heeled pedestrians and isolated policemen as was Navigation Street on the other side of New Street station, and the local roughs regularly carried life-preservers, which were batons of gutta percha (a hard substance also used for making golf balls) with an iron-covered knob. It was not surprising that by June 1873, the police relied on a plainclothes force of thirty men to check that landlords were keeping to the tougher licensing laws. Such work only increased the unpopularity and the risks of the constabulary, in plain clothes or uniform.

Prostitution was an over-crowded occupation and in early and mid-Victorian times it was a feature of the town centre, while the evil of child prostitution, to which the authorities were slow to respond, was prevalent around the two main railway stations. Girls as young as twelve years avoided starvation and appeared to casual observers to be earning a living by selling matches. The cabbies, from their wooden shelter behind the Theatre Royal, knew better. They kept a more constant eye than the police and saw the pimps and the punters, and much else which they kept to themselves. Campaigning journalists spoke to them and alerted the police, but the penalties even after the Children Act of 1889 were not likely to strike fear into those clients in the evil quest of 'purity'. The smarter brothels tended to migrate to the suburbs. The Calthorpe Park side of Balsall Heath attracted many such seedy businesses, with its good communications with the town centre and easy access for the genteel clientele from the southern suburbs. In time, Balsall Heath and Lower Edgbaston would acquire a reputation as the city's 'red light' area.

The streets on both banks of the little River Rea were amongst the poorest and most violent of Victorian Birmingham. *Showell's Dictionary of Birmingham* described the river as 'long little better than an open sewer' and the town's 'burial-place' for cats and dogs. Sun Street, south of the centre, was a street of shopkeepers and artisans, with a number of courts behind. It was well-known for its 'mob' of roughs by 1873, who the police claimed were robbing pub-drinkers of their coats. They even tried to put one man over Gooch Street bridge into the river. Across the river was Deritend, referred to famously by John Leland in Henry VIII's time as the 'pretty streete called Dirtey'. Although like the town itself its origins were mediaeval, with a mill and its own church, much of Deritend had a bad name in the late nineteenth century. By 1879 there were reports of 'the Bordesley gang' making the Watery Lane area of Deritend very unsafe for people on foot, especially those from Small Heath who had no choice but to pass through.

On the nearer side of the river were streets serving the town's markets and the canal at Fazeley Wharf. Digbeth was the name of the main street running down to the river, and leading to Deritend, carving through poor districts of St Bartholomew's and St Martin's on either side. In the twentieth century it would give its name to the whole area. Pubs had secret rat and cock pits. In April 1863, the police broke up a major bout of cock-fighting in the bowling alley of the Unicorn Inn, Digbeth, and found 'many cocks in various stages of fighting, some with their eyes out, some bleeding from wounds, some dying and some actually dead. Others were being prepared for battle in the pit, which was situated in the centre of the room.' Steel spurs for arming the birds and scales for weighing them were also found. About a hundred punters, including men from Darlaston and Wednesfied, scattered in all directions as the police broke in.

The children of St Martin's Ward, to the south of Digbeth, were described as of 'animal nature', with language which was 'peculiarly strong and full of expletives and adjectives' and required their own free school in order to avoid contaminating the better-spoken, in the view of the arch-spokesman for board schools, Dr Langford. Floodgate Street, once famous for its tanning industry, had a gang of young pickpockets. Cheapside was another of the longer streets with a reputation for all kinds of violence and crime. It was a starting point for organised slogging gangs in the early 1870s and was still a favourite place for confrontations in the 1890s. Off Cheapside was Rea Street where in one large lodging-house, five young thieves were living, in what the police described as 'a perfect barracks' or 'nursery of crime'. Rea Street South developed as a major centre of brass bedstead-making and had a large board school which helped crystallise the local identity. Highgate was a newly-built area to the south-east, in the 1870s: high-class on the hill, but badly equipped lower down towards the Rea, without much paving, drains or lighting. Fighting ability became a way of gaining a different kind of reputation.

St Bartholomew's Ward, to the north of Digbeth, was one of the most disorderly areas. Thirty or forty thieves lived in a single house in Bartholomew Street, emerging after dusk to 'work' the doors and windows of town centre shops.[3] The Fox public house in Freeman Street, off Park Street, once infamous as a den for coiners, retained its bad reputation. It was one of those pubs where strangers to the town would find themselves pitched from drinking into quarrelling and then into a fight, at which point coats were taken off and handed to bystanders, allowing the pockets to be rifled. In January 1875, the vicar of St Gabriel's, Barn Street, opened a soup kitchen and later made a special appeal for what he described as the 'poorest' parish in Birmingham. Close to the Digbeth Branch Canal basin, it was an area of hard-bitten navvies and labourers with a cream of brassworkers and others. In such an area there were lodging-houses where the young easily fell into criminal ways or joined gangs. Allison Street was already well-known for its rows and lawlessness in the 1850s and continued to erupt frequently into outbreaks of street violence.

To the east of the Gun Quarter, but still in St Mary's Ward, lay Bishop Ryder's District. It was seriously deprived and attempts to civilise it did not go down well. When the Bishop of Lichfield laid the foundation stone of its church in Gem Street in 1837, the 'low denizens of the neighbourhood' pelted him with mud. The parish was still described in 1874 as 'the most miserable in the town' with the children of its courts and alleys 'little, pale, ragged and stunted', according to the *Mail* in a report on the sanitary condition of the town. Gem Street had a ragged school and later a certified industrial school. Gem Street and Staniforth Sreet were the first board

---

3 According to calculations made by the Rev. Micaiah Hill, secretary to the Town Mission, there were, on a given day in 1880, 1,272 known thieves and 'bad characters' at large in the town, of whom 177 were under sixteen years of age. There were seventy-one houses kept by receivers of stolen goods, 118 others known to be frequented by the criminal classes and 188 brothels, in which 262 women were found.

schools in the city to be free to children, to ensure some degree of attendance.

Staniforth Street was the home of Posh Price, the pugilist, while the Stafford Street area had been the site of the archery butts in the Middle Ages and its martial tradition was as strong as ever. Legge Street had a gang of thieves who operated on Warwick racecourse. Lawrence Street was in an area described by the King Edward's Grammar School senior master, Rev F. M. McCarthy, as 'an awful plague spot', the 'Seven Dials' of Birmingham – as bad as its notoriously deprived namesake near Covent Garden in London. Some houses in Woodcock Street were falling down; new public baths were put up there, but a plan for model homes was abandoned. The *Mail* reporter however thought that Fazeley Street and Summer Lane were equally bad.

'The Lane', north of the Gun Quarter in St Stephen's Ward, was perhaps not originally thought of as one of the poorest neighbourhoods, but many skilled workers, including gunmakers and pearl-button makers, would be hit by heavy import duties imposed by the United States tariff of 1890 and forced into reliance on charitable soup kitchens by the bad winter of 1890-1. The Lane's families came from a diversity of backgrounds and attended a variety of schools, and its youth was willing to slog all comers, often on waste land nearby called the Old Peck. Harding Street, between Summer Lane and Newtown Row, was notorious for its poverty, violence and a gang of pickpockets and robbers with widespread and successful operations in the 1880s.

Across the whole of Birmingham, starting in the suburbs, the new board schools, twenty-seven of which were built between 1871 and 1883, many with fine towers, helped to promote neighbourhood cohesion among the young. Board school boys particularly enjoyed slogging church school lads, who were usually outnumbered, although in 1880 the schoolchildren of Birmingham were fairly evenly divided between board and denominational schools.

Ladywood, to the west of the town centre, was one of several areas of Birmingham where transport provided the main employment. The canals for which the town was famous employed any number of labourers, porters and boatmen. The last group was not to be underestimated. Two boatmen, aged seventeen and twenty-five, were more than a match for P.C.s Newman and Horton in 1873. They were said to be two of a gang of roughs who were the terror of the neighbourhood of Great Tindal Street. The elder, called Davie, was particularly menacing, as he had an iron arm, which he used to 'belabour' policemen, while the others in the group threw stones and brickbats. The two constables had to retreat into a pub and await reinforcements. Once arrested, the two boatmen were sentenced to nine months for assault.

Bargees and men in the arms trade in Aston also sought notoriety. Aston Manor, outside the borough, was growing rapidly in the mid-nineteenth century, with increasing numbers of new 'manufactories' and people. There were fears of 'pestilence' from cholera 'nests' such as Chester and Berners Streets, where children played close to stagnant water and piles of dead dogs. In 1871, four young men employed at Dowler's ammunition factory were arrested in the Lichfield Road on a Sunday afternoon, insulting passers-by and stoning the policeman who tried to disperse them. Unusually they were sent to prison for six months' hard labour without the option of a fine. One came from Ten Arches, Wainwright Street, which would be the home of a later gang.

Duddeston, on the border between Aston and Birmingham, was famous for its iron and glass and also produced many sloggers. Neighbouring Nechells, developing as a Victorian working class outer suburb, also acquired a slogging gang, based on Nechells Green. Saltley and Washwood Heath attracted visits by gangs of roughs on Sundays and the locals retaliated as necessary. Sparkbrook too had a slogging gang, centred around a family called Harper (see Chapter 13).

The area reputed to be the wildest and most isolated was the so-called brickies' colony, on the extreme eastern limits of the town at Bordesley Green, near where the St Andrew's ground would later be cleared and constructed for Birmingham's third football club in 1906. Here, north of the Coventry road as far as the railway to Adderley Park station, was a vast area of clay pits, next to which lived the brickies who made many of the bricks from which the city was built. They were said to be the only Birmingham workers to get into violent disputes with their employers. In the middle years of the nineteenth century, the trade employed women and children, although this changed with the Acts of 1867 and 1871. By the 1880s, women were no longer employed, the children went to the Garrison Lane Board School and Garrison Lane had its sloggers. The best-off, by 1889, were living in 'neat little bay-windowed houses' in streets radiating from Garrison Lane, but many still lived in a shanty town of homes clustered round the brickworks. These were single-storey huts or hovels, built by 'bedouin brickies' of any variety of bricks available, with switch-back roofs, crazily-leaning chimneys and glass windows riddled with holes caused by 'bulls' eyes'. All had custom-built pigstyes and gardens, with little shelters where their occupants sat smoking and consuming huge flagons of beer on Sundays in summer, and sometimes knocking each other out afterwards.

The men were employed in gangs or teams, often of casual labour. The most itinerant did not even have a hut, but coiled up near the kilns at night, careful not to get too close to avoid being found a charred corpse in the morning. These men caught birds and rabbits which they wrapped in balls of clay and then dropped into the kiln fire. When baked the shell was broken and inside was a cooked supper. The area was sufficiently remote for cock-fighting to go unobserved by the law. Brickies were said to be 'notorious fowl stealers' from chicken runs in the suburbs, but this form of urban poaching was not confined to them.

Certain meeting and fighting places became trouble spots. One was Cape Hill, across the boundary between Birmingham in Warwickshire and Smethwick in Staffordshire. Here the Cape of Good Hope Inn attracted criminals from both directions, thinking that they were beyond the reach of the law. There were various gangs called the Forty Thieves. One was based in Smethwick, another in Spring Hill, Birmingham. Highway robbery was much complained of on both sides of the borough boundary. Many of the youngsters concerned were ironworkers, who regarded themselves as particularly tough and inflicted malicious damage on their rivals' equipment. They were strongly territorial. In June 1872, three ladies happened to walk through a neighbouring field, past about twenty youths – mainly ironworkers – who were using 'filthy and indecent language'. The ladies stopped to share their indignation with a Smethwick 'gentleman' called Brown who unwisely went and told off the young men. They gave out more foul language and then followed Mr Brown, felled, kicked and robbed him.

EDWIN CHADWICK in 1845 described Birmingham's houses as 'small and of poor construction'. Most of the population lived in the courts, or yards, which lay behind every main street, approached through a narrow entry, the in-filling of gardens by nineteenth-century builders. Shared facilities such as washhouse and privy created common bonds between court-dwellers, but also led to arguments. In these courtyard homes and workshops, coal fires blazed at all times of the year. Many saved the cost of a chimney sweep by 'firing' their chimneys on a Sunday morning, preferably a foggy one – a breach of the law that was both a fire hazard and added soot to the atmosphere.

Overcrowding was the cause of Birmingham's main health problems in the mid-1860s, although the town's death rates were lower than in London, Manchester or Liverpool. Housing conditions were no better by 1875 when Joseph Chamberlain, the Liberal Mayor of Birmingham who would later have a career as a politician on the national stage, described, in lurid language to a conference of civic authorities, how criminals returned home from comparatively spacious and airy prisons to places where the air 'is contaminated by unmentionable impurities and filth. Hardly a gleam of sunshine ever comes into the dark and dreary courts. The dead and the living lie together in the same room for days.'

In view of the town's wealth and constant expansion, it was surprising what a poor state much of the older housing was in. Councillor William White, chairman of the new improvement committee, denounced the 'bowing roofs, tottering chimneys, tumbledown and often disused shopping [lean-to workshops], heaps of bricks, broken windows and coarse, rough pavements, damp and sloping'. In one house, 'the fireside of the only sitting room had to be deserted, owing to the noxious percolation from a privy penetrating the wall within a foot or two of the easy chair'. The moral effects of such conditions were not lost on the Victorians. No doubt Chamberlain was thinking of the violence on the streets, the magistrates' panic reactions, and public demands for more flogging, as he added, 'And when these people whom we have suffered to grow up like beasts behave like brutes, we rush to the Home Secretary in a blind paroxysm of terror and ask him to give us the humanising influence of "the lash."'

CHAPTER 4

Youth Gangs

BY 1870, A NEW generation was facing a new pattern of living. In Birmingham's workshop culture, many children would have helped their parents at work from as young as three or four right through their teens. Now school was breaking into this pattern and postponing work until the age of eleven or twelve, although not breaking the link with the family and the workshop or industry, whether gun, iron, or brass. More than half of Birmingham children would attend board schools by the 1880s. However their playgrounds were cramped yards with no trees and had a prison-like appearance behind their railings.

For many, the street was their home from an early age. As early as 1845, the *Birmingham Journal* had expressed concern about the large number of 'juvenile outcasts ...brought before the Magistrates by the police, and charged with sleeping in the open air on door steps, or perhaps in out-offices attached to dwelling-houses, with intent or on suspicion of committing a felony'. Those were the children of the street described as 'nobody's' or 'gutter' children. They were likely to be picked up by policemen or philanthropists to save them from people with less worthy intent. By the 1870s, there was a regular export of such children from Birmingham to Canada, where farmers were glad to receive free labour. This scheme developed into the Middlemore Emigration Homes.

Some philanthropists, like the Quaker Joseph Sturge, took a more enlightened view of child criminality. In mid-century, influenced by James Cropper and Mary Carpenter, Sturge set up his own reformatory in three cottages in Ryland Road and brought in John Ellis, a ragged-school teacher from London, to take charge. Sturge asked a police superintendent for 'some of the worst boys you have in Birmingham', and eleven were sent from the gaol. The experiment was deemed a success, and, with the help of the local landowner, Charles Adderley, two larger settlements were set up at Saltley and at Stoke Prior, where Sturge bought seventy-five acres, sixteen miles into rural Worcestershire, as a farm school for delinquent boys. There was space for fifty boys after enlarging the farmhouse and equipping it with dormitories, a schoolroom and workshops. On the staff was a superintendent, a schoolmaster, a labourer and a female housekeeper. It was one of the first seven reformatories certificated under the Act of 1854. The boys were set to manual tasks. The first inspector was impressed by the cleanliness, good order and spirit of industry, but criticised the food as 'too indulgent' and the boys as 'too rough and independent'. Sturge's Quaker conscience would not allow disciplinary cells or flogging; his concern was for reform, not punishment. Staff ate with the prisoners and there were treats such as railway excursions.

The treatment of children in prisons was very different. At Birmingham Gaol, Winson Green, Governor Maconochie had been dismissed for trying to modify the 'separate system', a form of punishment involving solitary confinement and labour on machines called cranks. The next Governor, Lieutenant Austin, had introduced a reign of 'pain and terror', used as material for Charles Reade's novel *It Is Never Too Late To Mend*, where the separate system continued and offending boys were strapped to the walls in strait-jackets and collars. Several incidents of suicide came to public knowledge and created a scandal about the regime in 1853.

Even after some reforms, the Warwickshire magistrates were still concerned that young children were treated just like adults in ordinary prisons. In January 1874, Stipendiary Kynnersley confessed to being shocked at finding a little child in the corner of Warwick Gaol, crying for his 'mammy'. Lord Leigh agreed and pointed out that children were sent to prison for sleeping under hedges, often because they were driven from home by their father's cruelty. In the same discussion the recently-knighted Sir Charles Adderley, the man who had helped Sturge but had also brought back flogging for violent highway robbery, thought that some child criminals, such as a juvenile gang leader called 'Captain Lewis', needed a good birching. However, as Kynnersley knew only too well, magistrates could only have the under-fourteens flogged if they were sent to gaol. Many thought that reformatory schools were the answer. Yet again many Birmingham children sentenced to prison were too young for reformatory school, being under ten years of age, such as beggars or those destitute because of criminal parents. The alternatives were local or convict prison.

One visiting magistrate reported of Winson Green Prison in 1877 that he did not think it was right that a boy 'should be strapped to two wooden posts, with a crowd of men round him and a strong man to give him a severe whipping', even if of only three or six strokes. By then there was much debate over flogging or imprisonment. Some preferred a week in prison to this birching, which Sam Timmins, himself a magistrate and an expert on social conditions, called a 'revolting punishment': the birch rod raised purple weals and even blood, if twelve strokes was the sentence. The gaol surgeon assured the justices that there was no permanent injury to the boys, but neither did the justices see any signs of a deterrent in the statistics they were shown.

Hard labour was delivered through the system of cranks and tread-mills. Although at least one crank was used for pumping water at Birmingham Prison in 1869, it was reported that on the whole the cranks and treadmill there continued to serve no other useful purpose than to provide the hard labour to which roughs were invariably sentenced. They might be expected to complete ten thousand or more turns of the crank handle in a single day in the 1870s. The alternative was stone-breaking or, for women, oakum-picking. Hundreds of sloggers would find themselves sentenced to such hard labour.

Many children on the verge of criminality, whose homes were described as 'depraved' or 'degraded' by charities such as Home Missions, begged in the streets. They spent the money, like adult beggars, on alcohol to deaden the sharpness of reality. Acrobatics and somersaults around horse-drawn omnibuses encouraged passengers to throw out coins in appreciation. If the tram conductor tried to stop them, he or his passengers might be hit by a stone. The advent of steam trams in the 1880s led to a spate of accidents in which children were injured or killed. The Watch Committee was concerned that urchins would cling to the back of tramcars and other vehicles and then jump off in the path of another moving vehicle. Many children became hawkers, some sent out by their parents with nothing to sell, effectively having to beg or starve. One boy, arrested for shouting his wares – perhaps evening newspapers – was told that it was illegal to shout in the streets. He asked if he could shout up the yards. The magistrates' clerk replied coldly, 'I dare say there are means of evading the law. I can't advise you.'

Street corners could be essential to making a living. Stephenson Place, outside New Street station, was constantly obstructed by boy shoeblacks, who tried to make a living by pestering passers-by in the hope of earning a few pence by cleaning their boots. The police saw them as a 'gang' breaking the law and occasionally fined or imprisoned them. At the Pinfold Street entrance to the station, another gang of boys annoyed passengers 'by clamorously asking to carry their luggage'. On company property they could be arrested by the railway police.

The police had strict instructions to arrest those who used the streets as a playground. Young people from very poor downtown areas could not afford fines for playing games such as bandy and tipcat – respectively throwing a ball to and fro, and hitting a pointed piece of wood with a stick or bat – or football in the street and went to prison instead. Yet there were few alternative playgrounds. The town's graveyards were amongst the few open spaces, but they were in a poor state, neglected and full to bursting with corpses. They still made exciting places for games, fights and gambling. St Martin's burial ground in Park Street had been split into two parts by the railway and abandoned as a last resting-place by better-off 'clients'. It had become the 'black spot' of the town. Most of the graves had been flattened and the headstones broken or thrown down. There was no grass, and any trees had been cut up for firewood. The iron railings had been taken for cash to the marine store dealer or used as weapons in street fights. Only the mutilated gates were left, probably because they were locked together.

In the summer, bathing in one of the canals which encircled the town centre was popular, in spite of the colour and stench of the liquid which passed as water. Irresistible in hot weather, bathing in a canal could still incur a fine for a teenager or, in default, a short term in prison. Few could swim before the development of the public baths. The result was occasionally fatal, as in the case of Samuel Earp, a sixteen-year-old who, in a crowd of boys from all over the town, was shoved into the canal at Fazeley Street, pushed about, deluged with mud and drowned, in spite of last-minute efforts to rescue him. The coroner's verdict was one of wilful murder, but the magistrates reduced the charge to manslaughter. At the Warwickshire Winter Assizes in 1874, a boy of the same age as his victim, called Sullivan, was found guilty. His history was said also to be 'very sad'. He had been sent to an industrial school at the age of nine, but this had done little for him and he had a conviction for street gambling. However, the prison officers were impressed by his behaviour while awaiting trial and he received a reduced sentence of a month's imprisonment, followed by five years in a reformatory school.

Birmingham's parks came later than in some Victorian towns and were small and overcrowded. The exception was Aston Lower Grounds, close to Witton Station, which provided a variety of entertainment from the 1860s and became very popular, especially after a theatre was added in 1879. More typical was Cannon Hill Park in Edgbaston, given by Miss Ryland in 1873, the 'misuse' of which moved one middle class owner of a villa overlooking it to complain to the *Post*. On a warm summer Sunday afternoon, from his window, he watched 'men run about the fields adjoining the river Rea quite naked and pelt anybody with stones who happens to interfere with them'. He could also see a dozen 'blackguards' chasing tame rabbits with dogs, while some were holding a 'regular stand-up' fight and others were playing cricket. An apple cart formed a stall just opposite his window and he had to 'order it off … amidst the jeers of the roughs'. Later another 'gang of black-guards' pelted each other with cow dung and swore. So downtown 'Brummies' were enjoying themselves in the ways they liked best, even if the elite in leafy Edgbaston was horrified. Chief Superintendent Glossop informed the committee that in fact the park was outside the borough and so technically beyond the committee's jurisdiction. Also, in his view, people were 'pretty well behaved'. However, in answer to the complaints, he put extra police there at weekends and suppressed the bathing. In this way parks became another no-go area for the young, unless they were under the supervision of nannies or other adults.

Another newspaper reader expressed an unusual sympathy for all these 'roughs' at play, who for over five days a week were treated as reliable 'mechanics' and 'artisans' at work. They had increased leisure on their hands, with very few opportunities to spend it anywhere than in the pub or on the streets. It was hardly surprising that, when released from some of the 'dismal dens called workshops', naturally full of 'animal spirits', they should start playing in the streets, grow resentful of the 'policeman's belt across their shoulders' and end up, after a row, in the police court. If Manchester and other parts of Lancashire could provide places for sports, why couldn't Birmingham? A positive response was slow in coming.

In the evenings and at the weekends, the streets were crowded with those enjoying their leisure. Saturday evening was the time when everyone was out. For the working class, it was shopping time and an evening for 'walking out', in New Street or Summer Lane, for shop-boys and factory girls. It was also a night for heavy drinking, which easily led to disorder. The prostitutes were also out in force especially in New Street. An anonymous observer described how, as the night drew on, they plied their degrading trade 'with despairing vigour, stopping the passers-by, laughing and shouting; some of them well-dressed and quiet; others shabby, dirty, painted, powdered and noisy.' Gangs also banded together and paraded. One boy, said to be 'one of the principals' in just such a gang, was sentenced to one month in prison for an unprovoked attack on another boy as they paraded on a Saturday night, in Broad Street, and the magistrate told him to pass on to others the message that the Bench was determined to stop 'the disgraceful ruffianism in the streets'.

Sunday evening was more of a chance for both sexes to eye each other up, link arms and jostle one another in a ritual sometimes called the monkey parade. It took place in New and Broad Streets for the many who lived near the town centre. Respectable people found themselves jostled into the shutters or the gutter and the better-off preferred to promenade in the Hagley Road, further out of town into Edgbaston. New Street habits soon spilled into the suburbs. An inhabitant of Clifton Road, Balsall Heath, in 1880 was reporting 'fellows' marching up and down on Sunday evenings 'insulting and assaulting every female who passes'. Hamstead and Birchfield Roads became popular with those who lived in Handsworth and Lozells, and the police were equally in evidence. In Aston, several thousand attended the entertainments at the Lower Gounds, where young men and women were observed daringly, in the free gallery, 'with their arms around each others' waists and necks'.

By 1900, the causes for Sunday complaints from the suburbs ranged from blazing away with guns 'at anything and everything'by 'gangs of hobbledehoys'[4] in Bearwood Hill Park to playing football on private property in Sparkbrook and breaking workmen's huts and road-making equipment at Gravelly Hill. Even in Edgbaston, Birmingham's 'West End', girls and boys were going up and down Calthorpe and St James's Roads using 'hooters' and reportedly making 'disgusting' noises. Youths also went around in large groups on week nights, partly for safety and partly because this was a young city. Their ways of entertaining themselves were not appreciated. A New Street tradesman complained in 1860 of a 'gang of fast fellows who nightly parade about doing all kinds of mischief', especially lighting their short clay pipes by striking their lucifer matches on his window panes, and scratching his glass. Such gangs would pick on and attack individuals and others of their own age who they came across as they moved about. The two hours before 9 p.m., between the

---

4 Hobbledehoy is thought to have Tudor origins and meant an untamed clown.

end of the day shift of police duty and the beginning of the night one, were said to be the worst.

Apart from Christmas, when gangs of boys and girls were reputed to go down otherwise quiet roads 'yelling or roaring carols', and New Year, Bonfire Night was the biggest celebration of the year. In spite of the carefree spirit of that night, health and safety regulations had made a tentative beginning. In 1873, eight shopkeepers were fined for selling fireworks to children under sixteen under the Gunpowder Act. Pistols were often let off as part of the 5 November festivities, with the inevitable consequences. The search for wood was ruthless. Empty houses were broken into and stripped of doors and cupboards, as more than one landlord complained to the police. It was a night for excess. In 1876, five young men were arrested for invading the house of a man in Chester Street, terrifying his family by letting off squibs and other fireworks, one of which set fire to a child's dress, entering his brewhouse and smashing plates and dishes. They told the Bench that they 'only did it for a lark' and were ordered to compensate for the damage.

GANGS OR close-knit groups outside the family circle were an important part of socialisation, necessary for companionship, learning and sometimes safety. Sometimes 'gang' meant only a loose group or collection of pals, at other times a tight knot of criminals; so it was a word with a highly flexible degree of meaning. Gangs provided entertainment and the means to obtaining it, for this was a society in which money was essential. For many, cash was obtained by hard work from an early age. For others, crime provided what was necessary for survival.

Mid-Victorian Birmingham, like other towns, was full of gangs of juvenile beggars and thieves. Coal stealing was a way of keeping a fire going and slack was easily picked up from the canal banks or dived for from the canal bottom. One little lad called Moses Palmer was described as the 'king' of a small host of coal-stealers and racked up dozens of offences. Some formed gangs of burglars. George Bird, aged fifteen, from Nineveh, though only small was well known as the 'captain' of a gang of burglars operating in Balsall Heath in 1859. They robbed the brewhouses and took the brass handles off gentlemen's doors. They slept in pigstyes and under hedges. No wonder as he left the sessions court that he appeared merely a 'tattered and neglected outcast'.

Gangs of juvenile shoplifters went in search of things to eat, smoke or pawn. One gang of ten boys aged between ten and seventeen crept about High Street in central Birmingham, barefoot – even if they could afford boots – to reduce the noise, breaking the side windows of shops with a hammer, carefully striking near the woodwork to deaden the sound. They stole a variety of food and clothing. Gangs of children swarmed around small shopkeepers, who often found they provided more aggravation than custom. Sometimes a shop's wares, especially fruit and potatoes, were thrown about the premises by a group of young people, either as a tease or from a grudge.

Big gangs were the ones most easily broken up. One gang of eight boys aged between thirteen and sixteen was soon exposed when one youth reckoned that he had been 'rounded on' or informed on by the others and so in his turn rounded or 'dogged on' others. Another boy rounded because he was angry that he had not received his share of the money raised from pawning some boots stolen in Navigation Street.

Older boys were often ready to combine personal violence with thieving. Three hotel ostlers were walking down Dale End when they were confronted by a gang and a fight ensued. William Edgerton from the Union Hotel was knocked down and kicked by a young grinder called Fox from Dartmouth Street, while the others urged him to 'gouge his eyes out'. In the scuffle one of the ostlers lost his watch. The Bench concluded that Fox was acting with thieves and sentenced him to two months' hard labour. If they were known to the victim, detectives would follow up the suspects and they would be committed to the assizes. Highway robbery with violence might evoke the exploits of Claude Duval and Dick Turpin for youths, but the law was now calling this garrotting and brought in the 'cat' to deal with it (see Chapter 9).

Juveniles were quick to take advantage of younger children. Often it was money they wanted, as when a Digbeth gang of fifteen-year-olds was stopped in Hob Lane for house-breaking and for demanding money at knifepoint from a girl on her way to school. In a letter to the *Mail*, the father of a ten-year-old boy who had been struck on the head with a buckled belt for not letting a gang pilfer goods from a shop, protested that even the '"Kentucky regulators" showed more mercy than the street ruffians of Birmingham'. (The regulators were a band of gunmen who roamed Kentucky shooting pro-Unionists in the after-math of the U.S. Civil War.) As the *Mail* newspaper grew in popularity in the early 1870s, the children who sold it around the streets were also a target not only of middle-class critics, but also of older children. One

January night in 1874, a fourteen-year-old tubemaker with a dozen other lads stopped one such little hawker in Digbeth, and while the leader put his hand over his mouth, the others stole the twenty-two copies of the *Mail* that he was carrying.

Rape was a recurring offence by young men in groups. One unfortunate victim was Clara Burke who, one night, was being escorted back to her home in Saltley, when she passed a group of ten young men who had just emerged from a pub in a quiet area near St Saviour's church. Her escort was the station master at Adderley Park station, who, after being attacked twice, unwisely abandoned Clara to go to get help. By the time he and his brother had returned armed with a poker and a child's sword, she had been raped and the men had run off. The men concerned were arrested and taken to the assizes. The victim declared that she had had no improper intimacy with any man beforehand and a nineteen-year-old was sent to prison for twelve years' penal servitude.

Yet juvenile crime, according to statistics, was in decline by the 1870s, and Sir Charles Reed, the chairman of the London School Board, was boasting that his Board, with over three hundred schools, had 'broken up every organised gang of boy thieves in London and that juvenile thieves as a class were fast disappearing'. In 1873, the editor of the *Post,* John Thackray Bunce, heard that a Liverpool theatre manager was employing real gipsies in a play. With a less triumphalist attitude than London's Sir Charles, Bunce announced, only half-jokingly, that Birmingham could offer eight hundred 'known thieves' for the parts of Fagin, Nancy and the Dodger and many others in any dramatisation that might be planned of Dickens' *Oliver Twist.*

The young, like their elders, had a passion for betting. Birmingham was said to have a reputation, probably exaggerated, for more betting than anywhere outside London. The streets attracted card-sharps or swindlers anxious to defraud younger men of their money. Youths who had some loose cash often played at pitch and toss, in which any number of players tossed copper coins against a wall to see whose could get closest, with the winner taking all. There was a large vacant space – a rarity near the centre of Birmingham – at Deritend Pool, or canal basin, off Fazeley Street, where pitch and toss was played with such passion in March 1859 that a detective who intervened had his jaw broken. Pitch and toss could often attract a crowd, especially on a Sunday, when most people were seeking relaxation and entertainment. Sometimes a policeman just heard some words in a crowd, such as 'head's a tanner' or 'head's a bob', and moved in. Near Moor Street station, there were complaints of 'crowds' of betting men supposedly taking advantage of clerks and shop assistants in their dinner breaks.

Some confectioners or provision shops provided what seemed a safer place for gambling than the street. At one such shop, 'billy' was played, in which a marble was rolled on a board bearing small numbered hollows. While the children staked money on getting the highest number, the shopkeeper would stake toffee or sweets. At another refreshment house at Gosta Green, boys diced for 'wet 'uns' (ice creams) or 'dry 'uns' (money). The Italian proprietor came into the room every few minutes, and, as one young customer explained, 'If you hadn't got no money he would throw you out.'

Gangs or groups of boys might adopt a pub or beerhouse for drinking and gambling. This happened to the Highland Laddie beerhouse in Park Street. Park Street, though close to the Police Court, was infamous for its poverty, rows and crime. One licensee of that beerhouse lost his licence in 1874 for infringing the new opening hours. The house was regarded as the den of a group of young brassworkers who passed their time gambling there illegally with the connivance of the landlord. In 1875, the new landlord, Joseph Haynes, a thirty-year-old former bedstead fitter from Bristol and his wife, Emily, told the magistrates how they had changed the policy and tried to 'go respectable' by expelling the boys and summonsing some of the most troublesome to keep the peace. In retaliation, the boys and their friends came back and smashed all the beerhouse windows with stones and brickends. Several constables were needed to restore order. Four youths were fined forty shillings and costs and the youngest, a chandelier maker, aged fourteen, was sent straight to gaol for fourteen days.

Unfortunately for the Hayneses, these prosecutions of youths alienated their older neighbours as well. A few weeks after the attack, a Park Street labourer called James Davitt was drinking in the pub one Thursday night. Seeing the landlady give some coppers in charity to an itinerant blind fifer (flute-player) who had just come in, he went over and took the money off him. The landlady protested, so Davitt drew a strap and buckle from his pocket and hit her so hard that she collapsed unconscious. He was later arrested on the evidence of the servant girl who had been watching, and whom he threatened to 'settle' when he came out of prison. Davitt admitted being drunk that night, but said that he had only thrown a stone. The magistrate was not impressed, and he was given the maximum sentence of six months' hard labour and was bound over to keep the peace when released or serve another month.

Joseph Haynes was thanked by the Bench for trying to keep his house respectable. However, this was not the sum total of his troubles, for two days later he was back in court prosecuting James Davitt's younger brother, Martin, a brushmaker of Digbeth. On the night after his brother had been sent to prison, Martin Davitt went along Park Street, saw the landlord standing at his door and cut him with a 'pop' bottle, before knocking him down and kicking him. Then his wife, Ellen Davitt, drew a knife and tried to stab Haynes. A witness called Thompson stepped in to help to stop her. He told the court, 'If they offered me half a million of money I would not accept [Haynes'] situation. He is not safe for a moment.' Haynes added that there were as many as four Davitt brothers who were constantly threatening him and putting him in fear of his life. There were indeed four Davitts. All four had been arrested for drunk and disorderly behaviour at the King's Head, Digbeth, the year before, and it had taken four policemen to take them into custody. At that stage they had an average of over twenty appearances each before the Bench, and Thomas and Martin had been sentenced to six months' hard labour. This time Martin received another six months and his wife got two months. These sentences hardly cleared the air for the landlord of the Highland Laddie.

The beerhouse keeper's policy had alienated the local roughs as well as his younger customers. Haynes' remaining clientele abandoned him. Five weeks after the Bench's commendation of his actions, he was declared bankrupt with debts of £217. He too had to transfer the licence to another publican and went back to the metal trades. Moral rectitude in Park Street seemed a lost cause.

WITH FEW alternatives, the street corner was the obvious place for people of all ages to gather, especially the young. Being neither in one street or another, it had a neutrality which was attractive to those who wished to observe the wider world beyond their own space or turf. It was also the site for corner shops and pubs, which provided a little more room on the pedestrian pavement and from which something new might always emerge, so it was a place for news, exchange and surprises. Groups tended to claim possession, with obstruction, dancing and sparring. Individuals might be picked on by a gang of such people, often apparently at random. Revenge was sometimes the motive, especially if someone gave evidence in court which led to a long gaol sentence and gained him or her the reputation of being 'a copper'. One lodging-house keeper in Thomas Street was knocked down and kicked near his own front door by a gang headed by an eighteen-year-old metal roller only just out of gaol. A similar act of revenge was wrought on a gun-implement maker in Sand Street in the Gun Quarter when a gang of roughs smashed four panes of his glass and some wooden shutters after a prosecution in the police court. In another case, a shell-fish hawker was assaulted and robbed outside the Gem public house in Steelhouse Lane for 'lagging' a man sentenced to penal servitude at the Warwick Assizes.

A similar case of assault started when a watch went missing outside the warehouse of Messrs Frazers', fender and iron manufacturers, in Highgate. A fire-iron forger, Timothy Gold, who was the uncle of the young man who had lost his watch, reported it to the police. That evening he went for a drink at the Vaughton Arms nearby. Shortly afterwards, seven men came in and started shouting at him for having gone to the police about the watch. Five men offered to fight him, so he drank up his beer and prepared to leave. Then one of them, Samuel Warrilow, hit him in the mouth, and three others, all fire-iron makers from Dartmouth and Garbett Streets, rushed at him. He was kicked and knocked unconscious by them. They knocked his brother down too, but finally allowed him to pick up Gold and take him home and then back to the police station to identify Warrilow. The next day Gold went to the Queen's Hospital where he was kept for eight days. He came out, but was soon back in hospital with a dangerously swollen thigh and was in a sufficiently critical state to have to make depositions about the incident, in case he did not survive. By staying in hospital another six weeks, he avoided having to have his leg amputated, but was still on crutches another four weeks later when he appeared to give evidence at the sessions. His chief attacker received five years' penal servitude.

To fall out with the street group or gang, for any reason, might lead to serious trouble. Thomas Russell was a sixty-one-year-old warehouseman put on trial in August 1879 for knifing Caroline Brooks, a nineteen-year-old electro-plater, in Fleet Street, not far from where she lived. At first her wound was not thought too serious, but the charge changed to murder when she died twelve days later of pneumonia resulting from the damage to her lungs. The evidence against Russell at first seemed overwhelming. He had been in the street that Saturday night in June collecting instalments for the clothing he sold. In court, one of his customers, Ann

Gourley had a sinister recollection of him in the poor light of a street lamp, 'feeling for the number on her door'. She went on to accuse him of threatening to 'chivvy'[5] somebody in the street that night. Later she had seen him and the deceased together. Caroline Brooks had put up her arm, called out 'Oh' and then fell. Mrs Gourley said she saw the blood flow from under her arm, and so she called out, 'Oh, he has stabbed her!' Then, she said, Russell ran away and a crowd of boys and men came up.

Caroline's 'young man', William Bruton, gave evidence that he had been walking with her when the mystery man came up and stabbed her. He had followed him as he ran away, but had lost sight of him. Then Russell was stopped in Summer Lane. Bruton's vision was defective in one eye, but he said that he could see very well with the other. The third prosecution witness, called Hubble, had seen Ann Gourley 'hooting and quarrelling' and confirmed her evidence. He claimed that Russell had a knife in his hand: 'I saw the knife as I ran by the lamp'. However when the judge questioned him again, he said he had only seen something shine that 'looked like a knife'. P.C. Pittaway, on duty at the time, had noticed that Russell, who had been shouting 'Police!' had been very much 'knocked about' by the crowd as they pursued him up the street. Russell was sober and denied stabbing anyone, but resisted going to the police station. On the way there he was struck twice by 'some persons in the crowd'. He had no knife on him. Russell told the policeman that his clasp-knife was in his desk at home as indeed it proved to be.

Russell felt himself to be 'a ruined man' after hearing the allegations of Gourley, Hubble and Bruton. However, if he had enemies, he also had friends. A clothier of Great Hampton Street had known him for twenty years and bought clothes from him. Russell had once told him that he never carried a knife on a Saturday when he was 'collecting'. Several other people gave him a good character reference. One of them was a woman who saw Ann Gourley follow Russell up the street and said, 'Thomas Hubble beat him about the head with his buckle.' When cross-examined, she maintained that Gourley had not gone far enough up the street to have seen the stabbing. According to another key witness, Gourley had followed Russell, 'blackguarding' him and then grabbing him by the collar and calling him a ' – tinker', but he just took no notice, walking

---

5 Chive, chivy or chivvy were variations of a word meaning attack, perhaps with a knife or strap. It had its origin in a hunting cry, perhaps deriving from the *Ballad of Chevy Chase*, describing a battle between the Percies and the Douglases in the Scottish Borders.

away from her fast. She then called 'Stop him' in a loud voice and a lot of boys came up from the canal and mobbed him. There were about fourteen of these fifteen or sixteen year-olds and they knocked him about and beat him with their buckles. Mr Justice Thesiger said later that it was clear from this evidence that Mrs Gourley's cry of 'Stop him' had been uttered before the stabbing occurred. The prosecution case collapsed and Russell was finally discharged as the victim of mistaken identity.

But for his friends, Russell, a newcomer to the town who did not live in the street, might have been found guilty of manslaughter, even murder, because of prosecution allegations and the 'deadly fear of the gang in Fleet Street'. A widowed witness admitted to being scared of the boys as 'a dangerous lot'. Such was the power of the street-group and the lengths to which victimization of a frequently unpopular figure such as a tallyman could go. One of Russell's supporters was obliged to 'bleed freely', or pay money, for agents to find witnesses to testify on his behalf, and two other gentlemen had paid his legal expenses. Russell knew that he had had a lucky escape. It was never established who killed Caroline Brooks.

Fleet Street had a bad reputation for its roughs, and the Watch Committee had noted a serious disturbance there five years before the Russell case. Many other streets could be said to have their own gang of young men, boys and others who were a potential threat to a suspected murderer like Russell, a stranger passing through, a 'copper' whose evidence had put someone behind bars or a bobby making an arrest. They also spelled danger to any passing stranger or weak-looking lad, and were notorious for their coarse insults to the old or to women. Parading on fine evenings, throwing stones, challenging and taking offence, such groups would easily develop into the slogging gangs of the 1870s.

CHAPTER 5

The Origins of Slogging

SLOGGING, OR SLUGGING, is a common word which once had special local connotations. The nickname 'Slogger' was often given to prizefighters, and received wide currency in Thomas Hughes' popular novel *Tom Brown's Schooldays*, first published in 1857, with its character Slogger Williams, a hard-punching lad who was quick to use his fists. Slogging had two traditional meanings in the West Midlands: it described the heavy battering administered and received in prize-fights, and it was an old Birmingham term for the merciless stoning of passers-by, with or without cause. Both of these meanings were eventually mixed together to describe the wild young gangs that emerged in the city in the 1870s and whose pitched battles would terrify the populace for the next thirty years. These sloggers were both stone-throwers and fighters, wielding heavy belt buckles and knives in toe-to-toe encounters.

Stone-throwing was something of a Birmingham tradition and was much complained of in the latter half of the nineteenth century. Windows and street lamps were targets, as were railway carriages. An inhabitant of Victoria Road in Aston complained in April 1864 that 'nearly all the day, gangs of ruffians from sixteen to twenty years of age, prowl about, swearing, gambling, stone-throwing and damaging property'. Such mischief could become deadly, as when four boys under fifteen stoned a horse to death in a field in Moseley. A contributing factor was that the Birmingham streets provided plenty of ammunition. Upturned road stones, described as 'petrified kidneys', sharp-pointed like 'parched peas' under foot, were a local joke. Originally rammed home by steam paving-engines, at least in the main streets, many of them became loose and were easily uprooted. New road surfaces made of stone 'Rowley setts' or vitrified blue bricks were slowly introduced after 1870. For years, courts and yards remained rough and coated with a layer of thick, black, greasy mud, which spread into the streets in times of flood. New areas like the lower parts of Highgate were at first not paved or drained and became hotbeds of disease as well as slogging.

Random vandalism could be extensive. A group of ten youths smashed nearly one hundred windows on a Sunday morning rampage through Highgate and Sparkbrook. More common was the use of other people's front doors for target practice, especially on Sunday evenings – sometimes not accidentally chosen but as a form of summons to a rival gang. But worst of all was the random violence against groups of people. Boys frequently stoned pedestrians coming in and out of New Street railway station, or a crowd gathered to watch a street spectacle, such as a fire, or even 'respectable' people going to and from church on Sunday.

For the young, their world was the streets of their town. It was there that they could seek reprisal for perceived injustices in their often harsh working lives. Often this involved attacks against employers, or folk villains such as bailiffs and policemen. Churches were sometimes the target, perhaps with an element of grievance against a man of the cloth or one of his minions. An eleven-year-old admitted to being one of a gang of boys who purposely broke forty-five window panes in St Stephen's, Newtown Row. He was let off with a caution and was taken to the lock-up to be shown the 'horse', on which he would be whipped if he were caught again.

Bailiffs were familiar figures, confiscating the few belongings still possessed by debtors and bankrupts. They were highly unpopular and referred to as 'bums'. Youths who lobbed stones at them thought of themselves as instruments of communal vengeance. In Farm Street, two young pearl-button makers went to the aid of a mechanic and his wife who had been given an hour by the bailiffs to raise twelve shillings and sevenpence or face the distraint of their furniture. When the time was up and the bailiffs started loading the furniture, the two young men collected a crowd of about sixty bystanders, who pelted the bailiffs with brickbats, threw pearl dust over them and damaged the furniture. And in Allison Street, Digbeth, a gang of boys filled their pockets from a nearby heap of Rowley rag stones and showered them on the court officers. When one of the youths was put in a police van, his mates surrounded it and attempted a rescue. He shouted to them that he could escape if only one of them could get hold of the horse's head. However the van moved away just in time.

Stone-throwing against the police had become a major problem. The year 1868 saw a peak of assaults on the police, and the following year it was complained to the Watch Committee that the police were finding it hard to control Saturday night disorders in the area of Thomas, John and Chapel Streets, where the roughs were hurling street paving stones at them; the public works committee was asked to have these paving stones removed as soon as possible. In Lancaster Street, by the Gun Quarter, Saturday night stone-throwing could easily be turned against any police officers who came to investigate. It was common for them to arrest the wrong man from a 'gang of about a hundred rough youths' and then cause a sense of grievance. Stones might also be used to attempt a rescue. John Holborn, aged eighteen, was being held in a greengrocer's shop for abusing a policeman after failing to disperse and dancing 'a double shuffle 'round him. He called out to the others the words frequently heard in such confrontations: 'Now lads, loose them at him, don't see a mate taken.' They tried, but Holborn remained in custody. Stones might give law-breakers time. One businessman noticed a group of young employees from the gasworks and metal firms at the bottom of Gas Street, near the main canal basin, playing cards for halfpence, each with his pile of stones, ready to pelt any 'disturbers of their peace', presumably policemen.

Not everyone was a passive target. Canal boatmen, for instance, were usually capable of vigorous self-defence. One July afternoon, some schoolboys fired stones from the Dudley Road over Lee Bridge as canal boats went underneath. Fifteen-year-old John Connor perhaps had too good an aim, for another boy heard a boatman passing underneath say, 'I'll blow his brains out,' and when Connor next appeared at the parapet, the boatman, William Boswell of Braunston, Northamptonshire, was ready for him and fired back with a gun loaded with small shot. No doubt this was normally used for shooting rabbits, but it had a devastating effect on Connor. He was taken to the Workhouse Hospital, which was nearest, and then transferred to the Queen's, the teaching hospital where the surgeon had more skill. He was found to have two pieces of shot in his nose, two in his forehead, one in an ear and one in an eye. Boswell was arrested at the Smethwick Stop, where a crowd had collected and tried to duck him in the canal before he was arrested. In court he complained that he had been the victim of stone-throwing for over seven years, from children aged as young as six up to eighteen. The prosecution was abandoned after he had paid compensation to the boy's parents.

*

FROM THE late 1860s, the new evening newspapers began to report juvenile gang activities. Reports in the *Mail* tell of how a gang of roughs from one street would take on a gang from another. One of the first such confrontations reported was on a Wednesday evening in April 1870. A group of twenty to thirty youths, shouting and swearing, armed with sticks and stones and led by two seventeen-year-old fender moulders, were accosted by a policeman. They came from Barford and Bissell Streets in St Martin's, just south of the town centre, and told him that they were going to fight a gang of the Sun Street boys, from the other side of Bristol Street, with whom they had clashed the night before. Their rendezvous was to be in Benacre Street. The local residents kept in their houses behind closed shutters as the boys marched up and down several streets like soldiers and the police had to double the beat to keep the factions apart. The two supposed leaders were fined the large sum of twenty shillings each.

Some street encounters were miniature riots, and were described as 'sham fights'. This term, said to have been used by the sloggers about their Sunday skirmishes in the early 1870s, may have been copied from a military term first used by the loyal volunteers for their exercises in the Napoleonic Wars, and the term was readopted by the rifleman volunteer movement of the 1860s. Sham fights may have taken place on the streets previously – the Franco-Prussian War of 1870–1 was an obvious source of inspiration – but it was not until 1872 that the phenomenon began to attract attention. Emerging from a stone-throwing culture, and already established as a means of annoying strangers and the better-off or a way of dealing with interfering figures of authority, it was a logical step for the practice of slogging to become more organised in terms of group against group or gang against gang. By 1873, slogging was, according to the editor of the *Birmingham Daily Gazette*, associated with 'lawless gangs of youths and boys of the lowest class'. Their age was described as of 'the hobble-de-hoy period of existence' between fourteen and eighteen. That implied that they had little to do with their spare time except loaf about, cause a nuisance and inflict terror on 'peaceably-disposed inhabitants' at dusk, especially on Sundays.

IN BIRMINGHAM, the trigger to slogging was not so much the war, but the heady atmosphere of the boom and the continuing aftermath of the Murphy phenomenon. Significant in its origins was the fact that the town had not suffered the last of Murphy's malign influence. A succession of tremors followed the major ethnic and social eruption associated with the Murphy Riots five years before, including the attacks on St Chad's Cathedral and St Alban's, Conybere Street. Park and Freeman Streets, which had borne the brunt of the mob's attacks, slowly recovered, partly with the help of a fund for 'the sufferers of Park Street'. No official attempt was made to identify their 'English' attackers, so any retribution had to be left to individuals or groups, taking action anonymously and in dark places.

Park Street remained tumbledown, overcrowded, embittered and prone to violence. Opportunities to get back at Murphy were not missed. When he was arrested in June 1869 for trying to attend a meeting in the Town Hall, in spite of a police ban, a bricklayer from Park Street, wearing a green ribbon, rushed up to him and called him an 'orange bastard', for which, being regarded as 'a violent, dangerous fellow' by the stipendiary, he earned himself six weeks in the House of Correction. When in Birmingham, and not on a lecture tour, Murphy was minister of his own chapel in Wrottesley Street in the Markets area. However, in April 1871 he went to deliver an anti-Catholic lecture at Whitehaven, Cumberland, and was beaten up by indignant Irish labourers. He was so severely affected by the abscess that developed from the kicks he had received that he retired to Sparkbrook, where he died on 12 March 1872.

His death reignited the old controversies. To many Protestants he was still a hero, and even to many moderates his demise seemed to 'mark a new era' – as the *Sheffield Telegraph* over-dramatically put it – in which the legal authorities abdicated 'in deference to the superior authority of the clog and the cudgel'. Two weeks beforehand, Queen Victoria herself had been threatened with a pistol by seventeen-year-old Arthur O'Connor. Perhaps this awakened memories in Birmingham of the first attempt with a pistol, albeit unloaded, against the Queen in 1840 by Edward Oxford, the eighteen-year-old son of a Birmingham jeweller. If so, they went unstated even by the town's republicans.

Murphy's funeral in Birmingham was the occasion of tension rather than violence. A huge crowd gathered on the Monday immediately after St Patrick's Day, to witness the funeral procession from Wrottesley Street to the General Cemetery, at Key Hill, but the police kept good order amid the cheering and jeering. Three pickpockets were arrested, along with a single stone-thrower, Henry Challinor, a sixteen-year-old gun finisher. Six weeks before, a policeman had been fatally injured in Bristol Street at the hands of an Irish labourer, Patrick Grady, who had been ejected from an ale and porter store after a row over the change from money for a pint of ale. P.C. Thomas Hardy, died in the Borough Lunatic Asylum on 3 April. Grady only spent four months in prison as Mr Justice Blackburn at the Warwickshire Assizes viewed the death of the constable as an accident.

It is possible that these events helped to trigger the outbreak of the first riot of 'the slogging gang', the so-called 'stone riot' which occurred five days later, and was another late convulsion from Murphy fever.

THE FIRST slogging gang to be identified as such originated in Cheapside, in the south-eastern part of the town. Stretching from Jamaica Row, close to the Bull Ring, through St Martin's Ward, this long street crossed the narrow River Rea into Deritend Ward and led up towards the more salubrious heights of Camp Hill and Highgate. It had a varied social make-up and a reputation for rowdiness. Like many Birmingham streets, its appearance was deceptive, for the frontage hid from view the impoverished existence of those who lived in the teeming courts down the narrow alleys beside many of the houses and shops. There had once been a famous Irish brawl there, in which a labourer called Kennedy had perished on the day after the St Patrick's celebrations, and the 1871 census identified a small but significant Irish enclave opposite the site of the old infantry barracks between Balsall Street and the river. The men from the iron trade who lived and worked in the Cheapside area were tough characters, and one died in an affray in 1871. The area was typical of many parts of the town in having a great variety of trades, from brassfounding and bedstead-making to wiremaking and stone masonry. Many of their employees were young, and when Breedens' the brassfounders celebrated a coming of age in the family they had a special dinner for their young workers. Cheapside roughs roamed up into the town and were often in fights; one attacked a policeman with a poker only a few months before the stone riot. It was a street which attracted others from the immediate vicinity in their leisure time as well as for work, but it seems that those 'others' – part of the floating population of Birmingham roughs – also liked to move around the town and claim possession of other thoroughfares in other neighbourhoods.

In the spring of 1872, the inhabitants of the Cheapside area and parallel Bradford Street began to complain about 'the large number of boys assembling there and breaking windows'. This might have seemed traditional Birmingham practice, but the signs were that it was becoming more organised. At the same time, gangs in the Gun Quarter also took to fighting on Sunday evenings. Something was going on. It is unclear who was fighting who, but it seems that the claim to be *the* slogging gang or band – originally perhaps meant as a collective name for all sloggers – was becoming a title of pride to be fought for by lads from different areas, whether from Cheapside, St George's, the Gun Quarter, Deritend or Duddeston.

The first use of the term 'the slogging gang' in the press was applied to a body of about four hundred roughs who appeared in Cheapside, without warning, between four and five p.m. on Sunday, 7 April 1872, 'to the great consternation of the inhabitants', according to the *Mail*. No doubt they were a mixed bag of men and women, boys and girls, although teenage boys probably predominated. They as yet had no sense of gang identity, uniform or style, although the men's belts were already showing signs of individuality. They included the poorer elements of the streets of south Birmingham, who had no Sunday best and whose clothing would have been worn and shabby, the men and boys in caps and mufflers, with a few women in shawls, and followed by the usual motley collection of stray dogs. Many of the crowd had emerged from the pubs – where poor people spent much of Sunday – some the worse for drink, many of them hungry, drawing in the youths from street corners and the urchins from court entries as they moved forward, without any strong sense of purpose.

First they smashed several windows in the Cheapside area. Then they moved up towards the town centre and into the neighbourhood of Hill Street, behind New Street station, where they stoned the windows of the hucksters' (sellers of cheap articles) and confectioners' shops which were open and forced shopkeepers to put up their shutters under a volley of mud, brickbats and dead dogs. In what became known as the 'stone riot', with its echoes of earlier bread riots, one Hill Street confectioner was hit on the chest by a brick and had to be taken to hospital. The rioters remained in the neighbourhood for some time, terrorising passers-by. A small body of police was sent to deal with them, under Inspectors Lomax and Wilcox, and the slogging gang quickly retreated to Cheapside, where they were met by a number of police of the third division. The officers dispersed the gang, making three arrests, and Inspector Lomax and several sergeants patrolled the neighbourhood until calm was restored. Those arrested included two very poor youths of no fixed home. One admitted to breaking glass and stealing herrings from the Market Hall, and the other to breaking the windows of a house and of St Jude's Church. The third, a polisher from Park Street named Callaghan, deliberately smashed a newsagent's window. The stone riot in Hill Street had elements of opportunism, vandalism and perhaps revenge as well as what the *Post* called 'shouting, horseplay and stone throwing'.

It remains unclear whether they were protesting about the prices and practices of small shops, the treatment of newsboys or evidence given in court against some of them, but the rioters were making a definite statement by pushing from the outskirts up into the heart of the town. No particular police action on street gambling can be identified as the trigger. When the police came with a warrant to arrest – as in Cheapside again a year later – a riot might well ensue, but this riot was different. No reference was made to Murphy and there was no sign of an opposing faction. Whether the stone riot was inspired as a protest in support of the local fire-iron operatives' strike for increased wages is impossible to say. Arguably it signalled a transition from communal riot to youthful gang activity in the sequence of street disturbances.

On the following evening, Monday, mobs threw stones in Rea Street South, a little to the south of Cheapside, and another five boys aged between thirteen and fifteen were arrested. Two of them came from even further south, in lower Highgate, and two from the Hill Street area, just to the south of New Street Station. This seems to have been an incident separate from the stone riot, but may have been some kind of continued protest or even a counter-attack, as these boys were also said to be of 'the slogging gang'.

Slogging riots and battles now took hold in south Birmingham. The chances of getting caught were slim, but the penalties, for the unlucky, were stiff: in the case of the Sunday stone riot, twenty shillings, with costs as well, amounting to three or four times a boy assistant's weekly wage even in such good times, or three weeks in prison. The magistrate, Alderman Henry Manton, hoped that in future the police would arrest some of the older offenders, but as the police would later say, perhaps there were none. The only indication that Monday's slogging occasion had sectarian undertones was that, as one councillor pointed out, there was also 'great excitement in the neighbourhood of the Inkleys' – an Irish area – on the Monday evening and two of the boys arrested had Irish names. The Chief Superintendent said that the riot originated in a 'sham fight' by a number of lads on a piece of waste ground.

On the same Sunday evening and at the same time as the stone riot, the Gun Quarter, three quarters of a mile across the town from Cheapside, and with a similarly significant Irish ingredient, also came alive. Youths in that part of the town collected together, again calling themselves members of the slogging gang, and paraded through the streets. Then they began rioting, smashing windows and injuring passers-by, although without reports of the deliberate attack on small shopkeepers that characterised the stone riot in Hill Street. The stone-throwing by the Gun Quarter broke out in Slaney Street and then spilled out beyond the Fazeley Canal into Cleveland and Pritchett Streets and the Aston Road. A magistrate, Dr Melson, stepped out of his house in Newhall Street, caught hold of one of the youths outside and thrashed him with an ash stick. His son also ventured out, chased after and caught the boys' leader, but returned home shortly afterwards with his ear split, his lip cut and a lump on his head. 'Have-a-go' tactics, especially by a family closely associated with the Murphyite Protestant Association, were unwise against the sloggers. Dr Melson had been an unsuccessful candidate of the pro-Murphy Protestant Association in the first School Board elections of 1870.

But if the gang had hoped to go unchecked, they failed, as seven arrests were made of youths aged between fourteen and eighteen, four of them from the Gun Quarter. Five of those arrested received sentences of six weeks in prison. One fourteen-year-old, a master shoemaker's son from Duke Street, was sent to gaol for three months for throwing a stone which injured a constable. Inspector Kelly said that they had been meeting frequently on Sundays for 'what they termed a sham fight'. The breakout from the Gun Quarter was, in the *Mail's* words, a 'military manoeuvre' by the sloggers. The press view in this case, in contrast to that of the stone riot, was of a fight rather than a demonstration of juvenile street power.

Suddenly the whole town seemed to echo to the sound of lads on the move. On the next evening, a Tuesday, seventy or more armed with sticks, bricks and large stones, gathered in Northwood Street, on the edge of the Jewellery Quarter. According to the police, they had come to 'slog' another gang. While waiting, they hurled stones at a policeman.

He held his ground and seemed to have managed to disperse them, but they reassembled around the corner. He next chased them across the canal into Lionel Street and, when another constable came up to help, they arrested two boys of about fourteen years of age. One of them was John Giblin, or Gibbon, an Irish-born engine driver from a court off Water Street who was to have a long career of slogging and violence towards the police. The fact that his mate was a filer from Hospital Street suggests that their gang was from the Snow Hill area, just outside the Gun Quarter, and was perhaps hoping to test out the virility of the jewellery lads, further to the north-west.

THREE SUNDAYS afterwards, a constable witnessed about four hundred roughs in Cheapside, again divided into two huge gangs equally matched in numbers. John Morris, a thirty-four-year-old bricklayer from a court in Barford Street, was leading one of them. Morris lived, unmarried, with his parents, who, like him were from County Galway, Ireland. He may have been the same man who had led a riot in Cheapside in 1868, on that occasion to 'square' the publican of the King's Arms, Barford Street, over some grievance. That same year had seen two revenge attacks on Murphyite landlords elsewhere in the town, in one of which an Irish attacker was shot dead (see Chapter 2). Morris' gang in 1872 would be identified by the *Post* as 'the Irish'. P.C. Harrison said that it was connected with the youths who had rioted previously in Hill Street. Morris was throwing stones and calling on others to do the same. Several people were hurt during the fighting, including a Post Office official who was brutally kicked.

A witness called William Hinton, a Protestant and member of Murphy's chapel, later deposed before the magistrates that the gang causing the trouble, and Morris, its leader, had threatened his life ever since he had attended Murphy's funeral five weeks beforehand. On one occasion, he claimed, the gang had stormed his house in Barford Street, where his wife and daughters were dressmakers, and would have pulled it down and perhaps have murdered him but for a small body of policemen who had driven them off. Morris was declared to be undoubtedly 'the ringleader of a dangerous and disorderly band'. In 1868, he had been fined five shillings with the alternative of fourteen days' imprisonment. This time he was ordered to pay forty shillings or, in default, go to prison for six weeks. So even if Hinton was exaggerating, there was some ethnic, Irish-versus-Murphyite element in this fighting. Most of the area around Cheapside was English but the small Irish enclave could call on allies from Park Street and the Inkleys.

THE EMERGENCE of slogging coincided with a time of prosperity enhanced by overseas warfare. After a dismal period for business following the collapse of the London banking house Overend and Gurney in 1866, most branches of trade were now enjoying a big recovery. The gun trade had flourished in the Crimean War and again in the American Civil War, during which time 800,000 weapons were sent from Birmingham, many to the Confederate forces. Later General Custer would use a revolver made in Birmingham. Wars in Europe were also good for business. In July 1870, after being riled into military action by the wily Count Bismarck, the government of Napoleon III had declared war on Prussia. Britain and other countries had not joined in, but instead benefited from the increased demand from the combatants, especially for arms. The gun trade boomed again: in 1871, a record 891,228 gun barrels were proved in Birmingham. However, the French were outgeneralled and outfought and the war was soon resolved, so the gun bonanza was shortlived.

The hasty military preparations of the French Empire and its army's new *chassepot* rifle had an obvious fascination. Once the war broke out in July 1870, the thirst for news triggered the launch of a Birmingham evening newspaper called the *Daily Mail*, which rapidly won a big circulation, as it sold at a halfpenny, half the price of its big sister the *Daily Post*. The war reached a decisive climax in the battle on 2 September at Sedan, where the French were trapped. Napoleon III tried to save his army by handing himself over to the Prussian king. In the whole of Britain, there was intense interest in the battles along the Franco-German border. At Worcester, boys from different parishes played rather too vigorously at 'French and Prussians', imaginatively pretending that the River Severn was the Rhine, and a policeman who tried to call an end to their fighting was wounded in the crossfire. Similarly in Liverpool and Manchester, Catholic and Protestant boys fought each other as 'French' and 'Prussians'. In Birmingham youthful imitation, if that was what was happening, was much less instantaneous and a slogging war would only ignite in 1873.

The rapid defeat of the French came as a big surprise to those who remembered the long years of the Revolutionary and Napoleonic Wars at the beginning of the century. The declaration of the Third Republic in Paris, immediately after the news of Napoleon's surrender and captivity, was very exciting for Birmingham's vociferous republican minority. The latest news headlines of the war and the subsequent siege of Paris were shouted round the streets by a large force of newsboys, and the police gave up trying to arrest them while the war fever lasted. (In the meantime, a controversial import from Paris, the can-can, increasingly danced by chorus girls as a highly popular and *risqué* 'leg' show, was facing the disapproval, and helplessness, of the law in London.) Once the Empress Eugenie had escaped to England and was joined by her terminally-sick husband, after his release from Prussian captivity, there was huge interest in their personal lives as England's latest and greatest refugees.

While the war did not last long, the boom in Birmingham's industries lasted through to 1874. There was spare money for leisure, especially drinking. The favourite beer was 'fourpenny', which cost a shilling a pint. For those who could not afford this, Birmingham's coiners produced counterfeit shillings which might sometimes pass unnoticed in the crush round the bar. There were also spare coppers, perhaps for the halfpenny newspapers and certainly for the favourite game of pitch and toss.

Eighteen seventy-two was a year of full employment and rising wages for workers of all ages, and, in this context, especially important for the young. Better trade led to a revival of labour disputes, as workmen tried to use the improved economic conditions to bargain for better wages from their employers. Small masters, as in the gun trade, were better placed to grant increases quickly, while some larger employers faced bitter disputes. It was also a year in which thousands of men, often quite young, were combining in strike action. The *Mail* identified an epidemic of strikes by 'the butcher, the baker, yes and even the apocryphal candlestick maker, in the guise of a brass worker'. This often meant violence against knobsticks or strike-breakers. In February, gangs of canal boatmen stopped bargees still at work, and in Garrison Lane hempdressers intimidated those still working at the Universe Works. In June, striking axle-tree workers used threats against a workman in Barford Street. Such group violence was the backdrop to the first signs of slogging in gangs. Workers' assertiveness extended to children, with a strike by newsboys in February. Over a year later some boys from Pritchett Street, led by a twelve-year-old brass founder, would break forty-three panes of glass in the spindle and screw factory of Jacob Dodd, where he lived with his family in Chester Street, Aston. Their grievance may have been also over wages.

The effect of the riots across the town in 1872 made the slogging bands, as they were sometimes called at this stage, more adventurous. The Aston Road and Gosta Green became popular battlegrounds. On Tuesday 14 May at 11 p.m., P.C. Day found a number of boys patrolling up and down in the Aston Road armed with pieces of iron and hard wood and stones. Tin kettles were being banged to summon support and as a preliminary to the fight. He managed to catch a fourteen-year-old printer from Drury Lane, who claimed that he had been forced to join the boys for a fight between the lads of Sheep Street, nearby, and Hall Street, over in the Jewellery Quarter. The boy's claim to innocence was treated with some scepticism when it was claimed that he had been up on a similar charge five years before.

The 'good' times seemed to have given the lads greater confidence. The Watery Lane area of Bordesley had a long history of fighting. Stone-throwing there, according to a press report in November 1870, was alleged 'to have had some connection with the dying threat of a girl who for some time resided there'. This ghoulish tale was given as a reason why a local blacksmith and his son threw stones at a brewhouse door, broke a panel and then ran away. The blacksmith accused the brewer's servant, whom he had seen through a window, of being the ghost. 'Yes I am Pepper's Ghost,' the man replied in court, without further elaboration. The two 'ghost-hunters' paid fines, costs and damages. More seriously, in June 1872 the constable found a group of twenty boys on a Friday night at the end of a disappointingly sunless May, standing at the corner of Great Barr Street and Watery Lane pelting passers-by with stones and shouting, 'We are the slogging band.' They ran away when they saw the constable, but he gave chase and caught the ringleader, a fifteen-year-old, button burnisher's son. The toughness of the area was shown again in the local elections two years later, when the roughs took possession of a polling booth in this part of Bordesley and stopped the voting until they were cleared out.

The police had hard work enforcing the new licensing laws which required pubs to close at 11 p.m. on weekdays and Saturdays, and 10 p.m. on Sundays and public holidays, and in the autumn of 1872 they increasingly came under fire from mobs of young men armed with stones. Some of the worst offenders were virtually unemployable because they were continually in and out of prison. Twenty-five-year-old Robert

Richards, of Lichfield Street, had only just come out of gaol after six weeks for assaulting the police when he was back in, this time for six months, for trying to rescue a man from custody in Thomas Street. Meanwhile Park Street was rendered impassable by two gangs of youths, reported by the *Post* to be 'imitating the Autumn Manoeuvres' by fighting with 'brickends, stones, mud and in fact everything they could lay their hands on'. As slogging fever now replaced war and strike fever, the state of the town's law and order threatened to get a great deal worse.

The First Peak

ON SUNDAY, 30 MARCH 1873, Birmingham erupted in an explosion of slogging that lasted for many hours. Five separate 'riotous outrages' broke out in different parts of the town, leaving the police stretched to breaking point and the townspeople in shock. What prompted this outbreak of mass disorder has never been satisfactorily explained, though there had been a number of violent incidents over the previous two or three months.

Just a week earlier, a major disturbance had followed the arrival of five constables to disperse a number of boys assembled in a ruined house in Livery Street. The constables were pelted with brickbats and only when six more officers arrived were they able to apprehend fourteen of the youths. A large crowd followed them to the station, hooting and throwing mud and stones, and in the evening, when a police van came to take the prisoners to the Moor Street lock-up, a mob of about a hundred men and women followed it along Great Hampton Street, Constitution Hill and Snow Hill, again pelting it with missiles. In the early evening of the same 23 March, Bagot Street, half a mile away, saw what was described as a 'small riot' between young men from the Gun Quarter and those who lived in the St Bartholomew's district, to the south-east.

Bad as they were, these incidents were nothing compared to the mayhem that broke out on the 30th. At 2 p.m., usually a quiet time on the Sabbath, Police Sergeant Parkinson and P.C.s Price and Tranter went to a house in Cheapside to arrest a man under a warrant. When the officers came out with their prisoner, they found themselves surrounded by a large crowd, which rapidly grew to over a thousand as it followed them. As they passed stony waste ground in Rea Street South, a number in this massive crowd picked up stones and hurled them at the three policemen. Various efforts were made to rescue the unknown prisoner, who kept yelling at his friends to 'pitch into' the officers, though he became noticeably more subdued when many of the stones intended for his captors struck him instead.

At almost the same time, officers were also stoned by mobs in separate attacks in Newtown Row and Great Queen Street, while in Farm Street and Great Hampton Street, passers-by were the main target for insults, mud and stones. The police must have cursed that year's efforts by the council to improve the streets with Rowley rag stones, which seemed everywhere at hand. Altogether they made fifteen arrests.

While the magistrates dealt with those arrested, the press, predictably, was outraged. An appeal was made through the media for 'every citizen to lend his aid to the police in their efforts to put down rowdyism', while the *Post* complained that there had in fact been 'eleven weeks of ruffianism in Birmingham' and summarized a number of incidents events between 26 January and 5 April as 'A Disgraceful Record'. It lumped together a series of unconnected but nonetheless disturbing crimes, including domestic assaults, stabbings, drunken brawls, vandalism, arson, garrotte robbery and attacks on police such as the previous riot in Livery Street, which had all taken place within the previous three months. It must have seemed, to many readers, that the town was in the grip of an epidemic of violence.

Certain streets, it emerged, were being used by sloggers as meeting places. Such a one was Bagot Street, with its various factories for making guns, ironcastings and nuts and bolts. The street's location was ideal in several ways. Alongside the Fazeley Canal, it lay in the Bishop Ryder's District; it linked to the Aston Road and was immediately accessible both from the Gun Quarter and Newtown Row. During that notorious March, Bagot Street had become a regular venue for Sunday evening stone-throwing. On Sunday 23 March, as mentioned earlier, a Police Sergeant Prosser found nearly forty youngsters flourishing sticks and throwing stones. Their chief targets were passers-by, but the the sergeant himself received a volley as he approached. The boys ran off, but he gave chase and caught four whom he called 'leaders', of whom one was a seventeen-year-old gunbarrel filer from Loveday Street in the Gun Quarter and three others were from Bartholomew Street and Old Cross Street. After they had been locked up, they were overheard to say to each other in their cell, 'We shall have two more Sundays at it and then we shall chuck it in.' This report smacked of wishful thinking.

A month later, the police were again on their mettle in the face of about a hundred boys throwing stones and smashing windows, again in

Bagot Street and neighbouring Staniforth Street, on a Tuesday evening. The local residents had to put up their shutters and one gentleman got caught in the crossfire and had to go to hospital. The two seventeen-year-olds who were caught both received good character references, probably from their employers, and were fined only five shillings. One came from Loveday Street, the heart, or rather fists, of the Gun Quarter, and the other from nearer where the fighting took place. The Gun Quarter lads seemed again to be 'playing away' against their immediate neighbours in the Bishop Ryder's District.

THE FIRST signs of slogging in Aston came shortly afterwards, on the border where Summer Lane, Birmingham, became Alma Street, Aston. Clifford Street, around the corner, had the attractions of the Alhambra Concert Hall and a fried fish shop close by. Fried fish and ginger beer were already becoming part of a young person's evening out; chips would follow on much later in Birmingham. Alma Street itself was still being developed, but was a popular venue for pitch and toss on Sundays. In the previous April, the inhabitants of Lennox and Clifford Streets had complained of 'drunken vagabonds' who infested the neighbourhood on Sunday and Monday nights. Over the next year, a gang of about sixty young sloggers routinely patrolled the area armed with stones and bludgeons, breaking windows and assaulting passers-by. On one occasion, they rallied on waste ground and fired a volley of stones at the police. A sergeant of the Aston force of the county police instantly rushed in among them, followed by as many as fifteen of his men from different points. The gang scattered, but two fourteen-year-olds were arrested with stones in their possession. Aston's Superintendent Gallaway said that on several occasions he too had had to use fifteen men to deal with them.

The trouble spread to other parts of this police frontier between Birmingham and Aston Manor. Farm Street, between Hockley and Lozells, saw a slogging match soon afterwards in which two dozen roughs fired stones and shouted obscene language. These streets on the edge of the police beats of the two authorities were also popular with street gamblers. Two years before, a police superintendent had referred to a group of youths in a much more remote spot, Bishop Ryder's Road in Saltley, and condemned 'the practice of playing at pitch and toss and the language used by the gangs who gathered together'. The link between the area's favourite pastime and throwing stones in gangs was very strong. Even after the police crackdown in Clifford and Alma Streets, it was said that pitch and toss had become 'general in the Manor on Sundays'.

Aston Manor remained poorly organised to impose law and order. It had no police van, so those destined for the sessions or assizes at Warwick were still being escorted by the police in a chain-gang through the streets to the station. One person wrote to the *Post* about the 'convict-like' degradation for those involved, regardless of how trivial their alleged offence. Traffic was held up and they were followed by up to a hundred people while 'chained to a number of other persons, some in our workhouse canvas suits, some in rags and often half-crazed wretched women'. Aston Petty Sessions met only every other Saturday and the county magistrates had a poor attendance record. There was no stipendiary and no local clerk.

OTHER AREAS were affected by the fashion for slogging. The fighting on the Aston border spread back further south into St Stephen's Ward. In Ward Street, sandwiched between Summer Lane and Newtown Row, local residents petitioned the Watch Committee, backed up by the police, against the trouble caused by 'gangs of idle and disorderly characters' on Saturdays and Sundays, including gambling and pigeon-flying, as well as shouting profane and obscene language, and creating 'wanton mischief'. In Bishop Ryder's District, indignation from the more respectable residents came to a head when, on the afternoon of Sunday, 8 June, a master gun-barrel maker, Edwin Cook, was beaten up outside his front door. Cook was something of a public figure, having been secretary of his trade's mutual aid association. He was sitting in his house in Potter Street, taking tea with his family, when he heard abusive language outside and someone throwing coins. He went out to investigate and found several roughs playing pitch and toss. He asked them to go away, but they jeered and swore at him. The ringleader was eighteen-year-old Joseph French, from Brewery Street, off Newtown Row, who had started his working life in the gun trade, but was now a hingemaker. 'If you come here I will put you through,' he told Cook. This was no idle threat. When Cook went up to him, French pulled out a heavy wagoner's whip-stock with an iron ferrule and struck at him. The weapon caught him on the forehead, inflicting a large wound which saturated his clothes with blood. When Cook, according to his own account, took hold of his attacker, French passed the whip-stock to another rough and told him to 'lay on'. The second man gave Cook another blow on the head and then ran off with the others. Cook managed to hold on to French until a constable arrived. He then went back into his house and was having his wounds dressed before going to the police station when the constable returned with the news that he had lost the man because he had been rescued by the mob.

However, Cook spotted French close by in York Street on the following Sunday and alerted the police. After a chase, French was taken back into custody. He admitted that he was in the gang but denied hitting Cook. Police Sergeant Millard marched him towards the station, again under a hail of stones. This time French slipped out of his jacket and again escaped, leaving the sergeant holding his coat. It was another two weeks before this slippery individual was re-arrested, charged with gambling, obstruction and violent assault and sent to prison with the exemplary sentence of two months' hard labour. The magistrate, Alderman Manton, warned any of French's companions who might be present in the public gallery that, if caught, they would get the same treatment.[6]

Cook did not leave the matter to the magistrates. Even before the court appearance, he had presented a petition at the fortnightly meeting of the Watch Committee from the inhabitants of five streets in the Bishop Ryder District between the Gun Quarter and Gosta Green. With his head still bandaged, he presented the complaints to the committee and the police chief. The petition, signed by sixty persons, called attention to 'the riotous proceedings' in that locality over the previous few weeks, and to the danger to their lives and property. The complaints had a familiar ring: gangs of youths assembling in the streets on Sundays, throwing stones, gambling and street-fighting with life-preservers and other dangerous weapons, all leading to 'mob law' and a 'reign of terror'. The mob had rescued several prisoners from police custody – not just Joseph French. The petitioners demanded measures to protect their lives and property. Cook had been savagely attacked; a Mr Boswell, who had caught hold of a youth taking part in a gang stone fight, had had his hand bitten through.

Cook explained how, a fortnight before his injuries, he had had a similar problem of a gang outside his front door, of ordering them off, of enduring 'disgusting' verbal abuse and of capturing one of them and handing him over to the police. Cook complained that the next day the

---

6 Unlike some Birmingham roughs, French would settle down with a wife and six children and the unenviable job of a corporation nightsoil man, emptying privies.

magistrates had let off the youth with the payment of a half-crown fine without costs. There had been a free fight between two gangs of youths in Potter Street on the Sunday afterwards and similar scenes in neighbouring Fisher Street. Every time the police appeared, the roughs ran off.

The police chief, George Glossop, in spite of over thirty years' experience, had no easy answer. He had already faced criticism for being over-active by arresting 'ragged and shoeless' newsboys and so preventing them from earning a living. He told the committee that on the same Sunday as the disturbance in Potter Street, there had been trouble in Macdonald Street in St Martin's. There, as many as ten policemen had been involved in chasing the roughs. This elicited the comment from John Thackray Bunce, editor of the *Birmingham Daily Post* from 1862 to 1898 and a close confidant of Chamberlain and the ruling group, that twenty or thirty police should be used in such exercises. Following Mrs Glasse's famous recipe for hare soup, he added that 'first catch your hare' was clearly the priority, before deciding how to 'dress' it.

Glossop agreed with Cook that those brought before the Bench were not being fined enough. Another member of the committee spoke of a similar disturbance in the area of Kenion Street, near the junction of Livery and Great Hampton Streets, an ideal meeting-place for Newhall, Hockley and St George's, as the police had realised by siting a station there. This was all the more of a concern in that the police had recently arrested a gang of fourteen from that neighbourhood. The Mayor promised to speak to the magistrates on the matter, and the Chief Superintendent[7] was instructed to take action and report back. The *Post* saw Gosta Green as the most worrying area and commented that although in Birmingham the Sunday diversions of local youths on the Green might be explained away as 'only their play', outsiders would not see it like that. More police would perhaps help catch the guilty, while stricter penalties might do something to deter offenders. Meanwhile the sloggers took advantage of the long evenings of an exceptionally dry June.

The situation worsened from the police point of view. Reporters reckoned that 'mob law' reigned on Saturday nights and Sundays in parts of the town, despite severe sentences handed down by the magistrates. Some fights attracted youths from a wide area. One mob of two to three hundred rioted in Milton Street, close to the Hockley Brook,

---

7 Glossop's successor, Major Bond, was in 1876 the first to be designated Chief Constable of Birmingham.

on the border with Aston, at the upper ends of Summer Lane and Newtown Row, and at another place where there was rough ground, close to St Stephen's School. This was on a Monday evening. The mob, which had probably gathered for a slog between various parts of Birmingham and Aston, was interrupted by only two policemen, so it was hardly surprising that so few were taken into custody. The four arrested were aged between seventeen and nineteen. Two were local to the Milton Street area, but there was also a labourer from the Jewellery Quarter and a pearl-button maker from Aston. The two constables tried to restore order, but the youths replied with stones and then their ringleaders assaulted the police as they tried to make arrests. The magistrates handed out six weeks of hard labour as exemplary sentences and proof that they were responding to all those complaints from the locality. Two days later, a young jeweller was arrested for leading a stone-throwing gang in a street off Hockley Hill.

The arrests showed the extent to which pearl-button makers and other fine craftsmen were being drawn into a practice previously associated with the metal trades. The mobs picked up some of the older, hardened offenders as well. Knowing the police were under pressure, fifty roughs collected in Park Steet to block two bobbies from carrying out their normal beats. One of the ringleaders came from as far away as Mount Street, Bordesley. When two hundred congregated in Brickkiln Street, between the Gun Quarter and Bishop Ryder's District, they were dispersed before fighting could start, but some took the opportunity to stone the two constables who were spoiling the fun. One of them was a twenty-five-year-old labourer with eleven previous appearances before the Bench.

Wherever sloggers were arrested, their mates developed the habit of stoning the police as they dragged their prey to the station, regardless of the strong possibility of missing their target and hitting those in custody. Occasionally a rescue was made, as when the unfortunate P.C. Tomkins tried to take a man who had been leading a disturbance in a street off Constitution Hill. He was followed by the rest of the gang, led by an eighteen-year-old hingemaker, called William Rowe, already well-known to the police for slogging and theft all over north Birmingham and currently resident in Slaney Street in the Gun Quarter. The constable's helmet was smashed by a brick and he had to be on the sick list for a fortnight. Rowe was picked up by another policeman later and given six months' hard labour.

Slogging by gangs was spreading out from the more central areas to new ones like Great King Street, off Hockley Hill, where a seventeen-year-old jeweller, the oldest of six children, from Kenion Street was arrested as a leader of a gang of stone-throwing roughs, after being pointed out by a resident fearful for his plate glass windows. Camp Hill, on the boundary between Deritend and Bordesley, was also affected and Mr Buckley, a magistrate, declared that the Bench was 'determined to punish boys who went about in gangs throwing stones'. By September 1873, a slogging gang was causing disruption in Little Francis Street, Duddeston, well to the east of Gosta Green. Boys were fighting, armed with gutta percha 'neddies' and sticks with iron at the ends. Of the two youths arrested one was a brass founder from Great Brook Street, Duddeston, and the other came from Woodcock Street, St Mary's.

A Sunday afternoon in September brought pandemonium in different quarters of the town. In the St Martin's area of Cheapside, Bradford Street and Moat Row, there was 'constant commotion' caused by a battle between two mobs of youngsters. One was apparently a mixed group from the suburbs of St Martin's and Deritend, including one whose address in the census was off Green Lane, Bordesley. The other mob included youths described as the companions of an enameller from the Smithfield Market area, nearer the town centre. Two or three hundred joined in, attacking each other, hitting passers-by with stones and dirt and finally turning their fire on two policemen when they arrived from Bradford Street station to restore order. After the police had made arrests, a crowd of a hundred or more collected outside the police station, threatening the officers, and then hooted and jeered as the police van was driven down Bradford Street to the cells at Moor Street. Stones were thrown at the officers and the driver of the van, and the mob followed all the way. The *Gazette* noted that the arrest of sloggers caused an uproar that same evening across the town, from Kenion Street police station to Ladywood, where people were just coming out of church.

The press was pleased that the Ladywood sloggers had been caught *in flagrante delicto*, a phrase used then in a more general context than today. The *Gazette* added, with exaggerated fear, that the Sunday in question, 21 September, had seen a concerted effort by ruffians to produce 'a general rising in various quarters of the town'. Such a comment seemed like a throwback to the potentially revolutionary days of the Chartists or a fear inspired by contemporary events on the Continent, where the French middle class in 1871 had lost control of Paris and had to fight its way back behind the artillery of government forces while the Prussians stood by and watched. This kind of catastrophe had never yet happened in England, although the Chartists had tested middle class nerves to the limit, but it was well known that the blue line of the borough police was only thin. At best, the widespread outbreak of slogging was regarded by Birmingham's Tory newspaper as a bad omen as to what the dark winter evenings might bring.

September did indeed end with a riot by a gang of sloggers in Bordesley Street, St Bartholomew's, two evenings running. Only one gang was mentioned in the press. It was led by a matchet (machete) polisher from Floodgate Street, whose stone-throwing on a Monday evening in late September forced many people to put up their shutters. A second day of this was too much for a master whitesmith in Little Ann Street. On the Tuesday evening, he was at work in his shop, when a large stone came through the window. He came out, pushed his way into the mob, grabbed the lad and detained him until the police arrived. The man told the court that the seventeen-year-old was one – the *Gazette* said the 'leader' – of a gang who congregated in the street and whose stone-throwing greatly alarmed locals. The youth was fined forty shillings and half-a-dozen extra constables were put on duty.

Disturbances were increasing so rapidly that the inhabitants of Bordesley Street talked of arming themselves with pistols to shoot the roughs down. The police, with a borough force of only just over four hundred, were at full stretch and suffering. At the Watch Committee meeting in early October, it was reported that twenty policemen had been injured in the previous three months. Those had taken an average of over ten days off each and six were still unable 'to discharge their duty'. Stronger punishment was required, but the powers of the magistrates were limited.

The demands on the police did not ease off. In mid-October, over fifty lads from the Suffolk Street area, close to the railways entering New Street and the Old Wharf of the canal, gathered in Bow Street with sticks and belts, and smashed windows and threw stones at doors while they waited to meet the gang from Cheapside. The police dispersed them before their enemy arrived, but they regrouped nearby in Horse Fair at the top of Bristol Street, where fighting ensued until six constables were able to disperse a crowd that had risen to about one hundred and fifty lads. A twelve-year-old boy of Irish parentage was arrested as he marched with the others along Horse Fair with a huge mallet in one hand and a stick tipped with iron in the other. He was bound over to keep the peace for six months, but the roughs' grip on Suffolk Street was not broken. A couple of months later, it proved impossible to find witnesses to convict a youth for assault and robbery in the street on Christmas Day, because, it was said, people feared for their windows.

This series of outrages by what the press still called 'the slogging gang' came in the aftermath of three major strikes: the defeat of farm labourers striking for recognition and a living wage, for which there was much sympathy in Birmingham; the victory of the Black Country nut-and-bolt makers in a long strike at their two principal works; and a victory for the chainmakers of south Staffordshire in their fight for increased pay. It is impossible to say whether the tensions of these three labour disputes affected the actions of the people of St Martin's and the Gun Quarter. Sloggers never mentioned the strikes to the police or magistrates, but the industrial action may have contributed to a more assertive popular mood. Wage increases in Birmingham itself during the economic boom, had been secured, in most cases, without the need for protracted strikes, but fuller pockets may have made 'young Brum' more uproarious.

The year 1873 had also seen the widespread charging of fines for non-attendance at school, following the visits by Board officers to 28,000 homes between January and June and the opening of the first five Birmingham board schools, including Farm Street, Bloomsbury, Ashted and Ladywood, as well as Jenkins Street in the growing suburb of Small Heath. Some historians consider that compulsory schooling stirred up a hostile reaction from youth. Be that as it may, board schools were very controversial among adults in the town, with special excitement surrounding the second set of elections of members of the School Board that year, the first under secret ballot. The main issue was supposedly for or against sectarian schooling, but it was really a party political battle. The struggle was fiercest in Ladywood and St George's, where the 'Liberal Eight', who campaigned for unsectarian education, had their biggest opposition from the 'Bible Eight'. In St George's Ward, church school children had a holiday to allow teachers and children alike to help with canvassing, and in Ladywood the St John's school children 'tore about the streets chorusing, "Vote for the Bible Eight,"' according to a report in the Liberal *Post*. The result was that the unsectarian Liberals topped the poll and took control of the board with the six churchmen in the minority and one Catholic, Canon O'Sullivan, supported by many in St Mary's Ward on the sidelines. However the St Martin's and Deritend areas, where slogging was shortly to claim its first fatality, appeared unruffled in this election and did not see board schools open until 1875. Aston had a school board from that year, but with fewer disposable resources than Birmingham's.

IT WAS only a matter of time before these violent fights caused their first death. In 1873, gangs from Park Street and Cheapside engaged in desultory fighting. Park Street was recovering from its Murphyite trauma. Its big houses, once the homes of the well-to-do, had long been converted into lodging-houses and had become dens of thieves, while among its many beerhouses the Duke of Cumberland pub had a special reputation for illegal drinking and harbouring thieves: on one occasion the landlord was even caught playing cards with them. The street was close to the town centre: its teenage robbers went on 'fishing' expeditions to other parts of the town, and in return adventurous youths came in from the suburbs. In one local attack on the police, about fifty roughs were led by a twenty-one-year-old from Bordesley. The street was famous for its fighting Irish, and in March 1873 a Park Street gang was caught going to take on rivals in Birchall Street, a locality off Cheapside with hardly any Irish-born householders. Meanwhile Cheapside, with its mixed population, conducted battles with the Markets area or exercised its muscles in evening sorties to the west, towards Sherlock Street and the Bristol Road. By 1874, Park Street was also at war with Milk Street, on the north side of Digbeth, with the action sometimes taking place in Cheapside.

On a dark Monday evening in early February, 1874, fifteen-year-old John Thomas Kirkham and fourteen-year-old Patrick Dunlavey left the factory where they had finished work and walked along the bottom end of Cheapside. Both boys lived in Milk Street, some way away. They were both from families of six, but whereas Kirkham was English and fairly well-off – his father being a skilled bricklayer and his mother keeping a shop in a front house – Dunlavey lived in one of the courts, the son of an Irish-born bellows maker and his wife. Their gang, Milk Street, were the deadly rivals of the Park Street gang, led by a violent thirteen-year-old called John 'Jacky' Joyce.

The Joyces were keen sloggers: another Joyce called Thomas was the leader of the nearby Allison Street gang. Jacky's family had moved from Rea Street, off Cheapside, to Park Lane, off Park Street, but Jacky was a tinner who perhaps, like his enemies, also worked in Cheapside. Perhaps he also had relatives there, as another Joyce family, with links to the same part of Ireland, lived in Court No. 45, one of the many long yards that stretched back at right angles on both sides of lower Cheapside and alongside the Gullet, a narrow passageway that connected Cheapside with Bradford Street. On the other side of the Gullet, and opening straight into it, was Court No 44. Together the two courts had a number of boys with at least one Irish-born parent who were no doubt involved in or highly interested in this gang rivalry. The Gullet was hostile territory for John Kirkham.

Patrick Dunlavey gave evidence later that, as they walked up Cheapside, he and Kirkham saw about twenty boys standing at the top of the Gullet. One of them, Prinny Mack, called out, 'Here, Kirkham. Why don't you try to square this slog with me?'

'I haven't got anything to do with the slog,' Kirkham was said to have replied.

Neither he nor Dunlavey had noticed Jacky Joyce among the boys. Kirkham later took up the story in a statement to the police from his hospital bed:

There were about thirty lads and some of them called me to them. I stopped and they came to me. The prisoner, 'Jacky' Joyce, got behind me and stabbed me in the neck by the ear and I pulled the knife out of my neck. I cried out and some men came to me and put me in a cab. Two of the men came in the cab with me…(and the knife) to Queen's Hospital … The boys ran away when I was stabbed. I know the prisoner and I knew his brother. There are two sets of boys in the habit of fighting each other. Joyce belongs to the Park Street set and I belong to the Milk Street set. All the others had gone away while I was looking through a window. There had only been a few of the Milk Street party there and no fight. Some of the boys carry knives and use them. Some carry buckles[8] and there is stone throwing. I never use a knife, but I am obliged to carry a belt with a buckle to it. I never had

---

8 The buckled belt was to become a major weapon for sloggers, as for Manchester and Salford scuttlers. In December 1875, Michael Coffey, a nineteen-year-old ex-militia man already a serial slogger, and with six prison sentences behind him, would use a militiaman's buckle to strike a man across the face in Summer Lane, cutting his cheek and knocking him out, before robbing him.

any quarrel with the prisoner by myself. The lads in different streets
are in the height of what they call slogging one another.

He identified Joyce when the suspect was brought to his bedside, saying,
'I saw you do it and run away, Jack.' Under cross-examination, he added,
'I saw him get behind me and stick the knife in me. I saw his arm
move.'

The knife had been left sticking out of Kirkham's neck as he lurched
about, covered in blood. He lay critically ill in the Queen's Hospital for
nearly four weeks, but died on 28 February. His 'exhaustion', as the
surgeon called it, had resulted from the severing of the vertebral artery,
caused by a three-quarter-inch wound two inches below the right ear. For
the Victorian public, who relished last words, those of Kirkham must
have seemed strikingly poignant and unusual.

The coroner's inquest heard from a shoemaker (one report called him
a chairmaker) named Thomas, who stated that he had heard cries of
'Murder!' and had caught sight of Kirkham staggering about in the road
'like a drunken man'. When he went to him, he found blood gushing out
of a wound in his neck, in which a knife was 'sheathed up to the hilt'.
Thomas described the knife as 'a large pocket-knife very much worn'.
Kirkham himself drew the knife out – although at the assizes, Thomas
claimed that he had done so – and the blood spurted over the shoemaker's
face and hands. Kirkham was carried into a 'doctor's' shop. This sounded
in court like a swift operation, but the nearest doctor's shop or druggist's
warehouse was over seven hundred yards up the hill in Alcester Street, so
it was hard work getting Kirkham there and from there by cab to the
hospital. Thomas was sulky at getting no reward for his efforts and even
at not being allowed to keep the murder weapon, but the coroner, Dr
Davies, told him that he would have been put in prison if he had not
handed it over.

At the police court hearing, Jacky Joyce, who was undefended, pleaded
not guilty but was committed for trial at the assizes on the charge of wilful
murder. When he appeared in court at Warwick in July, he was described
as a 'thick-set, well-built boy' with 'a determined expression' who had
been employed as a tinplate worker. He seemed wholly unconcerned, in
spite of his perilous situation, and simply pleaded that he didn't do it. It
was the view of the prosecuting counsel, Mr Adams Q.C., that Joyce had
no 'direct and express malice' against John Kirkham.

In Dunlavey's evidence he had said that Joyce had emerged from the crowd of boys, then run at them both, but Dunlavey stepped aside and it was Kirkham who bore the brunt. Dunlavey was clearly anxious to avoid any implication that he and Kirkham wanted a slog. Dunlavey himself was no stranger to the courts; at the trial he was only just out of prison after completing a sentence for stealing cigars through the broken shop window of a tobacconist's, and that was not his first conviction.

A second witness, Thomas Sheridan, gave a rather different account. A thirteen-year-old metal polisher, he said that he was also in Cheapside when the two boys came along, and that Kirkham had asked if there were any of the Park Street lads in the street. One replied that he didn't know. Kirkham then went a little further up the street. As he did so, a boy from the group stole up behind Kirkham, wrapped his left arm around his neck and then stabbed him with something he had in his hand. Kirkham called out, 'Murder! I'm stabbed,' upon which the knifer ran away, as did several others in different directions.

A key question was whether Kirkham was the innocent victim he had claimed to be in hospital. Sheridan, in answer to the judge, Mr Justice Denman, said that Kirkham was 'a leader of the Milk Street gang' ('Barn Street' according to the *Gazette* report, the latter being a continuation of Milk Street). In answer to defence counsel, he maintained, 'There was no fighting that night between the gangs. They were not looking out for a quarrel that night.' Kirkham, he thought, however, wanted 'bother'. He was standing alone when he was stabbed; then a great crowd of boys came around him afterwards.

The well-bred Mr Justice Denman, son of Baron Denman and Justice of the Court of Common Pleas, was anxious to get to the bottom of this 'slogging'. He had already ascertained that it meant fighting by street gangs and now embarked on his own cross-examination of Sheridan, asking him first about Kirkham:

'He wanted to have a slogging with them, did he?'

'Yes.'

'Do they fight and slog one another?'

'Yes.'

'To which side among the boys do you belong?'

'I am on the right side.'

Sheridan's last answer was met by a gale of laughter which annoyed Judge Denham, who threatened to clear the gallery. Sheridan probably meant simply that he lived on the righthand side of the street, from the direction of the town centre, with the possible implication that the boys on the right side of the street were in opposition to the boys on the left. He admitted that he and Kirkham were in the same group – 'We call ourselves the Milk Street lot' – but said he did not fight that night.

The defence case at Warwick was that Jacky Joyce was only 'a child', that the night was dark and that he had denied ownership of the knife, which in any case was probably thrown and hit Kirkham accidentally, as the hospital surgeon had said was possible. The judge reminded the court of the importance of Joyce's age. If he was over seven but under fourteen, he was legally responsible, but the jury needed to have evidence of personal malice and intention to take away life to find him guilty of murder. Joyce had given his age as fourteen to the police, but as thirteen to the county gaol, perhaps when he realised the implications for sentencing. The judge told the jury that if they thought him to be under fourteen and without malicious intent, they might find a verdict of manslaughter. The jury retired and returned after five minutes, with a verdict of manslaughter, recommending mercy on the grounds of the prisoner's youth.

The next day, Joyce went back into the dock to hear Mr Justice Denman pass sentence upon him. The judge acquitted him of wilful murder and sentenced him to a month's imprisonment and five years in a reformatory. Joyce was advised to spend his leisure moments 'not in quarrelling with his fellows but in self-improvement', and the judge hoped that his fate would be a warning to others. Arguably it was no such thing. Joyce may have thought that he had had a lucky escape from a murder verdict. If he did, he no doubt also felt that his reputation was established as one of the toughest of Birmingham's sloggers. When the press next reported his appearance before the law, aged nineteen, and fresh from the reformatory, it would be for an unprovoked attack with a heavy belt against two men in Digbeth on a Saturday night. His previous record having been read out, including several other convictions for assault, he would be sentenced to prison again and on this occasion to four months with hard labour.

Joyce's light sentence for manslaughter was probably more a case of an assize judge opting for leniency towards a boy rather than a conciliatory gesture towards the Irish of Park Street, seven years after that street's devastating and vindictive treatment in the Murphy Riots. Nevertheless the local authorities' cautious approach towards the Park Street community would continue. Soon after Joyce's sentence at Warwick the Corporation's Sanitary Committee was seeking a site for a smallpox hospital but was facing opposition from all areas. In some ways Park Street would have been an ideal site, central and with plenty of property ripe for redevelopment, but Alderman Manton believed that 'that street would have risen against them' if chosen. Park Street's sloggers may have regarded the Joyce verdict as a caution and so turned their energies for a while to stoning unpopular individuals or even the trains that passed across their street on the way to Moor Street station rather than other gangs.

Cheapside itself was still dangerous to youths on their own. One parent wrote to the *Post* about his sixteen-year-old son who was attacked on his way home one Friday evening at the end of February by a gang of boys, presumed by the newspaper editor to be 'the slogging gang', near the lower end of Cheapside – so, near the Gullet. For a time he defended himself successfully with his walking stick. Then a pack of about twenty young men, aged between eighteen and twenty-two, joined in stoning him. A policeman dashed in among them, striking out right and left with his staff, and a hairdresser came out of his shop to help, and so the youngster managed to get home. Afterwards, according to the parent, the hairdresser lost a number of customers because of his intervention and other boys had to run the same gauntlet, 'such is the terrorism exercised by this gang'. The chief of police admitted there were not enough men to guarantee the safety of those on foot in the lower end of Cheapside and Moseley Street. 'Has it come to this that we must carry life-preservers or revolvers with us to inflict a chastisement on street ruffians?' asked the parent.

At the quarterly magistrates' meeting in April, between the death of John Kirkham and the trial, Alderman Ambrose Biggs, a wealthy tobacco manufacturer with premises in the St Martin's area, raised the issue of 'organised gangs of boys aged from twelve to sixteen who went about and created a disturbance whenever they met, and loss of life sometimes occurred ... Belts and knives were used and steps should be taken to breaking up these dangerous gangs.' He was referring specifically to the death of Kirkham.

The suggestion from this case was that the gangs were not ethnically exclusive, as those with Irish-born parents could be found on either side. The two leaders, however, Kirkham and Joyce, looked to be clear standard-bearers for English and Irish. So perhaps ethnic differences still counted for something: Park Street after all was renowned for its fighting Irishmen, whereas Milk Street was mainly, although not exclusively, Birmingham-born. Cheapside, with its variety of employment including works for making tubes, tinplate, coaches, curtain hooks, bedsteads and wood screws, seems to have been the street where Milk Street and Park Street gained a living, recruited and fought. The lower part of Cheapside in particular was still a meeting place and battleground for gangs from different areas – in spite of the fact that Park and Milk Streets were both nearer to each other than to Cheapside. A stronger element of territoriality was emerging with that conflict. Now the Milk Street boys would seek to restore their dented reputation in other streets.

IN BIRMINGHAM, more than in Manchester and Liverpool, Kirkham's story was the exception rather than the rule. Knives were rarely used in gang confrontations at this time, although stabbings in streets and homes were frequent. As slogging developed, so did the weapons used. By April 1874, two months after Kirkham's death, the Milk Street gang from north of Digbeth was operating in Benacre Street and Vere Street in the St Luke's area, off Bristol Street. They were interrupted one Sunday evening while trying to summon up the opposition by throwing stones at doors, and turned on a plain-clothes policeman called Roden. His billycock hat was broken and his head reduced to 'a pulp' by attacks from behind. The eighteen-year-old who was arrested leading younger boys was a bedstead maker called James Timothy, from Milk Street. His Irish-born mother Bridget would later be described by P.C. Davies as a leading rioter and 'member of the mob' in that street who had tried to hunt and stone him off the streets. Timothy produced a letter of good character from his employers, which narrowly saved him from two months in prison. Instead he paid a forty shilling fine. Many of the young men who terrorised the streets in the evenings or at weekends were, during weekdays, not unemployed criminals, but valued employees. However, the Milk Street boys shocked the police by wearing rings on their fingers with spikes attached, which they had used in the same neighbourhood on the previous evening to stab their opponents. D.S. Seal agreed that such weapons were rather a novelty.

Stones and sticks were still the most common weapons in slogging, with buckled straps used at close-quarters. Birmingham craftsmanship, however, was nothing if not ingenious. One man, who claimed to have been attacked by three Irishmen outside a fish shop, carried a 'murderous weapon, a little longer than a life preserver, solid to the end'. According to the *Daily Post*, 'upon the handle being pressed as when the instrument

was used, eight small knives, sharp as razors and in the form of fish-hooks, sprang out of the sides, effectively preventing anyone from seizing the instrument from its possessor and calculated to produce fearful injury.' In view of the size of the gun trade, it is surprising that firearms were not used more in play and by gangs and perhaps indicates that, on the whole, the gangs were seeking recreation rather than the infliction of life-threatening injuries. The use of guns was not in the tradition of the 'fair fight'.

Close neighbours might be bitter enemies, as in the case where an ironfounder of Milk Street named John Roach was attacked and 'kicked twenty yards' by his neighbours, the Barn Street sloggers, led by a nineteen-year-old whitesmith. In this case there was an element of 'mob law', as the ironfounder turned out to have a violent past. This was brought out by Mr Cheston the defence solicitor in court.

'Have you ever been tried for a violent assault?' asked Cheston.

'Yes, for drunkenness,' replied Roach.

'For manslaughter?'

'Yes, but I was acquitted.'

'Did you get out a gun that night?'

'No.'

Cheston was referring to a manslaughter case of 1867, eventually heard in Liverpool in 1871. The man charged with kicking his co-habitee, Bridget Plowman, in the head and causing her death was a John Roach, who had absconded four years before and had been found in the Manchester area. His whereabouts may have been divulged to the police by his sister's husband called 'Curly'. Certainly Roach and his father, an equally violent man, had gone looking for Curly near Manchester and, on not finding him, knocked down one of his sisters and then kicked the other, Curly's wife, so savagely in the head that she was in danger of her life. When she was well enough to appear in court she pleaded with Manchester's stipendiary magistrate not to commit them to the sessions and instead they were bound over to keep the peace. Roach was acquitted ten days later of the manslaughter of Bridget Plowman. Now in Birmingham, he appeared to have met his match – or perhaps his run of luck still held, as his enemy the leader of the Barn Street sloggers was sent to prison for six weeks' hard labour.

The gang violence of 1874 was not exclusive to Cheapside and Milk Street. In Hockley, a gang of glass workers associated with Worrall's works terrorised the neighbourhood of Barr Street, assaulting opponents and causing a great nuisance to their employer. Another more typical gang paraded up and down Broad Street on the west side of the town on Saturday nights, assaulting rivals. Meanwhile, the Birmingham and Fazeley Canal acted as a bulwark for the Gun Quarter and across it sorties were made to the north by its fighting youth. In March 1874, a quarrel broke out between a Gun Quarter slogging gang from Loveday and Price Streets and the lads of Hanley and Cecil Streets over the canal. They were close neighbours, but in Hanley and Cecil Streets the social composition was different, with only a few Irish and not many gunmakers. After a number of evening battles, the Loveday Street crew crossed the canal on a Thursday and made for Cecil Street, where they smashed windows and stoned passers-by in order to provoke their opponents into appearing. Instead, a ten-year-old local schoolboy called Thomas Shelton, the youngest of a family that was half English and half Irish-born, happened to come down the street on his own – or was acting as a stalking-horse for older boys – and suffered a severe head injury from the volley of stones. He was followed by P.C. Brown, who arrested one of the leaders of the Loveday Street gang, a fourteen-year-old brasscaster, while the unfortunate Shelton was taken to the General Hospital nearby. The brasscaster was given fourteen days in prison with hard labour. The magistrates' clerk confessed that he could not explain why the town was 'in the possession of the boys and ruffians'. In June there was more fighting in nearby Newtown Row between boys from both sides of the canal.

Gosta Green was an open space in Bishop Ryder's District and a battleground where that rough area could be said to be 'at home' to incursions from its close neighbours, St Stephen's, Nechells and Duddeston, not to mention St Bartholomew's and Aston. It also marked the boundaries of several districts and so proved an ideal meeting place and battleground for all the gangs of the area. A total of six streets, as well as the Aston Road, fed into it, so it was a kind of Wembley for sloggers. A hub of many streets as early as 1795, the Green had been a popular meeting place long before the sloggers. The Chartists and the unemployed met there and later the Social Democratic Federation would stage their May Day rallies there. When charged with obstruction, the preachers of the Town Mission showed the magistrates on the map that the space was big enough to contain a large meeting and still allow cabs and other wheeled traffic to pass freely around the outside. The Green acquired a drinking fountain in 1871, but it was said to be placed too high for children to reach.

April 1874 saw a kind of knockout competition when over a hundred youths from different streets in the locality descended on the Green. In nightly contests, they slogged each other until a number of boys and other people had been injured. The police made two arrests, a clogmaker from Dale End, in the St Bartholomew's district, and an ironfiler from Dartmouth Street, across the canal. The gangs of Ashted and Duddeston were increasingly involved, and boys were put under pressure by their peers to take part. It was reported in the Dartmouth Street area of Duddeston that young urchins calling themselves 'slogging gangs' stoned any lad who refused to join them. If there were no youths to stone, adults were targeted.

Women were sometimes victims. One evening, Elizabeth Crook went out of her home in Rope Walk, in the Newhall district, to speak to her husband who was standing in the road. As she approached him, she found herself in the middle of a slogging match and was struck on the head with a stone thrown by a fourteen-year-old from London Prentice Street. She went to hospital and he went to prison.

On the weekend of 13-14 June alone, the General and Queen's Hospitals had to deal with over eighty victims of the violence. Some of the worst was in the Digbeth area, and on the St Bartholomew's side. Allison Street, off Digbeth, had some tough characters, and its slogging gang was under the captaincy of Thomas Joyce, Jacky's brother. Milk Street, further down Digbeth, remained active. P.C. Davies, in an incident already mentioned, had difficulty bringing three women from that street before the magistrates for riot and obstruction on a Sunday evening. He declared in court that the neighbourhood was 'so infested with roughs of both sexes that it is dangerous for a policeman to "work a beat" alone'.

Barn Street also remained a problem for the police. In July four men were sent to gaol for six weeks by the magistrates for breaking glass in the street. That evening, about a hundred roughs caused havoc in Barn and Fazeley Streets. One man threatened the landlord of the Brewers' Arms, and soon afterwards returned with about forty others. Fourteen panes of glass were broken in that pub, while windows were smashed at the Bordesley Street Independent Chapel, a shop and two more pubs. Two outraged landlords, George Guest of the Brewers' Arms and his brother Joseph of the Beehive, followed the mob. What they had done to deserve attack never emerged, but George was knocked down and kicked and Joseph was badly assaulted. This street brawl, with an element of a vendetta against publicans, gathered momentum, like so many distur-bances, and ended in a full-scale riot in Barford Street, until an inspector and two constables managed to disperse the crowd. The Guests later gave evidence, identifying the main offenders, and two were pulled from their beds at midnight. Six lads aged between fourteen and eighteen, from a wide radius of Fazeley Street, were arrested. Three were sent to prison for six months, one fined and two discharged for lack of evidence. The man who started it, aged twenty-five, was given two months. Yet the area remained extremely volatile, as the Bordesley Riot would show.

CHAPTER 7

The Bordesley Riot

A COMBINATION OF the familiar Saturday night attacks on police and the weekday slogging battles between gangs and street-groups culminated in what became known as the Coventry Street or Bordesley Riot, once again in St Bartholomew's Ward. It is hard to say whether the area around Digbeth had up till then been the most turbulent and law-breaking in the whole of Birmingham, but the question was settled on 13 July 1874, a Monday evening, when the whole area erupted in a major communal riot which would stand alongside the Priestley Riots and the Murphy Riots as one of the most eventful in the history of the town, although much less destructive than either of those.

It seems to have been caused by the sighting of a witness who had given evidence in the police court that morning – probably against Simon Ryan of Steelhouse Lane, a youth of Irish parentage named for throwing stones at a policeman on the previous Saturday night and sentenced to six weeks in prison. Street mobs had a history of picking on witnesses in the courts, derided as 'coppers', who in some way had helped the police. In this case the anonymous witness was hunted, it seems, to a house in Bordesley Street. His pursuers stoned first the house and then the police who arrived to restore order. The large plate glass window of the Wrexham public house was smashed and glass littered the pavements. At nine that evening, Inspector Shaw received a telegram, probably from Bradford Street police station, saying there was a riot in Bordesley Street. Sergeant Parkinson and fourteen constables were at once sent out, following the rioters towards Allison Street. The police moved up Allison Street from Digbeth but when they reached Coventry Street they were stopped by a hailstorm of stones and bottles from a shouting mob, estimated at over five hundred strong. The constables charged the mob and arrested three of the leaders.

P.C. Myott, one of the constables, gave evidence that he had been struck by five stones as he was running up Coventry Street. George Davis, a twenty-two-year-old from Gibb Street and allegedly a ringleader, was said to have produced a basket of stones, many of which were hurled through a bedroom window. Davis was inciting the crowd to 'come on' until he was taken into custody. Catherine Brampton testified that eighteen panes of glass were broken in her house on Bordesley Street. She had seen 'the girl Giblin' (Julia Giblin, aged fifteen, an umbrella maker of New Canal Street) carrying stones in her apron as missiles. Councillor Arthur Chamberlain, one of Joseph's younger brothers, was a partner in the brassfounding business of Smith and Chamberlain in New Bartholomew Street and a councillor for St Bartholomew's Ward. He said that riots were frequent in the neighbourhood and that it was not safe to leave his works before 10 p.m. because of the stone-throwing. The shutters had to be put up at 9 p.m. Neighbours were quite terrified and complained of their insecurity. The police eventually arrested five others apart from Davis and Giblin.

The next day's *Mail* called it a 'grand field-day for the slogging gang of Bordesley Street'. Over a thousand people were said to have been involved in the end. Chief Superintendent Glossop told the Watch Committee that in fact the disturbances had been going on for a fortnight. It was a row between the English and the Irish. Alderman Biggs expressed a common view of those in authority that only the boys were ever captured and the ringleaders who were older, managed to escape. In fact the seven arrested during and after the riots included three under the age of twenty-one: Julia Giblin already mentioned, the only female of the group, as well as a brasscaster and a striker. Three were in their twenties. The odd man out was James Riley, aged sixty-four. All seven were from the Digbeth area, and of these three were from Allison Street. Those three, who included Riley, claimed that they had been peacefully drinking in the Swan Inn and had been surprised to come out and find a riot of boys and girls throwing stones. Riley said that no 'big' ones were present. The other two, Moran and Manning, claimed that as they left the pub and went up Coventry Street they were accosted by the police and Moran was knocked down by their staves. No notice was taken of their statements. The four oldest were sentenced to four months and the three youngest to one month in prison. Of these, one was Irish-born and three had strong family links with Ireland.

Stipendiary magistrate Kynnersley warned them that any repetition would make them liable to a sentence of nine months' hard labour each. The lack of sympathy for and apparent prejudice against Birmingham's Irish population still lingered in the police and on the Bench.

In a later report to the Watch Committee, the police chief described the disturbances of St Bartholomew's Ward as an 'occasional' event, meaning that it was unlikely to recur. Glossop told the committee that this was not a revenge attack on a 'copper', but that the riots had been caused by boys 'turned out to play by the low Irish' – to 'play' on pieces of wasteland, not the public highway, and the police could not interfere with them for doing so. He produced a black and green paper flag with a skull and crossbones and a shamrock upon it. This had been found stuck on the railway bridge in Allison Street, implying that that was their territory. Then a rival band came up and fighting broke out. However Glossop did not go into any detailed identification of which gangs were involved or any theory as to what was behind it all, although he clearly thought that it was something to do with a 'party riot' involving ethnic animosity between the English and the Irish. This animosity certainly would have been felt if an Irishman or Irish-linked person had been sent to prison on the basis of evidence perhaps motivated by anti-Irish feeling. Glossop's view was that the large scale of that outbreak arose unexpectedly - which is surprising considering the the degree of tension already existing in that part of St Bartholomew's Ward. Glossop continued his statement that such disturbances were not confined to any one area but occurred all over the borough, suddenly and unforeseen, so that reaction to any disturbance was bound to be slow, without an enormous increase in the size of the force.

None of this explanation was very reassuring to the councillors on the committee, who had no reason to doubt Glossop's gloomy analysis of public disorder. However the Mayor, Joseph Chamberlain, was annoyed about the riot, as he said that he had been in the habit of boasting, presumably to Liberal friends, of 'the peace and quietude of the town'. In truth Chamberlain's sights were already well above street level; two years later, when an MP, he would admit to a political meeting that he was 'very seldom in Deritend Ward'. He went on to become Gladstone's President of the Board of Trade. Councillor Kenrick, the committee chairman, asked if a flying division of police would help, but Glossop replied that a body of men was always sent as soon as possible when a row had broken out. Alderman Brinsley, who was not a Chamberlainite and who was always concerned to keep the costs down, thought that a flying division was unnecessary, as these disturbances took place mainly on just three nights of the week: Saturday, Sunday and Monday.

He was wrong; there was a great deal of weekday slogging. He was also wrong to link Mondays to Saturdays and Sundays, as most weekend disturbances were over by Sunday nights, and hardly spread into Monday evenings at all. Alderman Biggs suggested binding over parents for a small sum of money to ensure the good behaviour of their children. Glossop said that he had been keeping a force in the Bordesley Street area since the riots. The trouble was that people would complain, but they would not come forward to give evidence before the magistrates, so it was difficult to convict – an old story and no less true for that.

It was easy for this to become a blame game. The press and the police blamed the magistrates for not being tough enough on the culprits. The magistrates either blamed Parliament for not allowing the youths to be whipped or the police for only catching 'little fellows'. The *Mail* at first favoured the 'most stringent measures' to avoid Birmingham becoming as disorderly as American cities. No 'metal' (meaning stones) should be 'thrown down' in the streets to provide ready missiles, and building sites and waste land should be fenced off, for the same reason. A bigger police force would soon make 'the guerilla war of our roughs' a thing of the past. A fortnight later, after hearing the discussions at the Watch Committee, and no doubt considering the extra cost to the ratepayers, the newspaper had changed its view. The *Mail* was now against any further increases in the force and was attracted to Kenrick's idea of a flying brigade to ensure sufficient force at moments when disorder threatened. Its diagnosis was that inter-family quarrels were at the heart of the problem, rather than the horseplay of children or the outburst of ethnic feeling.

One conclusion was clear to all: the police were on trial. The town council decided that the Watch Committee would in future receive a weekly report from the Chief Superintendent on any further outbreaks of 'rowdiness' or rioting. The police were promised no more support, in spite of depleted numbers, and were left with a double problem. Not only did they face much working-class hostility for trying to enforce unpopular by-laws, but also a duty to interfere in the battles between the slogging gangs.

August saw more violence. One constable got into trouble trying to disperse a Friday dinnertime set-to between glass workers, once again in the Hockley area. Their annoyance at his intervention was shared by the fifty-one-year-old wife of one of them, who asked him, 'What are you doing with these glass chaps?' A single stone from her knocked off his helmet, and at the second he ducked, before drawing his staff. Two more policemen were attacked on the corner of St Paul's Square by an angry, stone-throwing mob. Neighbouring Livery Street was a hotbed of disturbances, and P.C. Elliott was placed in the area to quell the disorder caused by the likes of the Rafferty brothers, two violent brass-casters in their early twenties who lived among other Irish with their widowed mother. Elliott reported that 'respectable people could not get to their warehouses and places of work without fear of molestation'. In the Sandpits area, two men were chased and attacked by a gang in Nelson Street.

Two reports, one unproven, of assaults on women by policemen may have stirred anti-police feeling to new heights. This was much more inflammatory than the usual tally of police drinking. Such complaints may have encouraged attacks on individual policemen in the course of their duties, usually while a man was being taken to the station. Staniforth Street in Bishop Ryder's District saw a huge crowd of lads in the street throwing stones and forcing householders and shopkeepers to put up their shutters. The *Mail* called it an 'epidemic of savagery' reaching right across the country which needed sentences of flogging rather than 'two penny-halfpenny terms of imprisonment'. One correspondent of the *Post* asked for mounted police action and a town's meeting before the winter dark set in.

There was no easy solution. Not only did the gross overcrowding of industrial cities provoke friction between neighbours – even without the Murphy legacy – but street honour or credibility expected you to pursue your quarrel or seek vengeance if you thought yourself wronged. There were often alcohol-fuelled. Stone-throwing started young and was an accepted part of Birmingham's street culture. The police were under-manned and had the unenviable task of enforcing draconian laws on the occupants of the streets. 'As unsafe as the Indian jungle' was how the *Mail* described the streets of Birmingham in September 1874. The 'riotous spirits' were 'in the ascendant'. In a kind of panic, the newspaper echoed the call for a town's meeting, because the police and the Watch Committee seemed at a loss as to how to cope with a worsening crisis of law and order. The alternative was simple: 'Otherwise every citizen will be compelled to carry arms.'

The cry was taken up by readers. One recommended a vigilance committee of 'twelve good men per street of average length', each to be armed with an 'ebony, ferruled walking stick' which, as it struck the cobbles, would act as a signal of warning to offending roughs. With memories of the Paris Commune only three years old, one letter-writer likened Birmingham ruffianism to a 'species of Communism like that which ruined and deso-lated France'. Calls came for martial law. It is doubtful whether this degree of panic was justified. Many of those arrested for slogging were not regular attenders at the police courts, and not many of the hardened criminals seem to have been involved at this stage. One example was Edward Lundy, a gunmaker from Slaney Street, who was handy with a knuckle-duster and was always in and out of the police court, especially for assaulting policemen. He was rarely arrested with sloggers, but it is noticeable that when he was being apprehended the following year, aged twenty-four, a large mob came to his help as he shouted, 'Don't let the – take me.' No doubt the sloggers regarded him as something of a hero.

In the gang-haunted area of south Birmingham, tension remained at breaking point. Thomas Joyce, who worked as a steel sashline binder, was a captain of the Allison Street gang and one of the best known slog-gers of the day. He was on his way home from work in Charles Henry Street with a friend just after 6 p.m. on a Friday in late September when they encountered twenty members of a rival gang from the other side of the River Rea in Deritend. Joyce claimed that he and his friend, an older man called Toy, were met near the Deritend Bridge and challenged with, 'What are you looking at?' They carried on their way, but eigh-teen-year-old William Smallwood, another steel worker from River Street, followed and struck Joyce on the head with a buckled strap, then assaulted Toy. Toy suffered cuts to his eye and hand which he said were from a knife, though the police did not find a weapon on Smallwood when he was arrested.

Defending himself before the Bench, Smallwood maintained that he used his belt only when the Allison Street lot tried to stab him. He knew Joyce as their captain. In the end Smallwood's actions were reckoned to be in self-defence, as an independent witness, a factory owner's son called Burton, saw Joyce and his mate wrestling with a youth near the bridge and heard one of them use filthy language towards Smallwood. There was even a suggestion that they tried to throw one of their rivals off the bridge. Burton saw Joyce and Toy pull knives, and a struggle ensued. Only after this did Smallwood use his buckle. P.C. Davis was at hand and overheard Joyce say that he would go into Allison Street and get his gang together; if they would not come he would 'chuck them up' and have them 'sneaked' to the police. Mr Jaffray, the magistrate, took the view that Smallwood had given Joyce and his fellow complainant a 'good thrashing – a taste of their own medicine and in self-defence'. So he was discharged. Smallwood's origins lay in Smethwick, while Joyce and Toy had Irish forebears, and that difference may well have prejudiced the decision.

Many, including the stipendiary magistrate, T.C.S. Kynnersley, and the *Mail*, put their faith in flogging. The question of the effectiveness of corporal punishment was hotly debated in the 1860s and 1870s. The Social Science Congress on the Repression of Crime in 1874 heard the view that flogging for garrotting had not diminished the number of highway robberies with violence. Yet the *Mail* wanted it introduced as an experiment in cases of extreme brutality.

However this panic died down sooner than many expected. At the early September meeting of the Watch Committee, its chairman, Joseph Chamberlain's brother-in-law, was able to announce that over the previous two weeks there had been a 'considerable cessation' of rowdyism and a fortnight later that 'the epidemic of ruffianism seems to have subsided', despite the attack on Thomas Joyce. The press was far from satisfied, but it was hard to contradict the official view completely. Glossop stuck to a narrow definition of rowdyism, encompassing assemblies of organised gangs of roughs but excluding street brawls and drunken rows. A concentrated police presence in the evenings in the hot spots, at the expense of night duty, seemed to have worked, at least for the time being. Tougher sentences passed by magistrates were also thought to be helping. Mayor Chamberlain refused one alderman's request to ask Parliament for the use of the 'cat', arguing that 'meeting one brutality with another ... did not put down crime'. At the beginning of October, Glossop told the Watch Committee that the situation was well in hand, with only three serious disturbances in the previous fortnight, in which two policemen had been assaulted, including one in Allison Street for which one man was given one month in prison and another four months. Elsewhere in the town there were several drunken brawls, 'but they were not of the character of rowdyism'.

It was a question of necessity. Birmingham needed to be calmed because a royal visit by the Prince and Princess of Wales was expected at the beginning of November. This was a matter of civic pride and competition with other cities. It was already felt that the town had missed out on a visit from the Shah of Persia the previous June because of the reputation created by its rowdies, though in fact the Shah had even shied off a visit to the Bank of England. When Mayor Chamberlain had laid the foundation stone of the Municipal Buildings there had been too much 'hustling' by the crowds. While Chamberlain proclaimed his great faith in the Birmingham population as 'one of the most orderly in the country', it was felt that precautions should be taken this time to reduce the likelihood of panic and crush.

On 3 November, the day of the visit, the sun shone with 'a radiance rare in November and rarer still in Birmingham'. Church bells rang from early in the day. Huge crowds gathered to see the royal couple, whose marriage had been such an occasion to celebrate back in 1863. Sightseers came from as far as Nottingham and Bristol, and the *Mail* reporter watched the Black Country pour 'its rough but loyal energy into the town'. Happily for the authorities the spectators were in a good humour, and this time, they were kept in bounds by strong wooden barriers, guarded by policemen.

Even in the areas most prone to slogging, there was a big turnout. Deritend Bridge held 'a dense mass of people' and in Digbeth they were 'packed like sardines'. Women and children from dirty courts and alleys were seen to 'shout and hurrah, as if they had no thought and no care for tomorrow'. Even the men sitting on window ledges and smoking 'meditative pipes' removed them 'for a brief cheer', as the prince and princess passed by. At night there was 'a general illumination' by gaslight, as there had been in 1863. Later there was a complaint about a mounted policeman who was seen to 'draw his sword and ride at the people in a manner both wilful and dangerous', but this was more the criticism of a military officer unimpressed by the amateurishness of the police than of any Birmingham republican disappointed by the amount of interest in the royal visit. In his report on the day, Glossop noted that six people had had to be treated for accidents at each hospital, but only one person had been detained with a broken leg and there were only seven cases of drunkenness. Altogether 'the crowd behaved most orderly'. Such conduct, however, would not be maintained beyond the great day. A month later, a *Post* reader from Sparkbrook complained of Sunday disturbances by 'gangs of respectably dressed lads, armed with catapults' practising 'interminably ... with swan shot, which from a catapult will perforate a window cleanly at sixty or seventy yards'. Early in 1875, two businessmen were complaining that Allison Street was again under-policed and 'once more in the grip of gangs'.

CHAPTER 8

Death in Navigation Street

IN FEBRUARY 1875, three months after the royal visit, a correspondent – perhaps the editor himself – wrote to the *Post* to express the view that there had been a 'relapse' regarding assaults in the town. It was all very well and safe, he said, for gentlemen who arrived in town at midday and went home at dusk, presumably referring to the elite who lived in Edgbaston or Moseley. For those who lived in the town, it was a different matter. The problem was thrown into high relief, a few weeks after this letter, by the savage killing of a policeman.

Navigation Street was one of the most violent and criminal areas of Birmingham. On a line roughly between the Old Wharf canal basin and the main railway station, it was a scene of constant coming and going, lined with small inns, beerhouses and dens of ill-repute. It was a place where men waited for new chances of casual labour and spent their few pennies quickly. The floating population passed beneath their waiting gaze. Men, women and children lived on the street, many of them without anywhere regularly to go at night.

There had been a fatal stabbing there in 1873. A twenty-three-year-old hairdresser, Samuel Bayliss, died in hospital three weeks after being stabbed in the early hours of 27 December. His killer, Frederick 'Bowey' Smith, was a twenty-five-year-old painter, who hung about in Suffolk Street with nowhere to live other than with his sister. He was rather too ready with his clasp-knife and had stabbed two soldiers just three days earlier, but had somehow eluded the police. He was not untypical of other violent semi-criminals, but his instability made him more dangerous than most.

Samuel Bayliss, with his younger brother Fred and two friends, who lived in the Islington area off Broad Street, had been spending the Boxing Day holiday in the town. By 12.30 a.m. they were on their way home by way of Navigation Street. Fred Bayliss was in front and as he turned into the street he accosted or bumped into a woman. At any rate Bowey Smith, perhaps her bully, was angered and came up and hit him. Fred returned the blow. Seeing the start of a fight, Sam Bayliss ran up from behind and said, 'Stop it, kid. Let's have no bother; there's a bobby coming.' Bowey Smith followed them on down Navigation Street, shouting, 'Stop him.' When they turned into Suffolk Street, they found, outside the Dolphin Inn, a crowd of cornermen, who stopped them in their tracks. Somehow Fred got away.

Edwin Southall, a son of the landlord of the nearby Greyhound pub, had gone to bed but was disturbed by a row in the street and went to the bedroom window to see what was going on. He saw two men running up the street towards the house followed by a 'ruck' or crowd of others. One of the men, Sam Bayliss, was tripped up at the pub door. The crowd called, 'Stop him, Bowey,' then, 'Let him have it, Bowey.' From upstairs the boy and his brother saw Bayliss being stabbed by Bowey Smith and then kicked by others underneath the Greyhound's window, with the scene being lit by the bright light from a brothel next door.

Sam Bayliss was taken to the Queen's Hospital. He was found to have been stabbed five times in the back, twice on the head and once on the shoulder. When arrested the next day at the Dolphin, Bowey denied his guilt. Later he tried to blame two other men. 'I am not going to stand for this,' he said. 'I don't mind the stir, but I am not going to get the rope to screen them.' He was not believed by either judge or jury, and was sentenced to death for murder at the Warwick Assizes. Four days before he was due to be executed, his sentence was commuted to penal servitude for life.

If that killing came from one moment of madness, the second, two years later, and notorious in Victorian Birmingham as the Navigation Street Murder, derived from drink-fuelled hatred of the police. The policemen involved were all experienced officers well versed in the challenges of the Birmingham streets: dealing with election rioters, murder suspects, housebreakers and pickpockets. They were used to physical assault by the drunks they hauled continually to the police station, and to the more dangerous scenario when they had to step in to arrest men fighting in the streets. Often they were attacked with fists or boots. Policing Birmingham was at best a wearying and bruising job. The shifts were still either the daytime circular beat, lasting nine hours, or eleven hours through the night. Many could not stand the battering they had to take and left the force. On the whole, constables earned their pay and could be excused for occasionally lingering illegally in pubs when on duty.

Shortly before eight o'clock on the dark, wet Sunday evening of 7 March 1875, constables Fletcher and Goodman were out in plain clothes in an attempt to avoid the hostile reaction of the downtown population to police uniforms. Their mission was to the Bull's Head beerhouse in Fordrough Street, close to the Gas Street canal basin of central Birmingham; their task was to arrest an eighteen-year-old chandelier maker called Billy Downes for burgling that house the previous evening. He and a boatman called Carey had slipped into the landlord's house next door and stolen some clothes and a cashbox from his bedroom. Now he was back brazenly drinking at the same bar.

The policemen found the front room full of drinkers, as was common even on a Sunday evening. At the constables' bidding, the landlord turned all the young men out – perhaps nineteen in all – although five, including Downes, stayed inside or slipped back in again. The landlord called to Downes, 'Billy, here! I want you.' Downes came over without any fuss, and was charged with the burglary and agreed to 'go quiet' with P.C. Fletcher.

A twenty-three-year-old brasscaster called John Cresswell was just behind the door and heard what was being said. He called to the others waiting close by. 'Come on! They are taking Billy.' As the two policemen escorted their prisoner out of the beerhouse and down towards Navigation Street, the drinkers followed them and stones began to fly. Among those at the front was Jeremiah Corkery, who urged the others not to let Billy be taken. With the rest of the pub customers following behind them, and a crowd in the street, the bobbies were increasingly worried at the prospect of an attempted rescue and moved Downes along as quickly as they could.

When they reached the corner of Navigation Street, they were relieved to come across P.C. William Lines, in uniform. Lines was no stranger to street justice, having once been knocked down with a poker by a group of late-night rowdies, and the others asked him to hold back the mob while they took Downes to Moor Street police station. Lines did his best, but the other two policemen could soon hear that he was having a tough time of it. When they reached Suffolk Street, they ran into another uniformed policeman, Sergeant Joseph Fletcher, and called to him, 'For God's sake, Fletcher, go back and help Lines.'

Lines and the sergeant, both in uniform, staged a brave rearguard action against a rapidly-building, stone-throwing crowd. The sergeant was the first to go down and was kicked repeatedly where he lay. Soon he was in a coma. Lines retaliated by knocking down the man responsible with his staff, but he too was set upon and stabbed in the neck just under his left ear.

Blood spurted from the wound. 'Oh, I shall die,' uttered Lines, as he staggered back. P.C. Lines was eventually conveyed to the Queen's Hospital. As he lay desperately ill on his bed, he managed to make a statement. Six suspects, chained together, were brought to his bedside and he was able to identify three of the four men who had attacked himself and Sergeant Fletcher. They were known to him from his beat. He had heard one, Aaron Rogers, a twenty-two-year old bedstead maker, urging on the others with 'Come along, you'll let any poor bastard get took.' Then as Fletcher fell, Lines had gone to get him up and hit Cresswell over the head. Cresswell was arrested on the night by P.C. Goodman and claimed that the blood on his head was from falling downstairs drunk. From his bed, however, Lines said, 'That's the man that dropped the sergeant and I then struck with my staff.' Thomas Whalin, aged eighteen, and Rogers had also attacked him – although Whalin denied it, complaining at his arrest 'If anything happens in our neighbourhood it's either me or our kid.' Lines also identified Thomas Leonard, also eighteen, who had earlier denied being at the scene: 'Yes, you were there and had me by the throat when I was stabbed.' Suddenly Lines had felt the stab in his ear from one of the four who were onto him, but from which one he could not say.

A number of witnesses testified that the fourth man was Jeremiah Corkery, or Corcoran, a twenty-year-old iron worker of Howard's Place, Tonks Street. P.C. Goodman searched for him on the night of the attack, but with no success. On the next day, Corkery was asked by his mates about a visible mark on his head. He admitted to one that 'he had got it hot', and to another, 'They will never find me out. I have been to the hospital. I gave them a wrong name and a wrong address and I got it put down the sixth of March instead of the seventh.' However the hospital treatment ticket with the correct details was found on him when he was arrested.

Mary Smith, the housekeeper at the Bull's Head, gave evidence that Corkery had no injury to his forehead prior to the assault. The four men had been amongst those who stayed on after the two plain clothes constables had cleared the house. Soon after, there was a scream in the street and she had closed the beerhouse. George Cunnington, the landlord, told the court the details of Downes' arrest. A crowd of about twenty had followed and run after them down the street, headed by Corkery. James Moore testified that he had watched Corkery run up to Lines, saw the blade of a knife which he held in his right hand and saw him 'put it up to Lines' face'. Lines had not seen the knife in the darkness. At the same moment, as he struck Corkery on the eye with his staff, Lines began to bleed from the left ear. Corkery had already run away up the street. Other witnesses corroborated Moore's evidence. One told the jury that as Corkery went along Severn Street after the event, he declared, 'It's me that chivied the bastard. Feel the blade of this knife. It's wet with blood now.'

P.C. William Lines died from wounds to the head on 24 March. Aged thirty, he had begun life working on a Warwickshire farm. There was a big turnout for his funeral and a subscription was started, publicized by the newspapers, for his widow and children. His death turned the accusation against Jeremiah Corkery into a capital charge. He was tried at the Warwick Summer Assizes before the notoriously irascible Mr Justice Field on the charge of wilful murder. He pleaded not guilty in a reportedly 'clear, but tremulous voice', but the judge told the grand jury that 'the evidence would leave very little doubt in their minds'. Wilful murder implied malice aforethought. Corkery was duly found guilty and condemned to death. From the dock he claimed that he had been framed. 'Not that I wish to gain mercy or anything of that kind, gentlemen,' he said, 'but you can see that there is a plot to put me into this case and get other people out ... but I leave it to somebody else's hands – to the Judge of Judges. No more, gentlemen.'

His defence counsel, the Honourable Chandos Leigh, highlighted discrepancies in the evidence, but they did not sway the judge. Mr Justice Field applied the dubious and pitiless logic that if there had not been such discrepancies, the evidence might have been liable to the suspicion of being 'arranged'. He was determined to make an example of Corkery.

The day after Corkery had been sentenced to death, it was the turn of the six other rioters: Mee, Cresswell, Whalin, Leonard, McNally and Rogers. The oldest was only twenty-three years of age. Three had previous convictions, but not Charles Mee, who was the youngest, aged seventeen, and nicknamed 'Barber' because that was his father's occupation; he was found guilty of trampling on a policeman's helmet in the melee. He had two testimonies as to his good character, but the judge viewed his action as 'indicating approval of the brutality which had taken place', so he was allowed no special mitigation. Leonard addressed the jury, pleading that he had only been in Birmingham seven weeks and that the only one he knew was Barber Mee. He and Cresswell admitted one previous conviction each, though it later transpired that Leonard had four previous convictions, all concerning theft, and Cresswell had two, one for stealing and the other for assault. The jury took fifteen minutes to find Mee, Cresswell, Whalin and Leonard, guilty of unlawful assault against a police sergeant and a constable, and the judge sentenced all four to penal servitude for life. The courtroom filled with the cries of the condemned: 'Oh! Lord, Oh!' Then they turned to their friends, who were shrieking and sobbing, to call, 'Goodbye.' Only Rogers and McNally were acquitted of the main charge.

Billy Downes was in custody, but the search for the other burglar, Thomas Carey, took over three weeks. He drew a knife on D.S. Black when he was eventually found in Newhall Hill, and Black took it off him with difficulty. The burglary had been observed by a servant, Sarah Ann Hyde, and she had given a full statement of this in a side parlour to P.C. Fletcher in front of her master, the landlord. The two men had ransacked the landlord's bedroom and then got away by means of a ladder. A third man, Thomas Kelly, had been arrested on the charge of riot and assault and had decided to give information. On his arrest he told P.C. Fletcher, 'I have suffered enough. I shall "round" [tell]. The room was broken into, but all the b– lot didn't realise more than seven shillings.' The proceeds from burglaries disappointed many Birmingham thieves.

Carey's appeal for mercy fell on deaf ears. The judge told him that his seven previous sentences for stealing in the past four years had all failed 'to make you a better man'. This time he was given fifteen years, while his accomplice Downes, with three previous convictions in the past three years, for riot, wilful damage and assault, got only five years, partly in view of his good conduct after his arrest. The same term was given to Kelly for assaulting constables Fletcher and Goodman. Kelly appealed in tears to the judge, 'Please give it me in a reformatory school, sir, and it will do me good.' The judge was not impressed and ignored him.

Local historian Thomas Harman called these assizes the 'Roughs' Reprisals' for their punishment of Birmingham low life, including the Navigation Street rioters. 'One was sentenced to death, four to penal servitude for life, six to fifteen years each (three of them were flogged as well), one to ten years, one to seven years, and four to five years each,' he wrote. The Victorians relished such exemplary retribution, and it was felt in Birmingham that the death of a constable from savage treatment in the streets had been likely for some time. The *Mail* pointed out that in the previous fourteen years, three other constables had been 'virtually murdered'.

Later two petitions were presented to the Home Secretary on behalf of Barber Mee, but after nine years of convict life, the 'weak-minded' boy who had repeatedly kicked a policeman's helmet had lost his reason altogether and had been transferred to Woking Infirmary and later to Broadmoor Criminal Asylum. Three others were released on licence after ten years.

HOW FAR the Navigation Street rioters had acted criminally together before the murder of P.C. Lines is impossible to say. Gangs had headquarters in pubs, and the Bull's Head beerhouse may have been theirs. The name 'Navigation Street Gang' was accorded to them with the passage of time and to support the view that the crime of that night in March 1875 was the most serious of all the group crimes in Birmingham in the late Victorian period. The death of Lines was not intended by most of the rioters, arguably not even by Corkery, and so cannot be regarded as a gang murder, but the circumstances under which the policeman was fatally injured became symbolic to respectable Birmingham of the dangers from the collective action of the streets.

The youthfulness of the rioters was typical of street crime and disorder in Victorian Birmingham. This was a society in which children had to grow up fast in a brutal and criminalising environment. Several of the rioters had previous convictions going back to their mid-teens, and so were held fully responsible for their actions. They were all too old to have benefited from public education and too hardened, in the judge's harsh view, to receive any mercy. The hope was that others would take note and that in future such patterns of behaviour would be reformed. Such optimism was slow to be rewarded.

A petition was also sent to the Home Secretary on behalf of Jeremiah Corkery, arguing that his mother's poverty had prevented him from having the services of a lawyer, both at the inquest into Lines's death and at the magistrates' inquiry which followed, and that he had only had legal representation at the Warwick Assizes thanks to the generosity of a clergyman and others. It also drew attention to the view of the surgeon at the Queen's Hospital that it was the surgical operation rather than the blow that had caused Lines' death. However the petition was to no avail. Corkery was executed on 27 July at Warwick Gaol. It was reported that he finally confessed his guilt to his brother, after earlier protesting innocence. His was the second 'private' execution at Warwick in the prison yard rather than outside in full view of the gawping public. A priest was with him at 'the drop'.

After his death, Corkery's life story was made known: how he was the son of a schoolmaster in Birmingham who had effectively abandoned his family and gone off to Ireland. He had been brought up by his mother, but had other relatives among the Irish in the slums of New Inkleys and Tonk Street. In his short life he had made nine previous appearances before the magistrates. It may be important that his first appearance before the courts, aged eleven – like his last, ten years later – was on a stabbing charge, although he was not found guilty then. In spite of being convicted on six later occasions, he was not regarded as a hardened criminal. After his first conviction, for stealing flannel, he was sent to a reformatory for five years. His offences quickly escalated on his release, from gambling and the theft of thread, to throwing stones at and assaulting policemen. His penultimate sentence, after trial in 1873, had been twelve months' imprisonment for stealing sweets. His violence towards the police was typical of many young Brummies of his class and time, but he went further than most. His particular mentality and circumstances set him on a collision course with authority for which he paid the ultimate price.

His execution was a warning to his contemporaries. The memorial for him was widely supported and an elaborate funeral card was sold by the hundreds after his death. The police were clearly worried by a backlash from the Irish community and others, and half a dozen constables were on guard at the family wake to prevent any disturbance of the peace. There was no uprising in the Inkleys, but the case left a ripple effect of bitterness towards the authorities. Policemen making arrests would for some time be threatened with 'another Corkery job' or, as in the later Hope Street riot by drunken roughs, with the promise to 'corkery the whole of the police'. The word 'corkery' became established in Birmingham street slang, designed to strike fear into any constable, but violence towards individual policemen had passed its peak and few, even when drunk, were willing to follow his reckless example to the scaffold.

Both Thomas Whalin and John Cresswell had been given life sentences, but this did not prevent bad blood between their families.

Whalin's sixteen-year-old sister Ann, who had given evidence at the trial, was quarrelsome after too much drink and easily started brawling with other women in a similar condition. One night she got into a row with Cresswell's wife and threatened her by saying that it was her husband who had chivied the policeman and she would 'peach', or tell, on him. In fact she had already done the damage and it was too late for any more 'peaching' in this case.

Perhaps Ann Whalin's behaviour can be understood as the result of the pressure she had been put under by the ordeal of giving evidence before a merciless judge. Intimidation of female witnesses, such as herself and Margaret Morgan, had become an issue even before the trials began. The very day after the murder, both were threatened and one was assaulted to warn them off 'turning copper' against a lamp maker called John Hamilton in another case. Six weeks later the other girl, Margaret Morgan, was again victimised for her evidence at the assizes against Barber Mee. Stones were thrown at her in the street and she was threatened by four youths. She obtained the protection of two detectives, and three of the four were bound over, but this was not the end of Margaret Morgan's punishment for giving evidence.

A few days after Corkery received the death sentence, his sister Margaret, a fourteen-year-old spoon cutter, tried to stab the same Margaret Morgan in Hill Street. Morgan, declaring herself a single person of Stafford Street who worked in the brass chandelier trade, told the magistrates that the evening after she had given evidence at the trial of Jeremiah, she had been going up Hill Street with a man. They saw Margaret Corkery and a lot of other girls standing at a corner with a Thomas Jackson.

'That's her, Margy, as went against your Jerry,' said Jackson.

Two of the girls added, 'No, that's her that went against our Billy,' perhaps referring to Downes the burglar. Either way, Jackson told Margaret Corkery to 'give it the cow!' According to Morgan, Corkery then struck two blows with a knife, but as Morgan drew back she missed and was pulled away. Morgan said that she walked off and Corkery followed her. On October 6, the police arrested Margaret Corkery in her mother's house. Also committed for trial for intimidating witnesses was Thomas Jackson, on the charge of inciting Corkery to wound Morgan.

At her trial, Corkery was reported as weeping 'very much' and being 'quite overcome' when reference was made to her brother Jerry. She denied even speaking to Morgan but neither she nor Jackson wanted to address the jury. Witnesses tried to contradict Morgan's evidence, but the jury found the two defendants guilty, asking the judge for mercy for Corkery on account of her 'tender age', for which she thanked them twice. Mr Justice Lindley did not take long to consider this advice and clearly ignored it when he sentenced them both to eighteen months' hard labour.

In fact Margaret Corkery had been up before the magistrates even while on bail, for gambling in the street. Then said to be aged sixteen, she was described as a newsgirl, one of the leaders of a number of boys and girls who sold the halfpenny evening papers in the streets and who congregated and gambled at pitch and toss, as so many street gangs did. She had been committed several times, so this time she got a month in gaol with hard labour, along with a newsboy of the same age. She was described as a polisher at the assizes; perhaps she was both, as Birmingham's industries began to move into recession. In any case, being in and out of prison prevented her from keeping down a steady job.

THE STABBING of P.C. Lines was an unusual event. Stabbing was a part of street life, but always attracted special notice because of its likely consequences. It was not part of the fair fight custom, and was described as a 'horrible practice' by T.C.S. Kynnersley, the stipendiary magistrate. Violence towards the police was endemic, but spinal injuries from kickings were much more common than stab wounds. Potentially most fatal was to receive a blow on the head from a brick, which might lead to concussion or permanent brain damage, such as the blow that led to the lingering death of P.C. Hardy in Birmingham Lunatic Asylum in 1872.

The Watch Committee, which controlled the police, was bombarded with demands for a new police station in Navigation Street. The landlord of the Greyhound Inn and a local taxidermist took the lead and prepared a petition to the Council. Alderman Manton, chairman of the Watch Committee, promised to consider the proposal. It was suggested that, since the demolition of houses at the back of the theatre, there had been a higher concentration of roughs coming to live in the streets close to Navigation Street, but it was not just there where property-owners were demanding more protection. The penny-wise Watch Committee decided against providing a new station, and instead it was recommended that Fordrough Street and some other dangerous thoroughfares be 'worked double', even though the Birmingham police force was seventeen men below its nominal strength.

A man called Millard, in Bath Gaol, later claimed that he had stabbed P.C. Lines in the chest on the night in question. The claim caused a stir, but the police did not believe his story, even though Sarah Ann Hyde, the servant girl who had spied the burglars through the keyhole of her mistress's chamber, said that Millard had been with Corkery on the night of the murder. The following year the street was back in the news with a clerk who conducted a Christmas hamper swindle, collecting money through newspaper advertisements. When a gang of roughs attacked and half-destroyed a man's house in neighbouring Wharf Street, the clamour for a police station was renewed.

British policemen do not die often in the course of duty. The attack on William Lines and Sergeant Joseph Fletcher by the so-called Navigation Street Gang, leading to the death of one and the severe wounding of the other in a neighbourhood described by the *Mail* as 'swarming with desperate characters', was a major event in the history of Birmingham. The fact that there was no repetition of this tragedy until 1897 (see Chapter 18) may have been just luck or it may show some salutary effect of the case and the sentences.

Attacks on police officers were then all too common.[9] Not only did the number increase, but also their intensity. In the fourteen years prior to 1875, three were said by the *Mail* to have been 'virtually murdered', four were 'cripples' and one was an 'imbecile'. So this tragedy was seen not only as a particularly savage murder of a law officer, but also as the climax of a period of increasing violence on the town's streets. Afterwards the town would become calmer and the death of P.C. Lines would become a byword for the 'bad old days'. The police had for once been found where they were needed, or so thought the middle classes, but for many of the inhabitants of the dark streets of inner Birmingham they were unwelcome visitors and all too often were greeted by a shower of stones and brick-ends. And it had all started with the investigation of a burglary at a public house. The local press had at last found a hero who, by the mortal wounds he had endured, had shown what the *Mail*'s editor

---

9 The pattern of summary assaults on policemen has been charted by Barbara Weinberger and has been shown to have reached peaks in 1868 (530) and 1874 (435). Continued population growth reduced the significance of subsequent peaks in 1878 (479), 1890 (433) and, after borough extension, 1894 (482) and 1898 (623).

called 'the bulldog courage of an Englishman' in standing up to the roughs. The incident was trumpeted as evidence that the members of the Watch Committee, the councillors in charge of the town's law and order, were wrong in claiming that rowdyism – their name for street battles and melees – was at an end. Nor was rowdyism the sum total of the town's criminal problems.

CHAPTER 9

Other Gang Crime

THE SLOGGERS WERE not the only miscreants to act in gangs. The world in which they lived was awash with crime and villains of all kinds. Conmen, for example, were always on hand to exploit the credulity of the public. The three-card trick was especially popular with tricksters or sharpers and needed only a handful of cards, of which only one picture card and two ordinary ones were ever seen. It was often played in the street or pubs to relieve the gullible of their money. A young man called Day recounted in court in1893 how he had been defrauded of a sovereign by a veteran sharper called Alfred Spriggins and his accomplices, who had placed before him and his friends in a pub two blank cards and a queen: 'Two of my friends began to bet on which one was the queen. One of the men turned one of the cards over and showed me the queen and I then put a sovereign on it. "You won't make it four pounds?" enquired Spriggins. "No," I said, "a pound is quite enough." Well, of course, when the card I had my money on was turned up it was not the card I had thought it to be.'

Another favoured location for this scam was on a train. The tricksters would get on a train, select a compartment and start playing the game, with the dealer inviting his two confederates, appearing not to know each other, to select the picture card and stake money on it. Once the two started winning and losing stakes, the idea was that naïve observers would want to join in. The game, which seemed so easy to win, proved much harder when an onlooker began to place money. Occasionally other passengers tried to intervene, but they rarely managed to do more than describe the sharpers to the railway police.

Out-of-town crime was easier. The age-old victim of the town sharpers was the farmer at market, flush with money and socially inexperienced. One such farmer, called Woolley, took a horse and a mare to sell at the fair at Burton-on-Trent in early November 1865. After selling the horse for £25, he came across two respectably-dressed men who showed interest in his mare. In conversation the two, who were Birmingham sharpers, claimed to know the farmer's brother well, and all three went to an inn to agree on a price. Woolley was given a promissory note for £26 payable later if the mare suited and then went off to a bank to obtain some cash. When he returned to the inn he found that his two 'friends' had been joined by a third man, who, unknown to Woolley, belonged to the same gang. The man said that he too had just come from the bank and urged the farmer to check his cash. Woolley did so and found it correct. Then the man passed round his purse for them to check his money and encouraged Woolley to do the same. Into this process one of the sharpers skilfully introduced a different bag, passed it to the farmer, and so 'rang the changes' (changed his good money for bad) without the farmer noticing. The next morning the farmer looked in his purse and found a piece of the *Gardener's Chronicle* and twelve fake sovereigns. He had lost his mare and £27 – rather more than most urban victims of sharpers.

Perhaps the most-reported type of mid-Victorian crime was poaching, and battles sometimes took place between gamekeepers and poachers. It was usually seen as a rural crime but in fact many townsmen took part and Birmingham had its fair share, often from the ranks of the poor or unemployed. A letter appeared in the *Post* in August 1860 from someone under the name of 'Anti-Poacher' of Erdington, describing how one morning he had seen 'five great hulking scoundrels tramping into town along the towpath of the Fazeley Canal, each with a sack upon his shoulders well filled with plunder and attended by three crafty-looking lurcher dogs'. The same gang could be seen going out on three nights every week and returning the next morning 'in broad daylight, undisguised, dirty and weary and laden with the spoil'. They walked in 'goose file', one behind the other, and 'the leading marauder is a long-legged vagabond nearly seven feet high'. The letter-writer protested that these were not poor honest labourers trying to stop rabbits from devouring their garden produce, but 'an organised system of robbery carried on by worthless wretches, steeped in crime'. Hampers of illegally caught game were sent up to London by train. Suspected poachers who were only stopped on the highway, close to Birmingham, after a 'shiny night', could not easily be convicted. They might be carrying nets and stakes, but this was not enough evidence for many town magistrates. This was why gamekeepers needed to catch them in the act. One of Birmingham's leading poachers, Thomas Biddle, a brickmaker of Highgate, was convicted a number of times across Warwickshire and Worcestershire in the 1860s and 1870s.

Many burglars operated in gangs. Break-ins were to be expected in a town where skeleton keys could be easily made. In the chimney of one den, a detective found a drill bit used for boring holes through locked doors, as well as a loaded revolver and thirty-seven skeleton keys, which he reckoned could open ninety per cent of all the locks in Birmingham. Shops were obvious targets. A junior member of one group, called the Vaughton's Hole gang, was detailed to watch out for unfastened cellar gratings. Three shops were robbed in this way in Booth Street, Handsworth.

One case, involving a gang of seven people, was masterminded by a famous thief of the day. Joseph 'Harry' Alexander was already notorious in the north of England when he came to Birmingham to coordinate the burglary of Robert Richards' draper's shop in the Bull Ring in June 1862. Supposedly once a tailor himself, Alexander was deemed 'the star among burglars' by the press. He prevailed upon the draper's assistant, David Williams, a hapless dupe, to lure away the night porter with an invitation to a liquor shop, broke in through a back door and stole £40 in cash, shawls and silk pocket handkerchiefs. Goods were left strewn across the floor and a pile of further items was apparently abandoned in haste. The shop's dog was found almost dead from poison.

The day after the break-in, Williams announced his intention to leave his job on the grounds that for some time he had not been trusted to serve the customers from behind the counter. He unwisely returned two days later to pick up a shirt. This time he was handed over to Detective Sergeant Kelly, who put it to him that he was the chief person behind the burglary. Kelly then searched him and found on him a pocket-book containing a drawn plan of the premises. Williams eventually confessed to his former boss, agreeing to 'round' on the thieves as they had not given him any money and had disappeared. The gang included 'Harry' (Joseph Alexander), and two others called 'Jack Sheppard' and 'Jack of Hearts'. While they were raiding the premises, a woman, perhaps Mary Alexander, had found the policeman on the nearest beat and got him drunk. The stolen goods were taken to a house of ill-fame in Grosvenor Street, where the gang had its headquarters, and the goods were divided up.

At the brothel, D.S. Kelly arrested the proprietor, called Leek, and his partner, Ann Jones. Once Leek knew that Williams had 'peached' he was anxious to tell his side of the story with the same hope of reducing his responsibility. The rest of the gang were eventually followed to Manchester, where D.S. Seal and two Manchester detectives made a raid on a well-known 'thieves' kitchen' in the Shudehill market district. They found Alexander drinking there, but the moment he caught sight of Seal he grabbed a heavy poker and made a 'desperate resistance'. One of the Manchester detectives was severely wounded about the head and body. As he fought, Alexander pulled a scarf from round his neck and another from his pocket, and gave them away, telling the people in the beerhouse to run off with them. The detective's right arm was disabled in the struggle, but he managed to stun Alexander with a pair of handcuffs. Some Manchester constables arrived in the nick of time to drag him to a waiting cab. Alexander was taken to the Manchester Infirmary to have his head-wounds seen to, and for a long time he was apparently unconscious. When he came round he told the police that the stolen goods had been fenced in Manchester's criminal district.

Alexander was brought back to Birmingham but managed to escape from the lock-up at Moor Street along with Jem Turner, in the first such escape for over twenty years. They had waited until the Saturday morning when other prisoners were being taken from the cells to a hearing in the Old Court. The policeman who had been escorting them returned to the cells and found a door ajar and the two burglars gone. It was thought that either they had been slipped a skeleton key when they had first appeared in court or that they had managed to force the lock with a piece of iron wrenched from a bedstead. Afterwards it was believed that Alexander had most likely dropped his shoelace into the lock and managed to open it that way. Access was in the process of being built to the new courts next door and from the cell they had quickly found their way down the unfinished passage, not yet shut off by an iron door, to the New Court, and up into the dock there. Then, unnoticed by the carpenters at work, they slipped out through the new building and into Moor Street. They headed for Nechells Green, where a beerhouse keeper gave them some money and Alexander found a hat to hide his face. Turner was recaptured soon afterwards in Leeds, with the help of photographs. Alexander was followed back to Manchester by Birmingham detectives. They found him and, after another damaging fight with staves and handcuffs, managed to stun him into submission once more.

All seven robbers were found guilty and sentenced by Baron Pollock.

Williams and Alexander, as the organisers, were sentenced to sixteen years' penal servitude, with Alexander's sentence later increased to twenty years. The three other men were sent down for fifteen years. Of the two women, Ann Jones got fifteen months' hard labour and Mary Alexander twelve months'. Harry Alexander's ingenuity continued to grab the headlines. He had received head injuries during his arrest at Manchester, and at one time he had appeared unconscious. In Warwick Prison he successfully feigned madness and convinced the doctor that the blows to his head had affected his brain. So, 'gibbering like an idiot', he was transferred to the County Lunatic Asylum at Hatton. There he managed to escape down a ventilation shaft and got to the basement, where he was confronted by three locked doors, which he managed to pick and then escape. A description of him was issued, and in the following January it was announced that he had been 'heard of' as finally caught and in gaol in London, either for felony or burglary.

A GRAVE national fear from the 1850s to the early 1870s was of garrotte robbery, or robbery with violence. Garrotters were especially active on roads leading into the town, especially the Pershore and Bristol Roads, as well as in the criminal rookeries of Slaney, Lichfield, John, Park and Allison Streets. Garrotte robberies were committed either by individuals or gangs, working by night or day. The thieves were popularly believed to operate in threes, a 'front stall' to walk in front of the victim to see that the coast was clear, a 'back stall' to walk behind to guard the rear and an 'ugly' or 'nasty' man to choose the moment indicated by the front stall to pounce on the victim from behind. In three swift movements he would grab the man's (rarely a woman's) forehead with his right arm and the adam's apple of his throat with his left arm, then releasing the forehead grab the victim's left wrist and pull it behind him, thus holding him half-choked and dazed or throwing him on the ground while the other two did the actual robbing. Sometimes rope was used around the neck.

In fact the word 'garrotting' was used to cover any kind of street robbery with violence or 'screwing', so the attack might come from the front. Highway robbery by prizefighters always attracted interest. The crime might attract a 'prizefighter of the lowest grade' such as 'Teddy Mush' Reynolds, of Livery Street. Another was Edward 'Ducky' Ingram, who was seen regularly in training at Ben Terry's establishment in Moor

Street. He was accused, with another, of the assault and robbery of John Breeze in John Street. The evidence was strong against him, as he had been overheard offering a witness £1 to keep silent or 'hold his click'. Some of the neighbours had seen the attack and called out of their windows, 'Don't kill the man, Ducky.' A servant at the Anchor Inn where 'Duck' had been drinking also saw the assault and was summonsed to appear as a witness at the assizes. Otherwise, he confessed there, he would never have spoken, 'for John Street is such a dangerous place that you would get your brains knocked out if you said anything'. The judge sentenced them to eight years' penal servitude.

The oddest-looking garrotter was a boot closer (who sewed uppers for a living) from Fazeley Street called Charles King, who also followed the profession of a clog-dancer. Street robbery was clearly his sideline, in company with a convicted thief called Martha Jones. However it was probably not a good combination of occupations, as both were easily identified and even appeared in court in their special dress, she 'a dirty-looking prostitute' in a white prison-type cap and a dress 'considerably extended by hoops', and he 'fantastically-attired' in 'a long-skirted coat, scarlet breeches and white stockings', according to the *Post*. She had tried to procure a slater's patronage in the early hours in Union Passage, and when he rejected her advances, an unseen arm was put round his neck and squeezed tight, while his trouser pocket was cut off along with its contents of £2 in gold and silver. P.C. Reden heard the cry for help and found the slater lying on the pavement with his head bleeding. The fancily-dressed garrotters both ran straight into the arms of P.C. Rourke and went to prison for six years.

One gang convicted of garrotte robbery – although for once not on a highway – operated in a well-known brothel in Cross Street. It was kept by Mrs Margaret Bell who had a long record of robbing men in her house, but had so far escaped being caught. One of her two accomplices was an ex-soldier called Wilkins who was probably a pimp or bully, living nearby. The other was a female prostitute called Hawkins who worked at her house. Their victim was a middle-aged man from Tipton, near Dudley, called Duffield with a wife and children – although they were not with him on this occasion. Duffield met this gang one night while drinking in the Engine Inn, Dale End. He did not need much persuading to go 'home' with them, but as he was going upstairs the other three attacked, bruised and scratched him. Wilkins turned out his pockets and then made off.

Duffield had the sense then to break loose from the two women, find a window, break it and call out 'Murder! Police!' He was in luck, for P.C. Buckfield was soon on the scene and spotted Wilkins dashing out through the back door. He said that he found Duffield and the two women in a heap on the floor. Duffield had lost his coat, neck and handkerchiefs, knife, boots and some money. However the bully Wilkins had not found the money he kept in his watchpocket, and the stolen clothes were found in the cellar. Wilkins was caught later in another brothel and protested that Meg Bell would 'lag any fellow to get out of it herself'. However all three culprits received prison sentences, ranging from four to ten years.

Garrotting produced a panic and the public was scared to such an extent that the Garrotting Act of 1863, introduced by the local MP Charles Adderley, brought back flogging only two years after it had been abolished. In December 1870 four young Birmingham highway robbers, aged between eighteen and twenty-two, had used considerable violence to obtain, in three separate incidents, a watch and two small sums of money. Baron Bramwell had them put in the dock together, at Warwick, and sentenced them each to eighteen years in prison and twenty strokes of the 'cat'.

The Visiting Justices decided to exclude reporters from this 'Birmingham' flogging which was attended by the governor of Warwick Gaol, a surgeon and six warders. The editor of the *Post* was so annoyed by this exclusion that he printed a detailed report on the event to give his readers a full sense of the punishment and provide a warning to other thieves. First the 'cat' was described as consisting of:

a straight wooden handle about a foot and a half long, to which is attached about a dozen thongs or lashes of strong whipcord, two feet or more in length, each thong being twisted, of considerable thickness and well knotted: altogether a most formidable weapon.

The article went on to describe the necessary securing of each prisoner:

Each prisoner was fastened… to a wooden framework, his hands being strapped to the upper part of it, his feet to the lower part and a strong belt, also fastened to the framework, or triangle, being placed round his waist.

Twenty strokes must have been terrible to watch, let alone endure, and it was added that 'indeed had not the prisoners been powerful, athletic, strongly-developed men it is doubtful if they could have borne the infliction at all.'

A garrotte robbery in Allison Street in May 1875 led to two sentences of fifteen years' penal servitude and eighteen lashes with the 'cat'. One Saturday evening two tube-drawers called Holyoake, uncle and nephew, were 'hustled about a great deal' by three young men. Both victims and attackers lived locally. The nephew Sam was knocked to the ground and robbed of money and his billycock, a felt hat with a low, rounded crown that was highly fashionable in the second half of the nineteenth century. After a fight with the uncle the three made off sharply down the street, but Sam recognized them, and they were arrested in the early hours. At the assizes, the three were sentenced by Mr Justice Field who had just dealt with the Navigation Street rioters. Two were clear cases of hardened men with previous convictions, but the third had no previous conviction and there was a memorial to the Home Secretary on his behalf.

After the trial Sam Holyoake and his family were given a hard time by their neighbours in Allison Street. They were threatened with knives, and he was afraid to walk home after work and instead rode with his master. The local gang of roughs had made clear that they wanted to 'make him suffer' and 'pay him out'. One of them, a striker by trade called Smith who was already drunk by 7.30 one Saturday evening, staggered up to Holyoake in the street, tripped him up and proceeded to knock him down with the insult, 'You – transport (informer) and lag'. Holyoake took the case to the Birmingham magistrates and told them that he didn't know Smith and thought he had been put up to it by other roughs. He told the Bench that he was in fear of his life. Smith apologised humbly in court, but the stipendiary still sentenced him to two months for assault. He was also bound over to keep the peace for six months after coming out of prison.

No Birmingham garrotter achieved quite the notoriety of the legendary 'Black Prince' of Lambeth in London, whose gang were said in 1873 to steal diamond rings by hammering the fingers of victims until their bones were broken and the rings could be pulled off with ease. By then, the heyday of the Birmingham garrotters was long over. As the detective force had improved from the 1860s, garrotters were hunted down by detectives such as Old Billy Hall and then suppressed by the use of the 'cat'. However, highway robbery was widespread and took time to be stamped out. In November 1877, Mr Justice Hawkins still complained that in some parts of Birmingham, such scenes of violence and cruelty occurred 'night after night'.

The press and public at first put much store by the use of the cat. However the exceptional brutality of one sentence in which a garrotter received forty lashes at Armley Gaol in Leeds led to a revulsion against it. By 1875, the editor of the *Post* was stating his definite preference for 'protracted terms of imprisonment' to flogging as a deterrent to inhibit the criminal classes. Some judges sympathised with this view, but Mr Justice Day, or 'Judgement' Day, was still handing out sentences including twenty strokes in 1887, in Liverpool – even to five youths aged under twenty. In parliamentary debates the view was expressed that such punishment would also be effective against burglary. The *Post* disagreed and came to believe with Lord Bramwell that penal servitude for life was a more effective deterrent for garrotters. However, corporal punishment would remain on the British statute book until 1948. (Detective Sergeant Garfield, on his retirement, declared by contrast that burglary and highway robbery in Birmingham had declined for lack of good fences or receivers. In his view the most successful fences had grown respectable and it had become too expensive to send stolen goods to London.)

Arthur Conan Doyle spent several months of each year from 1879 to 1882, while studying to be a doctor at Edinburgh University, as an assistant pharmacist to Dr Hoare of Aston. He lived with the family in Aston Road North and wrote short stories for the Hoare children. So it is perhaps surprising that none of these Birmingham cases seems to have beeen used as a model for the stories of Sherlock Holmes, although Conan Doyle probably noted carefully the exploits of the Birmingham detectives. Birmingham is used as the main location in one story involving fraud and impersonation called 'The Adventure of the Stockbroker's Clerk', first published in the *Strand Magazine* in 1893 and part of the collection called *The Memoirs of Sherlock Holmes*. In this story Watson and Holmes travel to an address at 126B Corporation Street and by timely intervention manage to prevent a suicide.

By the end of the century, tram termini, shopping arcades and entries to theatres had become popular with pickpockets, but they were all closely watched by the increased detective force. The same police, perhaps by reading Conan Doyle, were ever more ingenious in catching offenders. A successful raid on street bookmakers in Oxygen Street – inappropriately named, as Reverend Bass reported, when his eyes streamed from the emissions of its factories – was carried out by a policeman dressed as a corporation scavenger in a big slouch hat and a white smock coat. His prey was described as 'beautifully caught'.

CHAPTER 10

The Great Depression

STRONG POLICE action and heavy gaol sentences seem eventually to have discouraged the sloggers of the early 1870s. The former was spearheaded by the Watch Committee and by Chief Superintendent George Glossop, the latter by stipendiary magistrate T.C.S. Kynnersley. For a while, few wanted to admit to being in a slogging gang or to have anything to do with slogging. The riotous times of the early 1870s were definitely over. Meanwhile the local and national economy was in trouble, slumping after 1874 into what became known as the Great Depression, even if Birmingham was partly protected by its sheer diversity of trades. By 1877, its gun trade was registering only half the number of proofs it had recorded at the height of the Franco-Prussian War. Increased foreign competition, especially from Belgium and Germany, left the smaller gunmakers with little more than the birding trade. Brass and jewellery were also hit by the Depression, although both bounced back quickly. In the flint-glass trade there were complaints that it had become 'all tumblers and chimneys' – cheap glass covers for oil lamps – following the collapse in the demand for wine glasses. Growing unemployment left more lads on the street, though with little to spend. A resident of Macdonald Street in St Martin's complained in November 1875 that every afternoon 'about twenty of the Barford Street roughs assembled at the corner of Barford Street and Macdonald Street' and indulged in 'disgusting' talk, insulting female passers-by and obstructing the thoroughfare.

Prompted by a major smallpox scare, the town's attention was turning towards its sanitation and the *Mail* produced a series of articles in the autumn of 1874, pointing to the terrible state of much of the housing where the sloggers lived, including Bishop Ryder's District and the area around the General Hospital. The article on the Birchall (originally

Birchole) Street district paid tribute to recent improvements, but pointed out the infamous dwellings called the 'Devil's Rookery'. Birchall Street bisected Cheapside, where slogging had first broken out, and continued on into Charles Henry Street, which was badly drained. Its inhabitants were troubled by scarlet fever rather than smallpox, and it was not yet overcrowded, although it was always a favourite slogging ground. None of these were as bad as the London Prentice Street district, where demolition rather than improvement would soon be the answer.

Older properties had been flattened for the new municipal buildings, institutions and banks in the 1860s and 1870s around Colmore Row, Edmund and Newhall Streets, and the clearance of another five acres around New Street Station was already under way. Chamberlain-led improvements involved the destruction of some of the Inkleys, replaced by John Bright Street, and Green's Village, where previously 'the police could not venture ... single-handed; while no family could dwell there without destruction to the sense of decency, or peril to health and life,' according to J.T.Bunce in his *History of the Corporation of Birmingham*. Under a local act of 1876, many of the slums of Thomas and London Prentice Streets would be cleared away as part of forty-three acres designated for redevelopment. The new street driven through them, considered in itself to be a blow against squalor, violence and crime and at last named as Corporation Street, was begun in 1878 and its first stage completed in three years. Birmingham's civic pride was at its height. The impressive new department store of David Lewis was opened on the corner of Bull Street in 1885, and was meant to set the high-class tone. When the Prince and Princess of Wales made another visit that year, it was remarked that the smart and shabby ends of Corporation Street contrasted sharply with one another.

Yet no serious attempt was made to rehouse those made homeless in all this demolition. The sheer pressure on affordable accommodation in the areas closest to where people had lived before was probably one of the hidden ingredients behind the revival of slogging, added to the growing population and the continued preponderance of the young. The *Mail* sent a special reporter to see what had happened to the poor driven out of old slums such as the Inkleys. The council, having made such a success of taking gas and water supplies into public ownership, was reluctant to upset private landlords and builders by taking the next step of providing municipal housing for the working classes. The town's leaders could see no way of getting their money back. The council would build a total of only one hundred and sixty-eight new homes in Ryder, Lawrence and Milk Streets between 1889 and 1901. Instead of further rehousing afterwards, more light was let into old courtyards by the demolition of individual houses later on. The image of civic pride was severely tarnished in this way.

At least after 1876, no more back-to-backs or courts were built. From then on, every new dwelling was required to have at least two outside walls, and by the mid-1880s Birmingham builders were putting up long terraces of through-houses, called locally 'tunnel backs', for the better-off workers and lower middle classes. These had four or five rooms, a pantry, lavatory, cellar and even a front garden. However the next generation of sloggers and the 1890s cult of the 'peaky blinder' (see Chapter 16) came not only from back-to backs in Nechells, Highgate and Deritend, but also from tunnel-backs in Sparkbrook and Small Heath.

Declining economic fortunes in the Depression seemed to quieten the slogging gangs to some extent, as survival took up all spare cash and men had little left over to carouse with. This was just as well, considering the low morale of the police force, reflected in increased drunkenness, high turnover, under-manning and difficulties of recruitment. Complaints against the police grew but fines were preferred to dismissal in disciplinary cases. And when the police asked for an increase in wages, it was at last granted. The murder of P.C. Lines showed the pressure that the Birmingham police continued to endure.

Perhaps it was fortunate that so many children were being absorbed into the new board schools. Ten permanent new schools, designed in the 'Continental' style with gables and turrets, and seven temporary ones had been opened by the end of 1875. Not all were free, to the concern of many parents. Lower Windsor Street, Duddeston, charged as much as three pence a week when it was opened in November 1874. A year later, Mayor Chamberlain was boasting that the new board schools were obtaining better results than the church schools.

In spite of such efforts to civilise them, different areas of the town almost took it in turn to resound with anti-social street activity. In December 1874, Banbury Street, by the Curzon Street Station, was disturbed by a number of roughs who were throwing stones at each other but who decamped as soon as the police arrived. The following year, in which many trades began to experience a serious downturn, opened with a riot in Allison and Bordesley Streets among a 'gang of roughs' turned out of a pub at 10 p.m., the new Sunday closing time. There were similar rowdy pub exits and stone-throwing in Park Street and Oxford Street in the next few days. Likewise mobs continued to stone passers-by in New Street. The riot by the roughs of Navigation Street further showed how far off the elite's goal of civilisation still was.

ON A Sunday afternoon in late March, 1875, an organised slog took place in Holt Street, on the boundary between the three wards of St Mary's, St Bartholomew's and Duddeston. Over a hundred and fifty youths clashed, hurling stones and brickbats at each other. 'Some of the gang received severe hurts,' reported P.C. Morley, but only two, an electro-plater and a steel roller, were caught and fined. Ethnic elements in fights were by now played down, in contrast with the 1860s, but when the Recorder, A.R. Adams, Q.C., dealt at the quarter sessions with a riot among women in a yard off Hospital Street and a case of malicious wounding, he condemned the town for its constant rows and likened behaviour in Birmingham to the bygone era of faction fighting 'in some of the wildest parts of Ireland'. A fourteen-year-old with the Irish name of Mullaley, of the Cross Street slogging gang, near Suffolk Street, was sent to prison for six weeks for throwing the stone that put a man in hospital in October. Otherwise Irish 'faction fights', which seem always to have been rare in Birmingham, would become a thing of the past.

There were also incidents in the Parade and Broad Street, and constables continued to be targeted by small crowds, but by the end of 1875 police numbers and pay were up a little and Glossop reported no major cases of rowdiness. With such modest progress, he resigned as Chief Superintendent the following April. The new police chief, when finally decided upon, was drawn from the army, in the hope of improving discipline both in the force and on the streets. Major Edwin Bond was called on by the ratepayers to deal with gangs of ruffians on street corners – thought to be similar to Liverpool's 'cornermen' – and complaints of disorder in various parts of the town, such as Hill and New Streets.

Gangs continued to like to prey on individuals. In February 1876, a young solderer was attacked in the Gun Quarter by a number of roughs as he left a pub on a Saturday night. A hawker of no fixed abode caught him with a knife on his fingers and was taken into police custody. A general riot ensued and one of the crowd yelled, 'Come on, chaps, belts off; they shalln't take him.' Two more constables came up with staves, and one was knocked out by a brick on the back of his head. Twice the hawker was rescued, and he was only arrested later when things had quietened down.

Cheapside saw disturbances and assaults on four occasions in five weeks and in July 1876, the so-called Glory Hole Boys started a riot in Hope Street, off Sherlock Street, that drew a crowd of hundreds. The gang seems to have taken its name from 'Glory Hole', a ramshackle dwelling in Cottage Place, Hope Street, and perhaps its meeting place. They attacked Edward Davis, the landlord of the General Havelock beerhouse when he refused them more drink. Davis was injured and went out for a policeman. A woman heard one man at the corner of Hope Street say that 'they would go and demand a quart of ale at the General Havelock and if it were not supplied they would "knock the people's heads in"'. Armed with missiles from a half-demolished outhouse, they marched back to the beerhouse and shattered the windows. Hope Street was blocked by hundreds of people for over an hour and it took seven policemen to quell the riot. They managed to arrest only four young men, two of them from Thomas Street. The General Havelock seems to have been a beerhouse frequented by brassworkers, whose union leadership was less excitable than the rank and file.

There was disquieting news for the police that catapults were in fashion and that a full-sized one was 'deadly' at 800 yards. Favourite targets were plate glass windows. Joking allusions were made to the Balkan War between the Serbs and the Turks at the time, but shopkeepers were not amused. Some thought that too much police time was taken up by dealing with drunks. Physical attacks on the police did not lessen. Bond introduced a new eight-hour system, with night duty starting as before at 10 p.m. but finishing at the earlier time of 6 a.m., to reduce the length of a constable's beat. Even with this reduction the bobby still had to be down at the police court by 10 a.m. to give evidence. As to remuneration, Bond thought it would be hard to attract new recruits at the existing wages.

In February 1877, a wine merchant of Newhall Street approached the Watch Committee, concerned about a congregation of slogging gangs made up of forty or fifty boys throwing stones almost daily near his premises. Two were arrested; both were fifteen-year-olds, one from Fleet Street – perhaps the home team – and another from Suffolk Street – perhaps the visitors. Not many other such gangs hit the headlines at this time. In

1. Vale Court was once notorious as a den for prostitutes, while the Park Street area generally was one of the most deprived, and dangerous, in Victorian Birmingham. It housed a large Irish population and saw carnage during the Murphy Riots of 1867.

2. Allison Street, in Digbeth, was the home of a gang led by Thomas Joyce, one of an infamous fighting family and perhaps the best-known slogger of his day.

3. One of the first reported slogs was in 1870 and involved the lads from Barford Street (above). Gangs from here would still be fighting more than twenty years later, often against their sworn enemies from Park Street.

4. The Old Peck, four acres of waste ground beside the Hockley Brook, was a summer fairground pitch, with stalls, sideshows and rides. It was also a battleground for sloggers, some of whom extorted money from the stallholders.

5. Nechells Green police station, in the suburbs. The Birmingham bobby had a daunting job. Undermanned and poorly paid, he faced the constant threat of attack. Not surprisingly, many were given to drink.

6. A court off Navigation Street, where P.C William Lines was stabbed to death while trying to fend off a mob. After a sensational trial, his killer, Jeremiah Corkery, was executed.

7. John Adrian (left) was the leader of the highly-active Aston sloggers. James Grindrod (right) was one of his young lieutenants. Both were jailed for attacking a rival with weapons, and were photographed after sentencing.

8. Bagot Street, where Grindrod lived, was a gang meeting place and the scene of a small riot during the first peak of slogging in 1873, when lads from the Gun Quarter took on the neighbouring district of St Bartholomew's.

9. A sergeant at the stage door of the Old Theatre Royal. Part of his job was to keep out unwanted roughs, but theatres and music halls attracted gangs who often operated crude protection rackets.

10. William 'Bowey' Beard was a leader of the Digbeth gang and carried knife scars on his face inflicted by a rival. He was jailed for seven years for killing the manager of the Canterbury Music Hall.

11. Poverty, crime and violence were endemic in the Summer Lane area, the haunt of gangs of thieves, pickpockets and streetfighters.

12. The classic look of the peaky blinder. This young man, David Taylor, stole a gun at the age of thirteen and would spend much of his youth incarcerated.

13. Parts of Garrison Lane resembled a shanty town. It was also home to Henry Lightfoot, one of the first men to be referred to in the Press as a peaky blinder.

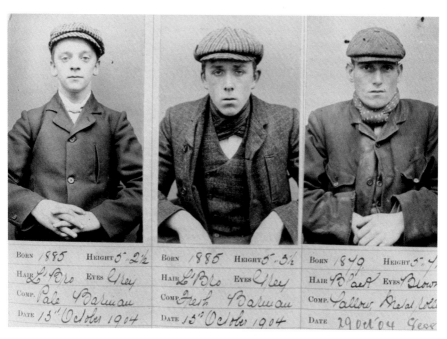

14. Three peakies, sporting the peaked caps which gave them their nickname. From left: Harry Fowles, Ernest Haynes and Stephen McNickle, all photographed while in custody for petty theft.

15. A small group of fledgling peakies amid the squalor of Clyde Street. With large families crammed into tiny, squalid houses, it was hardly surprising that so many spent their nights out on the streets.

16. New schools in Birmingham may at first have bolstered the neighbourhood identities that lay at the heart of slogging feuds. But by the 1890s, this one in Tilton Road was promoting the new craze for football, which helped to divert youths from gangs.

Photo credits. Birmingham Library Services: 1, 2, 3, 4, 8, 9, 11, 13, 15, 16; Warwickshire County Record Office: 12; West Midlands Police Museum: 5, 7, 10, 14.

Wolverhampton and Smethwick there were references to a gang or gangs called the Forty Thieves. A disorderly nut-and-bolt maker in Smethwick was said by a policeman before the West Bromwich Court to be one of this gang 'who some time ago were the terror of the neighbourhood'. A few months later, six youths gambling at dice and up before the same court were reported with the same name.

There was also a gang called the Forty Thieves in the Spring Hill area of west Birmingham. In October 1877, there was a confrontation at the Cape of Good Hope Inn between the landlord and four men belonging to this gang. The four, a boatman who was said to be the ringleader or 'king' and three ironworkers, were drinking there on a Saturday night and, after creating a disturbance, were ordered to leave, which they refused to do. They must have got word to their friends, and soon after, seven cabs loaded with thugs arrived from Spring Hill. The men laid siege to the inn, broke in and jumped over the counters, taking possession of the premises. It took seven constables to drive them out. Several pokers were found on them. Two years later, it was reported that another of the Forty Thieves, wanted for robbery in Birmingham, was caught in Wolverhampton trying to steal a watch and chain. Later in the same year it was said that gangs of men and youths from Birmingham were visiting Smethwick and assaulting the police there. Across town, about twenty of the equally mysterious but dangerous 'Bordesley gang' were attacking strangers with stones as they crossed the junction between Coventry Road and Watery Lane.

The year 1878 saw a new peak in assaults on police officers in Birmingham, but they were not reported as related to slogging. The town as a whole reverberated with street thuggery, from Charles Henry Street in the south to Allison Street in the east, and from Water Street and Farm Street in the north-west up Newtown Row to Harding Street in the north and Lawley Street in the north-east. The Gun Quarter also never stayed quiet for long. Loveday Street roughs entertained themselves by smashing windows on Saturday nights with loaded sticks and heavily buckled belts. In Slaney Street, in 1880, a gang made an apparently unprovoked attack on two policemen with stones; one was knocked unconscious and a youth was imprisoned for six months. And in 1882, in Vauxhall Road, Duddeston, two gangs were caught slogging with large sticks and stones tied in handkerchiefs. Meanwhile, individual hard men accumulated long records of convictions. James Cain, a brass caster of Wharf Street, was described by detectives, when he had moved to the Gosta Green area as a 'well-known member of the Cross Street slogging gang'. He was always ready to take part in any disturbance.

Travelling from Birmingham to Aston was always risky because of the chance of highway robbery, but it was like running the gauntlet when the gangs were about. Even after slogging gangs as such seemed less of a problem in the late 1870s, the streets round Gosta Green were subject to stone-throwing by gangs of boys, especially at the police, and continued to be so into the next decade. In 1882, one correspondent to the *Post* would complain of the trouble every Sunday evening because of 'gangs of young roughs who stood at the various street corners near Gosta Green, addressing offensive and obscene language to passers-by and in some cases throwing at them stones which lay conveniently at hand in heaps on the roadside'.

Birmingham roughs had always been employed at both parliamentary and municipal elections. They were even paid to go to other towns, like Evesham, Worcester and supposedly even as far afield as Brighton, to support or break up political meetings, whether for the Tory or the Liberal candidate. The Secret Ballot Act had not put an end to such activities. In the 1880 election, louts active around several polling booths were given free food and drink by the Tories. 'Gang' was becoming a vogue word in the political slanging match. In 1882 the Liberal councillor Powell Williams, in a local election speech, referred to the 'slogging gangs' of Moor Street police court, and in 1883 one of the Tory leaders, Lord Randolph Churchill, the father of Winston, demanded action against the 'Birmingham gang' of 'Messrs Nuttall and Co' – the Liberal registration agent and his clique of organisers who, he claimed, had used undue influence during the previous election. The political temperature rose in the 1880s, because of the keen competition between Joseph Chamberlain's Radical Liberals and Randolph Churchill's Tories, both ready to draw on the tough expertise of local 'roughs'.

In October 1884, a Conservative meeting at Aston Park, due to have been addressed by Churchill and others, was broken up before it could start by Chamberlainite roughs. A Liberal counter-demonstration had been held outside the grounds and, though the demonstrators were not officially allowed in, they made a breach in the boundary walls and poured into the park. The Liberal mob forced their way into the Great Hall and stormed the platform. Tory dignitaries were driven off, and over two hundred chairs were thrown about and broken. Fireworks were torn out of their frames and set off, and a riot broke out in the skating rink. A refreshment bar at Lower Grounds was invaded. Lads jumped over the counter, breaking table glasses and escaping with dozens of bottles of ginger beer and soda. More chairs were broken in the rink and in the meadow, where a dancing platform was also destroyed. (The Liberal newspapers the *Post* and the *Mail* claimed that it was the Tories' fault.) In the House of Commons, Churchill accused Chamberlain's Liberal 'caucus' of hiring the roughs concerned. Chamberlain blamed the Tories for inviting a demonstration of Midlands opinion and giving away tickets to the meeting indiscriminately. He claimed that the fighting had been started by Tory stewards with sticks and cudgels, which they used against those who went to the meeting wearing pro-Gladstone badges.

The arguments continued in the local courts, where the proceedings were sometimes reduced to the level of farce, reflecting poorly not only on the roughs and their political paymasters, but also on the lawyers, police and even the members of the judiciary involved. This was particularly so in the trial of 'Larry Mack', alias Peter Joyce, a blacksmith's striker of John Street, for a libel against Richard Corbett Jarvis, a grocer of Worcester Street and a leading local Tory. Mack had sworn an affidavit that Jarvis had given him an entry ticket to that notorious Conservative meeting at Aston Park, along with instructions 'to join the mob and do what they did'. Once inside the grounds, he had joined a gang of thugs. Together they spent some time enjoying free drinks and then went to the skating rink and stationed themselves close to the platform, from where a number of Tory leaders, most notably Randolph Churchill, would speak. Then the boundary wall of the park was breached and in rushed the Liberals, to find Mack and other Tory roughs ready to fight them. The following were the incriminating words of Mack's affidavit:

> About five o'clock the people came to the rink very fast. We noticed a lot of people come in with Gladstone badges on and we snatched them off. On the following day I went to Mr Jarvis's shop to be paid… Mr Jarvis paid me six shillings for my work on Monday. I asked him for ten shillings and he said he could not afford me more.

There were a number of affidavits of this nature, in spite of consistent denials by Birmingham Tories that they had ever hired such people to police their meeting against Liberals or given them money for free beer. Cases against the roughs were brought by those accused of such bribery, but Stipendiary Kynnersley, after hearing a few, refused to have anything more to do with them. The case of Larry Mack was different because the affidavit had been read out by Joseph Chamberlain, MP, in the House of Commons as evidence of Tory malpractice. So it had to go forward to the assizes, where it deteriorated into little more than a joke.

At the trial, the farce centred not so much on what was in the affidavit as on the identity of the person who had made the sworn statement. Two things quickly became clear in the initial proceedings before the magistrates. The first was that Larry Mack was a very elusive character. The second, once Peter Joyce had claimed 'Larry Mack' as his other name, was that Joyce was not the same Larry Mack as had appeared at Horton and Redferns, solicitors and commissioners of oaths, to swear the affidavit on 28 October 1884. The commissioner's clerk told the magistrates on 6 November, and the assize judge five months later, that the prisoner in the dock was not the same person from whom he had taken the statement for the affidavit. When called on to swear to his identity before the magistrates, he could not say that the prisoner was Larry Mack, and when Peter Joyce's brother John was pointed out in court and stepped forward, the commissioner's clerk declared that 'this man is so like Larry Mack that I should not like to swear the prisoner is he'. To this, John Joyce quipped, 'I have got another brother but he isn't in court.' Detective Sergeant Cooper intervened, 'We know all about that.'

D.S. Cooper said that Peter Joyce had told him that Larry Mack was his other name. There were three Joyce brothers and he knew them all. He had known Peter for fourteen years, but had never known him as 'Larry Mack' before. (Larry Mack was the name of a famous Birmingham prizefighter of earlier days.) Detective Mountford gave evidence that Joyce had been all too ready to admit his guilt when the charge was being read and had added, 'Then I shall have a bed.' Mountford claimed that Joyce had not been in custody for six or seven years and that he was sober when locked up, but other policemen who escorted him down to the cells gave contrary evidence that he was drunk.

At the assizes, the defence made much of the fact that Peter Joyce was not really Larry Mack at all. It was an assumed name, like 'the Tipton Slasher', another famous prizefighter. There was laughter in the court, but the judge, Mr Justice Field, famous for his severe treatment of the Navigation Street gang, did not see the joke: 'Why are we to have the

Tipton Slasher brought in?' he asked, to laughter. 'Pray don't laugh. If you would only look at this list [of other cases he had to try], you would find that half the prisoners here have got six names. Anyone who has lived in a Midland or manufacturing town knows the same.'

Next, the judge became annoyed by the commissioner's clerk who had originally taken down Mack's affidavit and clearly either wanted to forget the details of the case or could not remember them. The judge angrily denounced him as 'the most simple-minded witness' he had come across in the whole two weeks of the assizes. He sent him back to his office to fetch the relevant documentation. After the clerk had reappeared with the papers, it transpired that Mack had returned a week after his original deposition to substitute a statutory declaration for the affidavit. The commissioner had to give him ten shillings for the afternoon's and evening's work-time that he had lost in the process as well as sixpence for a drink at the Fighting Cocks. The clerk continued that the firm had been 'inundated with roughs for weeks' and that he could not swear that the Joyce in court was the Larry Mack in his office, although he was 'very like him'. His shorthand assistant was more forthright and gave evidence that Joyce was not the same person who had made the affidavit as Larry Mack.

The only witness who would swear that Peter Joyce and Larry Mack were one and the same person was a dubious former iron turner called Charles Caughtrey, alias Smith. Caughtrey said that he had known Joyce for twenty years and had heard him addressed as Larry Mack in the Leopard Inn, Dale End, and that he had tried to hide behind the fireplace when told that the police were coming after him about the 'Aston business'. This was good enough for the judge and jury. Joyce was found guilty of libelling Mr Jarvis and was sentenced to six weeks in prison, but, the judge added – perhaps from a troubled conscience – without any hard labour. It was Jarvis the political grocer who was off the hook and he wisely decided not to prosecute another rough on a similar charge.

Caughtrey's evidence was soon called into question in the letters column of the *Post*, in which the landlord of the Leopard Inn, itself a hostelry with an unsavoury reputation, called the disabled hawker a 'rough', a 'cadger' and a wife-beater and wrote that neither he nor his barman had ever heard Peter Joyce called Larry Mack in their inn. Joyce, he added, had been in Manchester at the time when he was supposed to have hidden behind the fireplace, which was in any case impossible because the space there was only fourteen inches wide. Another letter, this time from the Liberal party agent, McMartin, agreed that Caughtrey was an unreliable witness, and even alleged that he had injured himself in the act of assaulting his wife, but a third letter supported Caughtrey.

Joyce seems to have been the victim of a miscarriage of justice and of his own concern to protect someone else, possibly his brother. Chamberlain told the House of Commons that he did not know how Judge Field had come to his conclusion, but that 'in the absence of contrary evidence he accepted the denial of Mr Jarvis'. Yet Jarvis had admitted before Stipendiary Kynnersley that he had given tickets to roughs to go to Aston and the stipendiary had dismissed the charge against another man. Birmingham was a politically-divided town, controlled and manoeuvred expertly by the friends and followers of Joseph Chamberlain, labelled not only by the Tories but also by the radical MP, Labouchere, as 'the Birmingham gang', a jokey reference to three successful burglars in London at the time also called the Birmingham gang. In the town's politics they were in conflict with a hardened and persistent Tory minority. The roughs took their chance with either side, did the dirty work, got paid and, usually – if not in Joyce's case – got off scot-free.

WITH SO many roughs available for political purposes, it is not surprising that street violence and slogging continued in the early 1880s. A gang in Bishop Ryder's district was throwing stones apparently without opposition, until the constables breaking up their fun became their target on a Sunday evening in July 1880. The old haunts remained the same. In Allison Street, two policemen were sent to hospital. In Rea Street South, the new board school steps and neighbouring waste ground provided a ready-made gathering-point and platform for insulting passers-by. In 1882, Water Street in the Newhall district was said to be under a reign of terror from a gang. They were bolstered by a fighting 'cripple' from Fleet Street with twenty previous convictions who, with his stick and belt, knew that the only way for the disabled to avoid victimisation was to join the pack. He took part in an attack on a man who interfered with the kicking of a youth and was the one who did not get away, thereby receiving two months' hard labour. Coventry Street, the location of the 1874 riot, was obstructed every Sunday by men flying pigeons and betting on them. Yet it was for other reasons that Major Bond resigned as

Chief Constable and soon all these old centres of slogging would be overshadowed by those across the boundary of north Birmingham into the Manor, the redoubtable Aston sloggers (see Chapter 12). In the meantime the whole conurbation was rocked by a romantic tragedy which moved the hearts of even the sloggers.

CHAPTER 11

The Castle Bromwich Disturbance

ECONOMIC CONDITIONS DID not improve. After a slightly better year for trade in 1882, the Depression resumed, reaching a new low in 1885. The cycle industry was the only one to see any big expansion, after the invention of the safety bicycle in 1885. The last straw seemed to be the removal of the Royal Small Arms Factory from Sparkbrook to Enfield in Essex in 1888. Wives and daughters tried to make ends meet by 'home sweating' or tailoring for a pittance at home. 'Long after other work has died away you can hear the click, click of the sewing machine in the slums', wrote one *Mail* journalist, referring to the little dark streets around Small Brook Street and Holloway Head. The Black Country experience was the same, as unemployed ironworkers' women tried to earn a crust. Walsall was described to a committee of the House of Lords as a 'town of sweaters'; it also spawned a clutch of anarchists and the occasional participant in a Birmingham slog.

In spite of the Depression, which meant fewer coppers for pitch and toss and fewer shillings to pay fines, slogging gangs once more attracted public attention. The year 1884 saw slogging in new areas. One encounter in Hanley Street, off Summer Lane, led a reporter to explain – as if people had forgotten – that slogging gangs were 'composed of a number of boys who met each other simply for the purpose of throwing stones' and further that 'they were assisted by women and girls who took the stones in their aprons for the boys to throw'. West Birmingham was gaining unwanted public attention for slogging by boys from Birmingham Heath in Heath Street, off Spring Hill. In May 1885, a mob of one hundred and fifty youths fought with iron-pointed sticks in Ingleby Street, Ladywood, and in July there was fighting between the lads of Brookfields and the Newhall district with belts and sticks in Spring Hill. In Ellen Street, off Spring Hill, Cornelius and Christopher, the sons of 'Darby' Dockery, an Irish-born tailor, were emerging as the local leaders.

Even if board schools had their playgrounds, and recreation grounds were at last coming onto the council's agenda, the streets were still the main living space for young and old, and something of a refuge from conditions which were still, for many, equally awful at work or at home. C.R. Bowling, the sub-inspector of factories for the northern half of the town, had pleaded in the 1870s for the creation of model workshops. Such decent workplaces could be let out to the thousands of small masters, currently burrowing away in their human warren of 'hopelessly miserable' mills holding twenty to forty tenants, which must be so 'depressing and demoralising' on the poor people who had to work in them. There was a tendency towards larger workplaces and major factories, but the transition to large-scale businesses was only partial even by the end of the century.

Some people were starving. There were harrowing reports of new-born babies being killed because there was no food to give them. Free dinners were started for hungry children and kitchens were set up at schools to meet the huge demand. A halfpenny dinner, free for those who had charity tickets, consisted of a choice between bread and milk and bread and soup, followed by bread and jam. Some of the poorest, known as Birmingham waifs – an improvement on 'gutter children' – were still being 'rescued' and were now 'trained', or subdued, by the Children's Emigration Homes organisation and then shipped out to Canada as the best alternative to what was expected to be a life in and out of the police court and prison. Five hungry boys approached a policeman for something to eat and even asked the Bench to 'send them away' to the reformatory.

The adult unemployed sent a deputation to the Poor Law Board of Guardians, but they were told that the only work on offer was breaking stones. This was unacceptable to most men. They were asked not to march on the workhouse, as any violence there would alienate people's sympathy. Such fears of bad publicity may have caused a laugh when one member of the committee of unemployed, who kept the door at the Old Parish Office, was fined for keeping a brothel at his home in Severn Street. By 1888, 6,000 people were dependent on the poor rates in the town, and of those, 4,000 were in the workhouse or the lunatic asylum.

*

THE NEW Year of 1886 brought heavy snow and twelve degrees of frost. Then a violent gale wreaked havoc on the already dilapidated homes of the poor, adding to the misery of the unemployed and those on strike against wage reductions. The cold spell continued into March. Night-time conditions were horrific for the homeless: there were few options apart from the workhouse. A girls' night refuge had been set up two years before, but its reputation was little better. The Mayor's Relief Fund committee appealed anxiously for donations.

The atrocious weather helped to trigger one of the most notorious events of the decade: the Castle Bromwich riot or disturbance. This was initiated not by the gangs – although some prominent sloggers would become involved – but by a sensational death that gripped the imagination of the whole area. On the icy morning of March 11, after a cruelly cold night, the body of a pregnant young woman was found face down in a pond called Chattock's Moat, near Castle Bromwich, to the east of the town. She had been clearly there several hours, as the water had frozen over her. There was no mystery as to who the young woman was. She was Mary Jane known as Mary Ann Turner, of Cathcart Street, Birmingham, aged twenty, who worked at Warwick House, a big new department store in the town, as a dressmaker. Her family circumstances were unhappy. Her mother was dead and her father had been in Australia for nine months looking for work. She lived with her stepmother and her brother. For some reason her brother, reportedly unaware of her 'condition', had refused to allow her to stay in the house. One report was that she had not been at work for twelve months. Her family knew she was engaged. She had spent Christmas with the Bagnalls, a prosperous family of brick-makers, at Hodge Hill, Castle Bromwich.

At the pond that morning a man saw a hat and skirt in the ice and went back for a pole. On his return he met a boy from Bagnall's who had been sent out on the instructions of his grandfather, William Bagnall senior, the master brickmaker, to see if 'anybody had drowned themselves', while breakfast went on as usual for the rest of the family. The body was taken out of the water, and the local policeman had it removed to the Fox and Goose Hotel, Ward End, where the coroner's inquest was held.

The court was told that William Bagnall junior had left Mary Ann near the pond the night before she died. She had refused to go home, even though he had said that his father would not allow him to marry her and that he had no money to give her. Bagnall senior had affirmed this: he had told his son to send her home, even though Mary Ann had threatened to drown herself in the moat. Amongst the dead girl's clothes was found a printed consent to her marrying Bagnall junior, but it was unsigned. Bagnall junior told the court that he had obtained the form from the Registrar of Marriages at the end of November, but was told that, as she was a minor, nothing could be done until her father had signed it. They had been courting for three years, and six months ago he had bought her an engagement ring. One month ago she had informed him that she was 'enceinte' – in the French parlance that suited Victorian sensibilities. He had met her that evening at 9 p.m. near Ward End church (St Margaret's) where she complained of her lot. After a few minutes of this he had gone into the Barley Mow pub and was surprised to find her still waiting for him when he came out an hour later. She had reminded him of her condition and pleaded with him to take her back home with him: 'I have no work, no money and no bed to sleep on.' To her questioning, he replied that he would marry her in the course of a few weeks and would have done so already but his father had told him to 'wait a bit'. He had told his father of her condition three weeks before, and he had still told him that he must wait as he was not getting sufficient money to keep a wife. He had never given her any money even though she repeatedly asked him and, as he admitted in court, he had money on him. Outside Ward End church that night, she had threatened to drown herself. He had promised to marry her 'later on' and then left her standing near a gate and returned home. He had not asked where she was going to sleep. She said she was going home.

'Home – what home?' asked Joseph Ansell, the deputy coroner for central Warwickshire. 'You have said she told you she had no home.' Mr Ansell was appalled. 'You knew what this poor woman's condition was and yet you told her to wait – wait until her disgrace was known to the world.' The jury returned a verdict of 'suicide while temporarily insane', aggravated by the inhuman conduct of William Bagnall junior. Mr Ansell was unimpressed by any of the people in this tragedy, but he had especially severe words for the younger Bagnall: 'I cannot find language sufficiently strong to convey the utter contempt in which I hold men of your description. The death of this unfortunate girl lies at your door and must rest on your mind as long as you live.' He also censured the father for putting obstacles in the way of the marriage.

Pregnant single women did not usually receive much sympathy from the authorities or 'respectable' people, but in this case there was united condemnation of the Bagnalls' treatment of Mary Ann Turner. Suicide was a crime at this time, but the circumstances of this one infuriated local people. This girl had been savagely ill-treated, and the Bagnalls were seen as little better than her murderers. No-one would buy bricks from them any more.

Murder was thought to be a real possibility. There were rumours that Mary Ann's body was to be exhumed for any marks of violence. Yet no medical evidence at the coroner's inquest had suggested assault of any kind and only one track of footprints had been found in the snow near the pool where she had drowned. Her fellow workers at Warwick House had heard her talk of intending to take her own life. Reprisals were also rumoured. There was a plan to tar and feather the elder Bagnall. A Birmingham prizefighter had agreed to direct operations, and a subscription had been started with a hairdresser as treasurer.

The cortege from her stepmother's house in Cathcart Street, Duddeston, to the funeral at Saltley church, was followed by an estimated two thousand people, principally girls and women, in spite of the snow and it being a weekday afternoon. Two days later, a crowd of women were seen armed with sticks and beating tin kettles and hurling brick ends and tiles at the front of the Bagnalls' house. The next day, Bagnall senior complained of large amounts of hate mail and threats of imminent attack by an army of factory girls.

Ward End was under four miles from the centre of Birmingham and much closer to Saltley and Nechells. Although the Corporation Sewage Farm was nearby, it was still a rural area and a favourite destination at weekends for the working people of Birmingham. There were conflicting reports about the whereabouts of Bagnall junior. At the Fox and Goose, it was said that he had spent thirty shillings on Mary Ann's jewellery and clothing and was so passionate about her that he had all but drowned himself in the same moat. Meanwhile the rest of his family had stayed indoors on the Saturday except for his middle-aged father who, 'disconsolate' and 'with a stooping, uncertain gait', dressed 'like an agricultural labourer', wandered around his deserted brickyard, complaining of the apathy of the police, according to the *Post*. Another story told that he stood inside at the top of the stairs with a loaded gun in his hands. His house was described as isolated except for the sheds and kilns behind it, fenced off on the brow of a small hill. The front was open to the clay pit. The house was described by one newspaper as only a tall cottage, with two rooms end to end on each floor. The Bagnalls were employers, but not rich.

Hodge Hill was well outside the limits of the Birmingham police jurisdiction, so Superintendent Walker of Aston had sent a small squad of county policemen to protect the premises. It was rumoured that both male Bagnalls had gone away. Sunday brought an improvement in the weather – signs of spring at last – and those who expected crowds were not to be disappointed. Curiosity attracted sightseers, including some fashionably dressed women and girls, who came in their thousands by train, wagonette or on foot, many with their dogs, to see the now infamous house and pond. Rumours of planned retribution no doubt swelled the numbers. By 1 p.m., as Elizabeth Bagnall, the seventy-year-old mother of William senior, later testified, the crowd was shouting and making a disturbance. They went away at lunchtime but were back, in some cases fortified by strong liquor, by 2.30 p.m. in a 'huge, angry mob'. One woman was reported as saying, 'It won't take much to blow the place up'; to which another replied, 'No, two penn'orth of dynamite would soon settle it.'

At first the police managed to keep the crowd outside the boundary fence, but there were cries of 'Shove the police over' and both police and fence gave way before the mass of spectators. Soon the crowd was throwing stones and cheering lustily at the crash of glass from breaking windows. At this point, the more respectable members of the crowd withdrew to a safe distance, to avoid the missiles. A gang of men and youths, some wielding sledgehammers and crowbars, broke the police line beyond the clay pit and moved in closer in spite of two attempts by the Aston and Saltley police forces to charge them.

Inspector Hall told the court that the mob merely wanted to get hold of the two William Bagnalls and duck them. There was a cry of, 'We'll all lay a finger on him and then they won't know who did it.' More and more people surged in and soon the stable roof had been climbed and a stream of bricks and tiles were raining on the house. At the same time, a twenty-foot-high brick chimney was toppled. The stable was broken open, the terrified horse set free and the cart and trap sent careering off down the hill. Barrels were sent rolling into the claypit. The chickens in the yard were stoned or had their necks wrung and disappeared into the attackers' pockets. A fire was started with wood from the roofs of the sheds. One rioter was heard to swear, 'This will cost the – more than a night's lodging for a moll.' A fifteen-year-old girl from Saltley was knocked down and trampled in the rush and had to be taken to hospital with a broken leg.

The front door was heavily barricaded, but in due course men got onto the roof of the lean-to kitchen at the back of the house. Inside, the old lady was hit in the stomach by a brick thrown through a window, while the other women of the family, all on the ground floor, crouched behind furniture. Upstairs it was thought that Bagnall junior cowered under a bed, protected by a constable, but this was later denied. Four men burst into the back of the house and demanded to know where he was. When they saw only the women, they left, followed by three constables with drawn staves, who had not dared make any arrests but took careful note of their faces. Outside, the mob demanded that Bagnall junior should come out or they would pull the house down. There was no sign of Bagnall senior. His eldest son, the only man in the house, went out to implore the crowd to go away. Eventually, as night drew in, they began to disperse, though large numbers hung about the neighbouring pubs threatening to return and 'get young Bagnall'. The policemen stayed on, and the broken windows were boarded up.

There was no food for the Bagnall family and at dawn the next day they fled the district. It was later reported that Bagnall junior had gone to Derby, but was refused lodging by relatives and had to tramp back to stay with one of his family employees, with whom his father had hidden during the riot. Now half a dozen brickmakers whom they employed were out of work.

Monday had become a working day by 1886, but with many unemployed, thousands headed again for Castle Bromwich to gaze at the wreck left by the rioters the day before. The wheeled traffic jammed the lanes, while roughs were back again throwing mud and grass at the occupants of the carriages. The crowds were kept from too close a view by a police cordon, reinforced by fifteen officers from Birmingham whose task was to prevent further robbery. R.H. Kinchant, Chief Constable of Warwickshire, joined them. The sightseers brought food with them or bought from sellers busy moving amongst the crowd, and the scene was described as having the 'appearance of a gigantic picnic' or country fair – even of a carnival or wake. The Fox and Goose ran out of beer. A printer did a lively trade selling 'In Memoriam' funeral cards and sketches of the scene. There was an unsatisfied demand for photographs of the dead girl and the two men. Photographs were taken of the wrecked premises although the house itself had escaped lightly, as the roof was too tall to be climbed without ladders. Suddenly, at 4.30 p.m., a hay barn in an adjoining field caught fire. It soon blazed impressively, exciting those who lingered on. The Coleshill Fire Brigade arrived at about 7 p.m.and with the help of heavy rain put it out. The barn turned out not to belong to Bagnall but to a farmer called Bosworth. .

Of the fifteen men charged at Aston Police Court with riotous assembly with intent to demolish a house at Hodge Hill, eight were from Saltley, three from Aston, three from Nechells and one from Duddeston. Superintendent Walker blamed the press for the size of the affair. No doubt he was referring to the close newspaper coverage and the excitement over the idea of re-opening Mary Ann's grave. A stonemason and a labourer from Saltley were said to be two of the ringleaders. Earlier the police had arrested seventeen boys, aged between nine and fifteen, in an early morning swoop. They were charged with setting fire to farmer Bosworth's barn and causing £25 worth of damage on the day after the riot. They were all from Nechells, Duddeston and Aston. All pleaded not guilty and eight were discharged for lack of evidence. Nine were sent to the Warwick Assizes.

William Kemp, however, a twelve-year-old schoolboy from Duddeston, jumped bail and fled to America, so there were only eight boys at the opening of the assizes in May. Their story was hardly changed. Williams, a rivet heater from Nechells, described how before they went into the barn he had heard one of the accused, a schoolboy called Thomas Fownes Mansell, say, 'Don't light the barn. It isn't Bagnall's, it's Bosworth's. My father 's worked for him.' Williams told the court that he had only been in trouble twice before for stone-throwing and stealing some salmon. A thirteen-year-old called Robinson claimed that he had been given a match by a twelve-year-old schoolboy named James Thomas. Thomas's response caused laughter in court: 'I gie'd him a match to light his nose-ender.' Williams explained that this was a bit of a cigar. William Hinstone, of Duddeston, testified that, on going into the barn a second time, John Cambridge, a sixteen-year-old hawker, had asked a boy called Price for a match to light his pipe, but it blew out.

The judge's view was that the fire was not accidental but that the boys had done no more than act in a spirit of mischief. The jury found them all guilty except Mansell. Cambridge and a lad called Heap were regarded as ringleaders and sentenced to another month in prison, in addition to their two months already spent awaiting trial. The rest were sentenced to twelve strokes each of a birch rod. Mr Justice Mathew said that the sentences were passed on the recommendation of the jury as a warning to others. The arson attack was the result of the excitement caused by the riot; otherwise the boys 'would never have dreamt of behaving in such a way'.

The Castle Bromwich affair may well have been something of a sloggers' day out. Certainly two notorious sloggers, Alfred Whitehouse of the Whitehouse Street gang and William Rowe of Duddeston, joined in the riot. However, most of the men arrested were not known to the courts as sloggers; they took part through a genuine sense of grievance against the Bagnalls. Two of the boys arrested are also identifiable as leading sloggers. John Cambridge, the hawker from Nechells, seven years later led an attack with buckled belts on a group from Small Heath. A policeman described him as the chief of this Nechells slogging gang. Harry Tarpey, a thirteen-year-old from Walter Street, Nechells, was one of the boys who was said before the magistrates to have opened the barn doors to the rest, although there was some uncertainty over his involvement at the assizes. A William Tarpey of the same address was involved in a slogging gang incident in Thimble Mill Lane two years later, and in 1891 Harry Tarpey, now a labourer aged eighteen, again with a youth called Kemp – this time Robert – was involved in a suspected highway robbery in Rocky Lane. By 1900, Tarpey had not entirely made good: by then he was a furnaceman at Perfecta Tube Company in Aston, doing government contract work during the Boer War, and was fined ten shillings for being five hours late for work on a Monday morning and so keeping others idle while they waited for the furnace to be fired up.

At the trial of the adults for riot, neither the judge nor the jury were impressed that the two William Bagnalls had still not shown their faces. They were cowardly now, but had shown themselves as 'hard as a very millstone' on that night in March. Mr Justice Mathew told the jury that the riot was a case of misdemeanour rather than felony, in other words that the damage to the brickmaker's premises was the accidental result of the mob's fury rather than their deliberate intention. Of the fifteen men who appeared at Warwick shortly after the boys, nine were found guilty of riot and six not guilty. The judge said that the nine were all men of excellent character, so they did not merit severe punishment. Five were sentenced to two months' imprisonment without hard labour. A sixth man, denied bail previously, got six weeks, and three others who had spent two months in gaol already were required to find recognisances of £10 each.

Nothing more was heard of the Bagnalls in Birmingham. Their remaining possessions, including William junior's violin, were auctioned off. Later they were compensated to the tune of £181 for their equipment, and Christopher Chattock, owner of the freehold, received an additional £102 for the buildings under a new law allowing for compensation for victims of riot. By 1891, the Bagnalls were making bricks again near Lichfield and William junior, still living under his father's roof, was married to a woman from Aston. Ten years later, he and his father were still together and both widowers.

While bailiffs and policemen were the normal targets for the injured wrath of the streets and courtyards of nineteenth century Birmingham, men who were felt to have wronged their lovers were in a special category. The most famous case of this type had been the 'Tyburn Tragedy' of 1817 which had strangely occurred not far from the scene of Mary Ann Turner's death. Young Mary Ashford had been found apparently drowned in a marlpit at Erdington, and Abraham Thornton of Castle Bromwich, who had escorted her back from a dance there at Tyburn House the night before, was tried for her rape and murder at Warwick Assizes. He was acquitted – and again declared not guilty following her brother's appeal and his choice of the antiquated trial by battle to answer it. This historic case – the last of its kind - aroused huge public interest and again, although declared innocent, he appeared as a callous bully. His reputation was ruined and he emigrated to America. The Ashfords and many local people continued to maintain that Mary had been his victim, and the site of her death and her grave at Sutton Coldfield attracted many eager sight-seers over the years.

Mary Ann Turner's case was perhaps less infamous, but the immediate reaction to her death was more intense. Hundreds wanted to join in the revenge, and thousands wanted to see the spectacle. Over a period of several days, their action amounted to a major communal riot larger than even the Bordesley Riot of 1874. Estimates of the size of the crowd at Hodge Hill on the Sunday varied between sixteen and thirty thousand people.

MARCH 1886, the same month as the Castle Bromwich disturbance, brought a fear that gangs would start fighting with weapons more serious than sticks and belts. The scare started with the news that schoolchildren were playing at soldiers with bayonets bought cheaply, as cast-offs of the depressed gun trade, from local shops. Birmingham as a town where weapons and ammunition were made had always been at risk from these being used either in a revolt of the poor or in street fights. In fact guns appeared rarely as weapons with intent to wound or kill, but sometimes youths paraded with firearms and let them off in the street, and they were sometimes used in crimes of passion.

The headmaster of Allcock Street Board School, Deritend, noticed that some of his children were playing with bayonets. He advised against buying them, but his words had the reverse effect and it was said that the whole neighbourhood of Deritend and Digbeth went out to buy a bayonet. They had been on sale in the Lower Market for threepence each and had not gone very well, but when marked down to a penny by general dealers, they sold like proverbial hot cakes. The authorities could hardly believe it and asked the shopkeepers not to sell any more. It turned out that the bayonets were old stock, having been made at the time of the Franco-Prussian War, never sold, stockpiled and then eventually disposed of at auction and picked up by general dealers, who soon found that they could not sell enough of them. One Milk Street man was sent to prison for six weeks for assaulting his wife with one, but most of them seem to have been kept as trophies.

If the schoolchildren did not fight with bayonets they continued to fight each other with more traditional weapons. When a constable interrupted a stone fight in Albert Road, Aston, he was told that there was constant stone-throwing between King Edward's schoolboys and boys from board schools. Superintendent Walker told the Aston magistrates that although the police were continually receiving letters from the King Edward's parents, the grammar school boys dealt out as much as they received.

THE SALVATION Army took on the slums, in a way which demanded a reaction, sometimes positive, sometimes violent. Street parades led to verbal abuse, scuffles and assaults. Meetings were disrupted, such as at the Porchester Street 'barracks' in Aston, where a man assaulted a young cadet. Fighting sometimes occurred on the fringes. Seventeen-year-old Peter Hussey, a labourer of Staniforth Street, stabbed James Harrobin with a clasp-knife, blaming him for the fact that he had been thrown out of an Army meeting for disruption – a case in which it was said neither of them showed much commitment to Army principles. When Hussey blamed Harrobin in violent language, Harrobin knocked him into the gutter. Hussey got up, drew a clasp-knife and stabbed him twice in the chest. Harrobin's injuries were so severe that the surgeon, Mr Elliot, had to deal with him in the street, without waiting for him to be brought to hospital. Here was the great ability of the Birmingham surgeons once again tested to the limit. A jury found Hussey guilty of unlawful wounding but urged mercy on the grounds of his age and a degree of provocation. The recorder, J.S. Dugdale, while sentencing him to only fourteen days, told him that he had just had the 'narrowest escape he had ever heard of being put on trial for murder'.

As the sloggers of Newtown Row and Summer Lane went seeking the sloggers of Aston and Duddeston and vice versa, the Old Peck or Pleck[10] became an alternative battleground to Gosta Green. The Old Peck in its glory days was made up of four acres of waste ground in Miller Street, stretching along the Hockley Brook. Alderman Barrow called it 'a desolated and wretched spot', as the neighbouring zinc and metal works meant that nothing much would grow there. It was a place for much fly-tipping and where the poorest searched for firewood in hard winters. It was also a good location for slogging. Gangs of fighters could roam over a large area with little chance of being caught.

Another attraction of the Old Peck was that it had been the summer-time pitch of the annual 'pleasure fair' since 1875, when the fair was driven by the council from the streets of Birmingham and took refuge just outside the borough. Other traditional aspects of the fair had continued in the town centre, principally the sale of tripe and onions in the Bull Ring and the exchange of horses in Horse Fair and Bristol Street. At Aston, whelks and other snack food were popular, and with the sale of trinkets and sweets, and various sideshows and merry-go-rounds, the Old Peck attracted many day-trippers from the wider area. The supreme excitement came in 1889, when a lion escaped from Wombwell's menagerie on a Friday afternoon, ran across open land, past a large crowd and then disappeared into a sewer. It was claimed later that it had taken its 'negro' tamer, Marcus Orenzo, four hours to coax it back into its cage, but this was found out to be a lie to reassure the public. In fact the lion was still underground, and it required a major operation by the manager and two young men on the menagerie staff, equipped with lantern, revolvers

---

10 It was perhaps a difference of pronunciation. However in the *Post* and *Mail* the written form was 'Old Peck' until 1890, when the Corporation intervened and decided to turn part of the 'Old Pleck' into the Walmer Recreation Ground.

and noose and backed up by the police, to recapture it in the early hours of the Sunday morning from a manhole in Bracebridge Street.

To the young the Old Peck had always been an exciting wilderness where all sorts of dangers lurked. In particular by the 1880s it was the meeting place between the new centres of slogging.

CHAPTER 12

The Aston Sloggers

ASTON WAS BIRMINGHAM'S diminutive but hostile twin. Aston Parish sprawled round the east side of Birmingham, while Aston Manor, run by a local board, stood independently and defiantly to the north, hostile to any takeover bids by its big neighbour. New housing and industry there had created a vitality and an identity demonstrated famously in the formation of the Villa football team. This was both Birmingham's premier team by the 1880s and the first local team to win the FA Cup, in 1887. Aston had also asserted its new importance by becoming a parliamentary borough two years before that. Its next step was to become a municipal borough, which it achieved in 1903. One witness at the government enquiry into Aston's application for borough status in 1888 stated almost proudly that there were 'a number of slogging gangs' who fought 'pitched battles as between Aston and Birmingham'. The growing importance of Aston was reinforced by the movement of the population away from Birmingham town centre, caused partly by redevelopment, like that of Corporation Street, which slowly ripped the heart out of the older slums, and partly by the decline of the gun trade. Ten thousand children attended its board schools.

Aston's slogging gang had re-emerged by the summer of 1882. The new fighting grounds were now the Old Peck, for skirmishes between boys from Aston or Duddeston against those of Newtown Row or Summer Lane, and Aston Cross, which was favoured in any clash between Aston and Nechells. Both the Old Peck and Aston Cross had the advantage of being far from the centres of normal policing. On Friday, 2 June, the fair was on at the Old Peck and two youths were heading home at about 10 p.m. when they drew near to a large gang. One of the gang shouted out, 'Here's Muff!' the nickname for one of the two, a seventeen-year-old polisher from Harding Street, Summer Lane, called Thomas

Dan. The Aston gang leader, John Adrian, from Thomas Street, accosted him and accused him of being involved in a fracas the previous evening. 'You were there last night,' shouted Adrian. On hearing this, Dan began to run, with the whole gang in pursuit down the Aston Road. His friend saw a half-brick thrown at him, and then Adrian hit him on the head with a stick which had a heavy piece of brass on the end. A third man struck him with a pair of buckles. Dan fell, was kicked on the ground and was left bloodied and unconscious.

When he regained consciousness, his friend helped him to walk to the hospital. Surgeons found he had a fractured skull, a compound fracture of his left thumb and extensive bruising. Adrian and his associate, fifteen-year-old James Grindrod, were arrested. The latter produced alibis before the Birmingham magistrates, and Dan was not sure whether his other assailant was the same Grindrod – as this James lived with his uncle and aunt and their three sons of a similar age in a big household in Bagot Street. Adrian was also charged with assaulting another youth called William Simpson, a wood-turner of Gee Street, St George's. One of the two was overheard in the cells saying that he expected to be 'fullied', meaning committed for trial, and that if they had chivied him he would not have rounded on them. The case was adjourned to the quarter sessions, where Dan denied being with another gang. Simpson said that he had known Adrian for a few weeks. Grindrod had hidden his weapon, but a shoemaker who found it in an entry in Miller Street produced it as evidence. The jury disregarded witnesses' alibis for both youths. Adrian was sentenced to twelve months' imprisonment for malicious wounding and Grindrod to three months for common assault.

The case showed that the Aston sloggers were not exclusively from Aston itself (the *Post* called it 'collecting partisans from certain streets to engage in combat'). Grindrod may have been the same fifteen-year-old from Bagot Street who four months earlier – when a highly-thought-of errand boy at a luncheon bar – had led a gang of six in assaulting a lad walking with two friends in Bishop Ryder's District. Bagot Street was close to the border with Aston. Later the Aston boys would attract even more determined fighters from other parts of Birmingham, often wanting to retain earlier loyalties formed perhaps before moving home or to fight alongside renowned individuals.

Nearly three years later, in February 1885, an encounter on the Old Peck proved fatal. 'They came on me with a rush,' a young wiredrawer named Whateley told his father as he lay dying from head injuries at the

General Hospital. 'But I don't know who they are.' Whateley, from Dartmouth Street, Duddeston, had been attacked from behind on a Saturday night after leaving his fiancée. They had spent the evening at dancing rooms and the Royal George in Summer Lane and he was probably on his way home. The perpetrators had not only beaten him but also taken his money. At first it seemed that nothing could be found out about Whateley's murder, but the police arrested Thomas Dan's elder brother George, and he was sent to the Spring Assizes of 1885 at Warwick. However Mr Justice Lopes was so struck by the lack of evidence against him that he insisted that Dan be acquitted without trial.

This non-trial may have encouraged the resumption of slogging in Lozells on Aston's borders with St George's and St Stephen's, causing rage among the ratepayers, especially shopkeepers and factory owners. The magistrates decided to increase fines for stone-throwing to five shillings after being reminded by a police superintendent that the sloggers 'clubbed their halfpence together' to pay their shilling fines. According to one fairground showman, reminiscing about the bad old days on the Old Peck to a *Mail* reporter in 1898, there were more than halfpennies at stake:

> ...cliques of them would go round the ground blackmailing the proprietors of the shows. Their dodge was to say that one of their pals had lost his child or his wife and, producing a book, would ask for a subscription towards the funeral expenses. To refuse to give half-a-crown or so meant more than any of us dare risk. If you withheld money you were marked and might as well shut up shop and clear out, for if you stopped, your show would be 'queered' and a row created by the roughs.

Further north-east in Aston itself there was a series of new gang formations. One of the first was the Ten Arches gang, named after the place on the Lichfield Road near Aston Station where three railway lines met and were carried across the canal and the road on a viaduct. A policeman had dispersed a gang under the railway arches there back in 1874, so this gang was possibly a revival. One of its leading members was a boatman from Sycamore Road, who was sent to gaol for two months in 1883 for assaulting two constables and fined again six months after coming out of prison for blocking the footpath on the Lichfield Road. In spite of its intriguing name, the gang seems to have been little more than a group of canal bargees making a nuisance of themselves on the highway. Their leader was William Newman, a dangerous, twenty-year-old toolmaker from Clifton Road who was regarded as a kind of madman for the misuse of his physical strength. He broke a man's arm in Rocky Lane when his victim, a householder, came across Newman and others stealing the fencing from his garden. On another occasion he broke a grocer's plate glass window in Phillips Street simply with his fist.

Slogging became so frequent in Aston that the newspapers gradually moved from referring to 'the' slogging gang fighting with 'another gang' and instead began to differentiate specific groups: first the Ten Arch, and then the Wainwright Street and Whitehouse Street gangs. These names might be seen as centres of activity rather than exclusive groups, although in due course reports reaching Superintendent Walker suggested that there were a number of young gangs, who 'infested the neighbourhood'. An Aston magistrate declared that 'the slogging gangs were intolerable nuisances'. Nevertheless the *Mail* usually preferred to employ the phrase 'the' slogging gang when referring to the Aston mob, who often acted together as well as with allies from elsewhere.

The more serious battles took place on the eastern side of the Manor in an area less well policed, in Aston Road and Whitehouse Street, near the gas works, where Avenue Road crossed over the canal and railway into Birmingham's suburban ward of Nechells. The Aston lads' foes were any gang from Birmingham willing to test them, and they now reckoned themselves *the* slogging gang, as once had the Cheapside and Gun Quarter lads. In an encounter in Park Road in July 1886, a local person was knocked unconscious by a flying stone. The young man responsible was Alfred Simpson, a seventeen-year-old from Whitehouse Street who worked at a forge. He was the second youngest of a notorious father who lived with a woman twenty years younger than himself, the mother of his five ruffianly sons. Alfred was sent to prison for twenty-one days for stone-throwing and assaulting two constables as they tried to arrest him. Superintendent Walker of the Aston force complained that 'scarcely a day passed but the Aston slogging gang met a Birmingham gang and held a pitched battle …with stones and brickends'. Extra police had to be put on duty. The next night, a Saturday, an ammunition worker from Vicarage Road called Shaw, who was said to be a member of the Wainwright Street gang, was fined for throwing stones at a policeman when asked to go home. The *Mail* was not impressed by that sentence and thought that only three months' hard labour would have any impact.

In such ways slogging was defying the Depression, although the political excitement caused by two general elections in consecutive years may also have stimulated street disorder. There was a particularly rowdy election in Aston, where householders now had the vote, in July 1886. It was characterised, at least on Chamberlain's side – now a Unionist – by hired ruffians dealing out intimidation. Aston was also one of the more prosperous parts of Birmingham, with its newer factories and greater diversity of employment than some of the older areas.

By the autumn of 1886, the sloggers attracting most attention in Aston were the gang from Wainwright Street. Here, roughly parallel to the Lichfield road and the Birmingham and Fazeley Canal, close to the Ten Arches at Aston Station, the Wainwright Street boys took on their rivals from the St Matthew's District, next to Duddeston. They also kept lookout to head off any police interference, and in the end the Aston police had to send in plainclothes officers to catch the fighters. In December, a labourer from Adams Street was among a gang of sixty or seventy who were throwing stones in Wainwright Street, having crossed the canal via Dartmouth Street to attack the Aston gang on their home ground. He was arrested by P.C. Baxter in plain clothes and hit and kicked him all the way to the station. The defence argued that the man from Duddeston did not know that Baxter was a policeman, but Superintendent Walker replied that he was a young ruffian and had been fined twenty shillings for assaulting a man six months before.

Not surprisingly, in view of this spread of slogging to the suburbs, a Nechells gang, mainly from Nechells Green, had also taken to the streets, apparently for the first time. Once again the Fazeley Canal was the frontier, with its three crossing places in Avenue Road, Rocky Lane and Sandy Lane/Thimble Mill Lane as the lines of attack. Rocky Lane, which wove its way between Aston and Nechells and was lined with a mixture of factories, newly-built houses and waste ground, became the scene of greatest turmoil.

By the summer of 1886, the Nechells gang, possibly strengthened by an element of Catholic identity based on St Joseph's, was reaching as far as Gosta Green, with raiding parties of forty to fifty strong. Its centre was perhaps close to Rocky Lane, in Charles Arthur Street, where some of its members lived. The street contained a number of rough characters. On Easter Monday of that year, fourteen-year-old William Embrey, whose elder brother Edward was a convicted slogger, was found quarrelling with and hitting the sister of John Simpson, a neighbour. Simpson, aged twenty-one, came up with another man who lived in the street, called

Pollard. Both had been drinking beer. They grabbed the boy, knocked him over and kicked him over the eyes. William went to work the next day but was very sick and came home. He fell into delirium and died ten days later. Pollard claimed the boy had thrown a brick at Simpson. The outlines of the incident were laid before the coroner, but in the end the police court abandoned the case through 'absence of evidence'. Many such deaths from injuries on the streets were treated as accidental.

The residents continued to complain of the fighting and language of a crowd of youths. They were easily labelled the Charles Arthur Street gang. (A year later, one of them, aged sixteen, was caught stealing pennies from a fruiterer in New Canal Street. He asked the shopkeeper's ten-year-old daughter not to tell, but she followed him for half a mile, grabbed his coat-tail and clung on until she spotted a policeman.) A youth from there was caught taking part in a riot in Legge Street, Gosta Green, with a heavily-buckled belt in his hand, but was fined only half-a-crown for his first offence.

A week later, on the afternoon of Sunday, 15 August 1886, hundreds of people fought a running battle along Rocky Lane, between Nechells Park Road and Aston Cross. The police estimated that, at first, two hundred were involved, in a fight between the Aston gang and another, presumably Nechells. By 5 p.m., the numbers in the affray had increased to nearly 2,000. The addresses of two who were arrested indicate that Gosta Green and St Matthew's had joined the pitched battle, perhaps in retaliation for the Nechells attack on them a few days before. Those involved ranged from boys aged thirteen up to men of mature age, armed with heavy belts, sticks and brickends 'which they freely used in all directions', according to P.C.s Wale and Barratt, causing considerable damage to the windows of the factories in Rocky Lane. The full available strength of the Aston police force was sent out, while the Birmingham constables on the borough boundary had to be greatly increased. However, the police were better at collecting the heavy straps and belts dropped by the sloggers than making many arrests. The *Post* commented that 'what were at first small groups of disorderly youths with no legitimate outlet for their splendid physical energies seemed to have swelled into small armies…' and that the roughs were like 'an escaped steam engine without a driver'.

Though the battle involved exceptional numbers, it was typical of the kind of skirmishing that was now a weekly problem. It seems that the Nechells gang was concerned to establish its fighting credentials both in the old Gosta Green arena and against its Aston neighbours. Both Rocky Lane and Thimble Mill Lane were dangerous to non-sloggers after dark. Local factory owners in the Rocky Lane area – one also a magistrate claiming that he had endured £20 worth of damage in a single year – were up in arms about the risk to their property. One complained to Superintendent Walker that his caretakers had been driven off the premises by the sloggers and another that he dared not enter his factory on a Sunday because of the showers of stones and brickends into his premises. The Birmingham police, who were responsible for Nechells, and the Aston force, who were still separate, both struggled to cope, each on their own side of the borough boundary, which between Nechells and Aston ran roughly parallel to and on the eastern side of the Fazeley Canal. A deputation of Aston residents went to see their Superintendent of Police and the magistrates were called upon to treat culprits severely. The two sloggers arrested, Foster and McGuire, were both older roughs, boatmen in their twenties, and gave Birmingham addresses. McGuire was well known to the police for heavy drinking and minor crimes and was shortly afterwards giving his address as Cuckoo Road, at the top end of Nechells. They were both given the choice between heavy sureties or two months' hard labour in the county's House of Correction. These seemed light sentences, but the Warwickshire police at Aston had not caught enough people in the fight at issue, and nobody would admit to being seriously hurt.

Another favourite street for slogging was Chester Street, a long straight street running from Dartmouth Street, Duddeston, up into Aston. On a Sunday in late September, P.C. Baxter caught two sloggers there, one from Bloomsbury and the other from Nechells. One was George Pimm, a labourer with aspirations to prizefighting and the army; the other was called Emery. When Pimm said he had been a militiaman for two months and wanted to join the regulars, the magistrate, Mr Rowlands, looked up.

'You didn't come here for a character [reference], did you?' he asked.

'No, sir,' said Pimm. 'I came to see Emery tried.'

'And found you tried yourself,' remarked Rowlands.

Both Pimm and Emery had a long list of previous convictions, principally for stone-throwing. Emery was given two months' hard labour, while Pimm's sentence was delayed while investigations were made as to his fitness for the Rifle Brigade. He acquired the nickname 'Gunner' but would never realise his military ambitions. He fancied himself as a bully and nearly three years later would find himself in prison again for making bloodcurdling threats against a man called Wood and his family for giving evidence againt two of his friends. The threat came in a written note:

> Your – sons, Enoch and George shalln't live after June. We will let their gutzes right out for sending those two fellows to prison. You have some money and we will have it and your – life as well.

For a time, the Aston sloggers confined themselves to standing around in Tower or Lichfield Roads waiting for trouble. They often made their own by picking on any solitary lad or by stoning a bobby who had come to interfere with a game of pitch and toss or to tell them to move on. Fifteen minutes was regarded as the maximum time for loitering on busy roads and pavements. One lad complained in Aston Police Court how he and another were taking leave of their young ladies when two policemen came up and said, 'Now you young mashers, move on.' A 'masher' was a young man about town, often characterised by his bell-shaped, shiny silk hat. His friend protested that they had only been there ten minutes, to which one of the constables replied, 'Why, you've been there long enough,' and the other said, 'Let's summons them.' The magistrate was sympathetic and told the constables that it was better to move people on and only summons them if they refused, though he fined the young men a shilling each. Yet even if there were no more reports of pitched battles, the sloggers still seemed to be in the ascendant, and 'Lounger' in the *Birmingham and Aston Chronicle* was not impressed by police efforts to deal with them. In December 1886, he wrote, 'In the face of the outrages we have been hearing of lately in Aston – and Birmingham too – Charles Lamb's oft-quoted remark about "the sweet security of the streets" sounds like a ghastly piece of irony.'

When another battle with a rival gang was reported in June 1887, it was on a Tuesday evening at the corner of Phillips Street and the Aston Road, well away from Rocky Lane. The encounter became notorious. A bystander, Thomas Read, was mistaken for one of the opposition by the Aston mob. He was brutally beaten about the head and body with buckles and finally his skull was fractured by a flying brick as he bent down to see if another man had been injured in the fighting. He was conveyed in a cab to the General Hospital and stayed there as an in-patient for three weeks, finally appearing in court, with his head bandaged, to give evidence.

Five men were arrested, two from Whitehouse Street, including Alfred Whitehouse – there were a number of people of that surname in that street – who had been one of the rioters at Hodge Hill. Another was William Newman, who had been already named four years earlier by the police as the leader of the Aston sloggers. William now described himself as an edge tool maker and was accompanied by his elder brother Joseph, a painter like their deceased father. Read had identified two of his Aston attackers, namely the two oldest: Newman, who had struck him on the head with a buckle, and a glassblower called Perrins from Upper Thomas Street, who had thrown the brick. Both subsequently confessed to these offences. This was helpful, as a defence solicitor said that there had been about forty people present at this particular slog. Not all were sloggers, a fact that confused those who were. A witness called Smith was told in court by the glassblower that if he had thought he was one of the opposition gang he would have 'done for him' as well. The main culprits both confessed their guilt and one blamed the fact that he was drunk at the time. When bail was requested, the magistrates' clerk replied, 'Oh no, the man may die.' Fortunately, Read survived. At the assizes, it emerged that the glassblower had admitted throwing the brick at Detective Winkless, who had appeared at the scene, presumably well disguised, as the glassblower was 'under the impression that he was one of them'. He was sentenced to eight months and William Newman to five months, both with hard labour. Mr Justice Wills[11] in his judgement expressed himself 'very sorry to see that there was being imported into Birmingham and the neighbourhood that kind of savagery which he thought was confined to some other large towns with which unfortunately he had considerable judicial experience'. It was, he opined, a new phase in the history of Birmingham crime, but he was behind the times.

However, the impact of the case led to an increase of twelve men in the Aston police force. The junction between Phillips Street and Aston Road, on the boundary between Birmingham and Aston, was a key point for gangs to assemble and 'buckle' any youth who challenged them, and in the past these boundary areas had been poorly policed. They were at the far end of the beat for the Aston bobby, who, in

---

11 Sir Alfred Wills (1828-1912), a judge of the Queen's Bench Division of the High Court, of 'austere integrity'; famous for sentencing Oscar Wilde in 1895; also a mountaineer (*Oxford Dictionary of National Biography*, 2004).

uniform, could be seen coming. By April 1888, in response to endless letters of complaint, plainclothes men were being placed in the Aston Road to deal with the gangs, and arrests followed. Stone-throwing became more subdued, but in one incident in Phillips Street a nineteen-year-old girl called Minnie Hewson lost an eye. She was walking up the street with her sister and another girl on a June evening, when three lads began throwing dirt at them. She turned round to strike one of them and was caught in the eye by a brick thrown by a thirteen-year-old. In June, a Lichfield Road shopkeeper was wounded in the head with a blunt instrument by one of four young lads, two of whom were from Wainwright Street, after a tussle over a farthing-worth of sweets and a broken window blind.

The Lichfield Road continued to be plagued by the sloggers. In August of that year, a so-called 'King of the Sloggers'[12], a nineteen-year-old filer called Edward Emery, from Nechells Park Road, was caught slogging with twenty others, near the Lichfield Road, by two policemen. A tram conductor joined in the chase and succeeded in capturing, in the *Mail*'s words, 'the fugitive king'. Emery, as an old offender – although less of a household name than some sloggers – was given the maximum sentence for slogging of three months. A month later, another thug from Park Lane in Aston was given six months on the grounds that he had knocked down a passing gentleman on the corner of Lichfield Road. The lad was pointed out but denied that it was him, calling the gentleman 'a – liar', and it took a constable and two detectives to drag him to the lock-up. The magistrate, Mr Wills, declared that he had never seen anything like it in all his travels in France or Germany.

The Nechells sloggers, like their Aston counterparts, tended to tread more warily after their battles in Rocky Lane. Like sloggers elsewhere, they had learned that it was often safer and grimly more satisfying to pick on an isolated policeman. Older Nechells roughs, like the moulder John Husselbee, now aged thirty-three, already had long records for assaulting all comers, including the police. Husselbee would get six months for attacking a policeman who was trying to arrest him for robbery in a Nechells pub by hitting him with a large stone he kept wrapped up in a handkerchief in his pocket.

---

12 The London hooligan boys also had their 'kings', as did the scuttlers of Manchester and Salford, most famously John Joseph Hillier, who was a highly active in the 1890s and reportedly wore a knitted pullover bearing the words 'King of the Scuttlers'.

In spite of such police attention, the Nechells sloggers continued to terrorise those who passed along Thimble Mill Lane. One leader of the Charles Arthur Street sloggers was a nineteen-year-old axle-filer from Cromwell Street called 'Chass' Frith, another young rough described in a *Mail* headline as 'the king of a slogging gang'. The son of an iron moulder and brought up on the Aston Road, he was well suited to his position. One Sunday night in December 1888 he led his men in search of action in Great Lister Street and Duddeston. John Healey, a twenty-one-year-old glass blower from Rupert Street, noticed four men outside a pub at the corner of Great Lister Street.

'Here he is,' said one of them.

As Healey walked towards them, Frith pulled out something which 'glistened like silver' in the light from the pub. Healey was struck in the face, knocked down, kicked and later taken to the hospital, where he was found to have an 'extensive wound on the right side of the face, his nose and lip severed' and was detained for a fortnight. The perpetrators fled, but Frith was found during a festive gathering at home just before Christmas 1888. He shinned over the back wall, only to fall into the hands of two policemen. He was found guilty at the sessions and was sent to convict prison for five years.

Girls of course were not always passive supporters. In June 1889, the Aston sloggers were aided and abetted by Lizzie Hands, a fourteen-year-old from Vicarage Road, who stoned P.C. Rogers, shouting obscenities, as he arrested some other members of the gang in Church Street. Her turn was next and she was sentenced to twenty-one days in prison and five years in a reformatory. In Bordesley Street, a girl threw a ginger beer bottle at a man, who came over and struck her in the face, breaking her nose. His violent act led to a free fight between the friends of both sides and a joint visit to the Queen's Hospital. Indeed once slogging gangs got back into their stride it was hard to think that anything had changed.

William Greening, a member of the Whitehouse Street gang, as it was now called, was a tube drawer who in fact lived in Duddeston. He was active in the Whitehouse Street riot outside the London Museum Concert Hall in 1889 (see Chapter 15). Five years later, the same Greening, who worked as a brassfounder, was up before Baron Pollock[13] at the assizes for

---

13 Charles Edward later Baron Pollock (1823-97), son of the Lord Chief Baron of the Exchequer who had presided in the Digbeth burglary case; became Baron of the Exchequer in 1873. He became a Baron of the Court in the Queen's Bench Division in 1879.

a far more serious wounding of a policeman near his home in Windsor Street, Duddeston. He was lucky to be put away for only ten months. Greening's involvement reinforces the impression that the Aston sloggers drew recruits from a wider area. Two others from Duddeston also identified themselves with the Rocky Lane gang in a foray into the Gun Quarter on a Saturday night in May 1889. One used a buckled belt and the other a knife.

Another such recruit from outside Aston was John Casey, of Pritchett Street, Birmingham, close to the Aston border, who also seems to have decided to join the Aston sloggers as no doubt the 'premier' team. Superintendent Walker of Aston, who was in a good position to know, said in 1889 that Casey, a glassblower by day, was by night 'a member of the slogging gang and when out of gaol was always with the gang'. By the age of eighteen, he had been eleven times before the Aston court. He was not alone among the Aston sloggers as being a thief by the age of sixteen. His mother was no example to him. On one occasion when they were both taken into custody for assault and disorderly behaviour on a Saturday night, the two of them quarrelled in the dock and Sarah Casey, an Irish-born laundress and the widow of a labourer, spat in her son's face. Her other son, James, had a similar propensity for hard liquor, violence and slogging with the Aston boys.

Street fighting drew in some very unsavoury minor criminals. One of the worst was a sociopath called George Deveridge, of Lichfield Road, Aston. A jeweller by trade, Deveridge had a very violent record, as much against women as against men. In December 1885, he assaulted a policeman who had been called in to stop him chasing his sister with a poker. Three months later, he was in prison again for striking and kicking his father, who suffered a three-inch wound on the forehead. It emerged that this was his fourth attack on his father and his nineteenth conviction at Aston Police Court. Later he tried to burgle a former employer who had kindly given him some food. When arrested in June 1888, once more for assaulting a policeman, he was described in the press as 'a well-known member of the Aston slogging gang'. He was always ready to involve himself in any kind of 'turbulence' or fight, especially with the police, and his favourite boast to each one he confronted was that he 'had already killed forty policemen'. Yet he was a solitary individual, usually incapable of social interaction or of taking part in any concerted group activity. By 1890, in his late twenties, Deveridge had notched up thirty-six convictions at Aston alone. By then he was just another violent drunk of no fixed abode or trade. By 1893, he was in court once more as the most troublesome occupant of a lodging house in Duddeston Mill Road and he continued to spend most of his life under lock and key. As Superintendent Walker concluded, 'he was not fit to be at large.'

Unlike Deveridge, the formidable Simpson brothers were well integrated with the other Aston sloggers. There were five Simpsons: John, George, Alfred, Charles and James. John, the oldest, was a wireworker who went to live off Newtown Row, but frequently returned to Aston. He was very violent when drunk. Superintendent Walker said of John Simpson that he was one of the best workmen in Birmingham, although he and his brothers were among its worst characters. In the mid-1880s, the other Simpsons still lived in Whitehouse Street, between Aston Road and Chester Street. Alfred was an iron filer and George and James were hawkers. George was a one-time mate of William Newman, viewed by police as the leader of the Aston sloggers, while Alfred was the best known member of the slogging gang which 'infested' Whitehouse Street and the Aston Road and which in 1886 was engaged in daily battles with a Birmingham gang. The Simpsons attracted their mates to join their crew, which was still being called the Whitehouse Street gang after they had moved. One of them, a labourer called English, was described by Superintendent Walker as a 'little terror when in beer'.

By 1890, the third Simpson brother, Alfred, then aged twenty-two, had drifted from job to job – tin roller, hawker, steel roller – and moved to Tower Street, Summer Lane. Soon after, George and Charles had moved too and were living in New John Street, also in Birmingham. Alfred had made eighteen appearances at the Birmingham police court, and perhaps a similar number at Aston, for assault and disorderly conduct. He was quick to quarrel with neighbours. One Saturday night, he argued with two men who lived close to his sister's, where he was staying in a court off Ashley Street. An evening's simmering row reached a climax when the two men invaded about midnight and there was a fight in which all the crockery on the supper table and the ornaments on side tables hit the floor. Someone threw an oil lamp and his sister's clothes caught fire. Simpson rushed into the yard after her and they both suffered burns as he helped her dowse her dress. Meanwhile the two invaders had run back to their own homes and bolted the doors.

The Simpson assaults were usually to do with women, drink and the police. In April 1892, P.C.Boutell instructed the landlady of the New Inn, Aston Road, not to serve Alfred and his mates, whereupon four men followed him out, wrestled him to the ground, tore his clothes and kicked him in the ribs. Simpson then held him down while the others stole his watch and some handcuffs. The stipendiary magistrate later said that George, Alfred's brother, had started it. He added that he was the 'worst of the lot' and so deserved his six-month sentence. George had been at the centre of the Whitehouse Street gang and had been involved in petty theft since the age of fifteen, but his record shows him a more wary streetfighter than James or Alfred. He certainly spent less time in prison.

Another of Simpson's Aston rivals, well known to the police, was an ammunition worker of Vicarage Road called George Guy. Like Deveridge, he had drunken rows with his father, one of which landed him a month in prison for smashing the windows and furniture and refusing to return his father's 'half-dollar'. In 1889, he created mayhem in the Upper Grounds Hotel. After a quarrel involving the landlady, Guy went out and returned at the head of a gang armed with stones. He picked up a glass and threw it at the landlady. She cleared the counter of glasses, so he knocked all the jugs off the tables in front of the bar. A policeman was called and Guy and two other roughs were arrested, but gave fictitious names and addresses – as one of them later revealed, in the expectation of being let off. Guy gave his name, sarcastically, as 'George Simpson'. The three were only taken with great difficulty, after brutally making 'footballs' of the constables in front of a large crowd of whom only one man was willing to aid the police. With his help, the three constables in time got the better of the men. One of the three was finally frogmarched to the station, while Guy himself had to be taken up Park Road on the front of a tram engine. Superintendent Walker said that they were all prominent members of the slogging gang – in a loose use of the term – and that their degree of brutality made it impossible to keep good men in the constabulary.

Meanwhile the future of slogging on the Old Peck seemed uncertain. Building plans threatened to reduce its size and there was talk of its use for football pitches. Some sloggers from the Newtown Row end migrated east. One was George Betts, a metal drawer of Moorsom Street. He was another who was constantly in and out of prison. He was the third of four brothers, of whom Charles, the eldest, also got into trouble for slogging. In 1881, when George was twelve, they lived next to the Simpsons in Whitehouse Street, which must have provided the Betts boys with their role models. Although George now lived just in Birmingham, in a part of the Newtown Row area that was well-known for its slogging encounters, his offences often occurred in Aston. One conviction was for the theft of mackerel from outside a shop in Tower Street. The value of three mackerel was only a shilling, but because of his criminal record he was sent to prison for three months' hard labour. In January 1888, by which time he was probably aged twenty, he was sentenced to six months for throwing a large stone at P.C. Hickens, which smashed his headgear and cut his forehead, and for striking P.C. Wale in the eye, while being at the centre of disorder in Aston Road on a Saturday night.

As soon as Betts was out of prison, without anywhere to go, he was on the streets raising money for his upkeep. There had been complaints from stallholders on the Old Peck about extortion from the gangs, so Betts looked elsewhere for funds. On a Saturday afternoon in July 1888, James Russell, a bicycle maker, was in his garden in Catherine Street, Aston, when Betts, Alfred Simpson and another of the gang came up and asked what he was going to give towards a fund for Betts, who had recently done six months in Winson Green for assaulting the police. Russell replied that he could not afford to give anything, as he had a wife and a large family to keep. Thereupon the three attacked, kicked and beat him with their buckles. Russell managed to take refuge in a neighbour's house but his neighbour, Mary McCarty, was also set upon with boot and buckle. P.C. Harrison came up and the three ran away. One escaped by jumping in the canal. Only Betts, described as a labourer of no fixed address, was arrested. He was sentenced to a fine of forty shillings and costs or two months' hard labour.

The magistrates grew wise to the sloggers' fund-raising. Four weeks later, Alfred Simpson was finally caught and brought before Aston Police Court. He asked for another chance, promising to leave the country, if he was leniently dealt with. The magistrates had heard such stories before, and Mr Hill, the magistrate, explained that Aston roughs were being sent to prison to prevent such extortion of money to pay their fines. So Simpson was sentenced to two months, like Betts, and this time without the alternative of a fine.

Betts, like many hardened young gang leaders, learned nothing from his time in prison. The very day of his release he was back on the Aston Road, Birmingham, flaunting his reputation, this time with James Simpson and James Casey. Their gang by now felt that they owned the streets and could do what they liked. Laura Solloway, an Aston press worker, told the Bench that about two o'clock on a Tuesday afternoon in October 1888, Betts had spoken to her in a 'blackguardly manner'. She asked if he were addressing her and he responded by hitting her in the eye with such force that she went reeling into the gutter. Betts and several of his companions then started kicking her, but luckily a chemist came to her help and she took refuge in his shop. The men then stood round the shop, 'bent on smashing the windows and fetching her out to murder her'. It took three quarters of an hour for the police to arrive.

Two detectives eventually appeared, and the rowdy mob retreated along Chester Street, towards Aston. Detective Thomas seized Betts, and Detective Brown went after Casey and Simpson. Casey struck Brown with a brick, but he managed to get handcuffs on him before he was felled by a stone from Simpson. Exhilarated by his success, Simpson then threw another big stone at a passing cyclist and knocked him into the road. He seemed to revel in the fact that 'he was not in Aston where the Bench gave it them so hot'. Detective Brown recovered enough to drag Casey into a nearby house. Then the 'cavalry' arrived from Duke Street police station, Gosta Green, in the shape of Superintendent Sheppard, three other officers and about a dozen constables. The roughs, about thirty in number, took up positions on some waste ground in Chester Street, well supplied with bricks, and showered them at the constables as they approached. However they were soon ousted and five arrests were made. Chester Street, connecting Duddeston and Aston, was fast becoming as famous for slogging and violence as haunts like Allison Street in Digbeth. It also had a similar reputation for squalor and deprivation. In court, it turned out that Betts' grievance against Laura Solloway was that she 'dared' to answer him back when he fired words at her and 'he wasn't going to stand any woman talking to him'. Betts and Simpson were sentenced to fifteen months in prison, an outcome billed by the press as 'A Warning to "Slogging Gangs."'

Two years later, Betts, by now aged twenty-three, described as a caster, and living again in a court off Moorsom Street, was once more before the magistrates, accused of theft and assault. This time his victim was an icecream vendor crossing the fairground at the Old Peck. By 1890 many small stallholders had gone from the fair, but the icecream man, George 'Dancer' Owen, was thought to be fair game. Betts was one of several men who accosted him and asked him for fourpence one Saturday night in September. When Owen refused, he was struck, allegedly by Betts, and knocked to the ground. Then he was hit across the head with a pair of buckles and lapsed into unconsciousness. When he came round he found that money was missing from his pockets, and a policeman took him to the Workhouse Infirmary. Betts was arrested by Detective Heffernan, but he denied the charge and his lawyer, perhaps paid for by his fund, said that he was in a pub at the time. Stipendiary Colmore, a member of a leading local family, decided that he could not convict him on the evidence shown, and so he was discharged.

Although under threat from developers, the Old Peck was still regarded as the territory of the 'Aston slogging gang', who frightened those respectable citizens using it for meetings. It was said by the *Post* to be covered with stones 'from the size of a pebble to that of a granite sett', which could readily be used as ammunition. When the young radical David Lloyd George, M.P., addressed over 8,000 people at a temperance rally there in June 1890, he was largely inaudible due to the cheering, groaning and singing of a 'hundred resolute rowdies'. Yet the much-feared danger that the roughs would seize the wagons before their use by the speakers did not materialise.

Moorsom Street, close by, remained a slogging ground. Six months later, six plain clothes officers had to be sent to stop a 'war' between two gangs on three consecutive nights in May. Inspector McManus's efforts to stop the feuding were successful for a while, but perhaps the proximity of the Old Peck made it too difficult to catch anyone. In July, a melee involving one hundred lads stopped the traffic in Moorsom Street, and McManus this time sent in a dozen plainclothes officers, who succeeded in arresting three of the fighters. One was in his home street while the two others had come from New John Street and New Summer Street to the south, all in St Stephen's. A month later, a Moorsom Street resident wrote to the *Post* complaining that things were even worse when the school holidays brought 'batches of these young roughs' who were 'continually indulging in stone-throwing tournaments across the road'.

Rocky Lane, between Aston and Nechells, also remained dangerous. In February 1891, two Nechells sloggers were disturbed at about midnight throwing stones up an entry at someone running away from them. A man called Hartley, approached them and was soon made to wish that he had not. 'Here is one of the Summer Lane birds,' said a labourer from Long Acre, called Tarpey – perhaps the same man as at the Hodge Hill barn. The other, a stamper from Cook Street, said that he would have his suit of clothes or money or would knock his brains out. Hartley told them that he only had tuppence. He gave them what he had and was allowed to pass on. Then he heard them stop a young woman. At the assizes, they were charged with trying to extort money from six different people. However Mr Justice Wills was not impressed by the evidence against them and thought that a charge of common theft would have sufficed, so they were acquitted with a caution. The judge added, in support of the police action, that it was very necessary that they should exercise firmness in a district 'infested by unruly boys'. These unruly boys, however, were not restricted to one area of Birmingham and Aston.

CHAPTER 13

Mob Law

IF ASTON WAS now where the sloggers were most active, they also began to make their presence felt in other parts of the conurbation. A lengthy battle was reported in Oxford Street, off Digbeth, in November 1886, after which several had to take their wounds to hospital. One of the injured was twenty-year-old Edward Joyce, who was also fined for attempting the rescue of a man in custody, as, unusually, was seventeen-year-old Ellen Carroll. She was a flower seller and charged with being drunk and trying to rescue Joyce. A frequent slogger, he also led his gang in a late-night raid on a provision shop in New Canal Street for luxury items such as tinned salmon and jam. (It was he or possibly a namesake who, a few years later, was prosecuted, with his wife, by the Society for the Prevention of Cruelty to Children for the neglect of his four children under eight, 'nearly naked and covered with vermin' in a house off Cheapside, largely devoid of furniture and with only a heap of sodden straw for the children to sleep on.) The Parade area was haunted by a particularly vicious group of roughs, centred around the Brannan brothers of Holland Street, who seemed to specialise in attacking lamplighters and old men. And in May 1887, the inhabitants of Warwick Street, Deritend, presented a petition against a gang of boys who stoned anyone who complained about their gambling and obscene language.

In the hot, dry summer of 1887, street-fighting was in full swing in Duddeston, partly because of its proximity to Aston. Living in the wrong road was enough to spark an attack. One man was accosted by another as he was going towards Dartmouth Street, with the challenge, 'You live in Coleman Street.'

'I live there,' he replied, 'but I don't streetfight.'

His challenger, however, struck him on the head with a stone, with the words, 'Whether you do or don't, cop that.' A similar exchange took place in Broad Street on the other side of the town, where a man was suddenly challenged and struck with a pair of buckles for admitting to 'know' Sheepcote Street, in the same neighbourhood. The town's authorities may have been preparing for city status, but its working youth in their leisure time had a different agenda.

Stiff sentences for street crime were handed out at the 1887 autumn sessions, but the *Mail* expressed fears that the 'old fashion' of ruffianism was 'once more running rampant in our streets'. By November 1887, another gang was active in St George's. A brasscaster with fifteen previous convictions led other roughs in an attack on a policeman on a Saturday evening. The bobby blew his whistle and his attacker was arrested by another constable as he and his mates ran into Farm Street. Across the town, Watery Lane, linking Deritend and Bordesley, was the focus of the Bordesley gang, who were often blamed for highway robbery in that area. In April 1888, the same month in which a Bordesley labourer was being charged with stabbing a man to death in Duddeston, nailcasters on strike at Messrs Shaw's factory in Glover Street attacked the premises in protest against the employment of non-union men. They had to be dispersed by a number of constables sent from Moseley Street and Small Heath police stations. In the neighbourhood was also a group of thieves who were handy with their buckled belts and were referred to as the (Great) Barr Street slogging gang.

Meanwhile trade was improving and, in spite of the endorsement of the birch rod for punishing 'bad boys' by the new stipendiary magistrate, Thomas Milnes Colmore, slogging gangs were spreading. Balsall Heath was a new area to face a serious slogging problem. Perhaps because it was in Worcestershire, beyond the jurisdiction of the Birmingham constabulary, Balsall Heath attracted incursions by the Highgate Street gang from neighbouring lower Highgate. Twenty-two-year-old Henry Butterworth, who worked variously as an iron filer and a brasscaster, was described by Superintendent Tyler as the gang's captain and 'a very dangerous character with a bad record'. He was the third son in the family of nine of an advertising agent who lived on Highgate Terrace. When Sergeant Gwilliam tried to arrest Butterworth and another man for being drunk and disorderly in Longmore Street, a number of the gang tried to rescue them and one stabbed Gwilliam in the hand with a knife.

In spite of its name, the Highgate Street gang recruited from as far away as Bordesley. It was involved in a particularly notorious incident triggered when Thomas Cox, another brasscaster from Warwick Street, Deritend, brutally kicked a woman as she lay on the ground in Longmore Street. Two policemen witnessed the attack and arrested the nineteen-year-old Cox. They were about to take him to the station when he called to a couple of dozen companions to rescue him. The gang had just been expelled for drunken conduct from the Saturday night shows at the two Balsall Heath concert halls, the Caledonian and the Sherbourne, and was ready for trouble. Under a storm of stones, the constables managed to handcuff Cox, but only on one wrist. A man ran to Edwardes Street police station for help and along came more constables, led by a sergeant. Yet they proved powerless against so many assailants. P.C. Sadler was knocked out by a large stone. He was picked up, taken to a nearby inn and later to the Queen's Hospital. Cox managed to escape, but was spotted later on, hatless and increasing his speed when he saw the sergeant. Close examination showed that he still had on his 'darbies', one handcuff still on his wrist and the other hidden up his coat sleeve. Cox already had a record for shop-breaking in Birmingham and Small Heath. Sentenced with him at the King's Heath Police Court were a polisher from Bordesley Park and a nail-caster of no fixed address, called North and nicknamed 'North Pole'.

Fighting with buckles was an increasing concern for the courts. When a heavily buckled belt was produced as evidence after one courtyard brawl, the magistrate, Sam Timmins, declared, 'We mean to punish people heavily who use these things.' The defendant, a Camden Street slogger, excused himself with the words, 'I only wore it, sir, because I hadn't got any braces.' Timmins replied, 'Well, we shall do our best to change the fashion.' When a young woman from the Jewellery Quarter called Ellen Giblin cut through a policeman's helmet with her belt, a pair of buckles used by one of the gang, in the Gosta Green area, was found to weigh half a pound.

In May 1888, a gang answering to the name of the 'Nova Scotia Street kids' from near the Curzon Street goods station in St Bartholomew's was attacked with buckled belts after venturing into Tower Road and Potter's Hill, Aston. One of the interlopers had to go to the General Hospital for treatment, and the Aston gang – whose numbers included a seventeen-year-old labourer from Birmingham with the battle-cry 'I'll kill 'em!' – were arrested the same Thursday evening in the Swan Inn, Tower Road. In the same month, the 'Milk Street rowdies', as the *Mail* called them, were responsible for the stabbing of a man from Duddeston outside the Ring of Bells pub in Milk Street, near Digbeth.

The *Mail* newspaper, strangely unaware that belts were used every bit as aggressively in Manchester and Salford as in Birmingham, mused that although the buckled belt was less deadly than the seaport knife (presumably referring to Liverpool) and less likely to disfigure than the Lancashire clog, it would be better if the Birmingham slogger could leave off 'the cowhide strap and its formidable clasp' altogether. This was wishful thinking. Buckles were used with devastating effect. If none was available then a worse weapon was used. One Monday evening in September 1889, one of the Nova Scotia Street lads was turned out of the Gaiety Concert Hall in Coleshill Street, along with a local rival, for fighting. In the street, the Nova Scotia lad met a mate from his street and asked him for a belt, but he was not wearing one. So instead he borrowed his mate's knife and finished off the fight by using it to strike his opponent above the eye. Fortunately the General Hospital was able to stitch his victim's wound, while he went to prison for twenty-one days.

Prison sentences were becoming almost automatic for the use of belts and knives, and victims were often approached by their attackers, sometimes with money, to stop them pressing charges. When a man was struck with a buckled belt in Charles Henry Street, St Martin's, in July 1888, probably in a slogging encounter, the perpetrator's friends visited the victim's house to try to 'square him', but without success. Taking on the police was still the ultimate excitement; there was no chance of squaring them. The police were not usually sought out, but if they interfered in a slogging encounter they were considered fair game.

The power of the incitement to fight and its often awful consequences was shown by the case of Alfred Oxford, a young brassworker who lived in a court in the Markets area. On the night of 8 October 1888, a Monday, Oxford was in a free-and-easy, or licensed singing and dancing saloon, in Jamaica Row when he was told that he was wanted outside. He later admitted, under cross-examination, that he knew that it was for a fight and that he said, 'I'll fight him; I have never been beaten yet.' He went out and walked up to the top of Digbeth, where he saw Benjamin Mee, an eighteen-year-old carter, and a number of his companions. One of them asked Oxford if he wanted a fight.

'What do I want to fight you for?' he replied.

At that point a policeman came up and they all dispersed. Oxford headed off down a dark lane off Digbeth but suddenly felt himself struck from behind. The thud of the belt on the shoulder had become the city's latest form of challenge to a fight. Oxford turned round and saw Mee with a buckle-ended belt in his hand.

'Hello, that's got one home, has it?' said Mee.

Oxford, despite his earlier bravado, walked a little further, then felt a heavy blow from a brick on the back of his head. He felt ill and had to sit down by some railings outside Smithfield Market. When he came round, he dragged himself off to the Queen's Hospital. He was kept there as an in-patient for over three weeks, with a badly fractured skull and a small puncture wound penetrating the brain cavity. Mee was identified by another man to whom he had promised to lend his 'straps', or buckles, that night. Mee's father, apparently a Digbeth fruiterer, and his brother-in-law, a nailcaster, seem to have been those caught earlier for running two major illicit whisky stills in Sparkbrook which the police had been trying to track down for some time.

Slogging, like crime, ran in families. Such affiliations were linked to turf, but might supersede it as men moved round the area. To be called Joyce in Birmingham seemed almost to mean that you automatically enjoyed slogging. It was certainly true of Jacky, Thomas, and Edward Joyce – perhaps also of Peter, the election mobster. Now Patrick Joyce, a seventeen-year-old chairmaker of Blucher Street, off Holloway Head, formed or revived a slogging gang. They attacked youths who ventured into their territory and expanded into Park Street, where they robbed and kicked a lad in November 1888. In the following March, with as many as three or four dozen at his command, Joyce stabbed a lad named Reuben Cooper, or Cosier, in his right arm three times with a penknife. The case did not come to court unti June, and the new stipendiary warned him he was heading for a heavy sentence. Joyce had five previous convictions and was unaffected by these words. He told Mr Colmore that he was going abroad soon, to which the stipendiary replied that 'the city would be glad to see the back of him'. For the present he would have to go to gaol for six weeks. At this, Joyce turned to his mother nonchalantly and said 'Let's go and have some dinner,' which produced laughter in the courtroom. Joyce's next affray was the stabbing of a man in Bellbarn Road, near Lee Bank, well outside his territory. By the end of 1891 he had moved to Bradford Street, from where he was thieving close by. Birmingham had not seen the last of him after all.

Cosier was no angel either. The oldest of five sons of a Barford Street blacksmith, he was said to be something to do with 'rival villains', probably based in his home street. In July he was caught, with others, stealing roses from a garden in Selly Oak. Later he was described as a hawker and in 1893 was imprisoned for a month for trying to sell bad eggs from a barrow of eggs and chicken. The health inspector declared that his egg shells were two-thirds empty and that the rest of their contents was 'a dirty yellow substance'. So he became a carter. He was the victim of another assault, by a brassfounder from Bromsgrove Street, and by January 1894 he would be one of the six Barford Street boys involved in the death of John Metcalfe in the Digbeth stabbing case (see Chapter 17).

Girls were rarely arrested after a slog, except when they sometimes intervened to stop the police making an arrest. In February 1889, two girls were apprehended after a gang fight in Legge Street, Bishop Ryder's. They had aided a man as he attacked the unfortunate P.C. Long so savagely that he suffered a compound fracture of the skull. While the man was sentenced to three months' hard labour, the girls got away with a twenty shilling fine or fourteen days.

Gangs from Birmingham had always been attracted to the suburbs and adjacent neighbourhoods, often on Sundays; sometimes to thieve as in Cosier's case, or in search of trouble. Now there were complaints of Birmingham sloggers moving into Smethwick as well as Balsall Heath. Two seventeen-year-olds from Icknield Port Road attacked two younger Smethwick lads as all four came out of a show in Grove Lane; they knocked one unconscious with a poker. Other gangs were visibly on the move. In May 1889, a Moseley Street and Cheapside gang of six eighteen-year-olds, four of whom were brassworkers, assaulted passers-by in Victoria Street, Sparkbrook, with belts, bricks and sticks on a Sunday afternoon. One man lay in the Queen's Hospital for three weeks after being knocked unconscious by a buckled belt and taking a knife in the shoulder blade. The case went to the Worcestershire Assizes, where Baron Pollock gave two of the brassworkers six and three months' hard labour.

Meanwhile the Aston gang was still determined to show its supremacy by journeying south across the new city to fight the Charles Henry Street gang. Perhaps the high Irish-born element, noticeable in the 1881 Census, gave that street a special sense of its own identity. A change of address by certain individuals was also a factor in such an 'away' fixture. A boy called George Langford was struck on the head and put in hospital by eighteen-year-old Alfred Vincent, who was just out of a reformatory, in Charles Henry Street on a Thurday evening in May 1889. It was said that Langford happened to be in the street talking to some of the opposition side – believed to be the 'rowdies of an adjoining thoroughfare' – when Vincent and his crew made their attack, and battle commenced with sticks and buckled belts. Langford was hit on the top of the head, staggered a few yards and then fell unconscious. Vincent later admitted using a stick but pleaded provocation from Langford on the previous night. Langford had to undergo a trepanning operation for a compound depressed fracture of the skull. Once more the Birmingham surgeons surpassed themselves and three weeks later he was fit enough to appear at the quarter sessions.

There it was stated that Langford had been involved in the quarrel between rival gangs on the day previous to his injury, when 'his side' had used catapults. A policeman gave evidence that Vincent belonged to the Charles Henry Street gang. His denial was ignored and he was sentenced to fifteen months' hard labour. He did not take his sentence calmly, denying belonging to the street's gang and shouting at the constable as he was removed from the court, 'I'll kill you – swine; see if I don't. I'll knock your bleeding head off when I come out.' The assistant barrister in charge of the case remarked that 'these gangs were the pest of the Birmingham streets'.

In all this courtroom drama, Langford's role and his connection with the opposition in the fight could easily be overlooked. His age was unclear: he was said to be eighteen at the police court hearing, when first reported, and then at the sessions as in fact 'about fourteen', which was more likely correct. Moreover he was accused in court by Vincent's mother of being himself the leader of a gang. This allegation was not challenged by the defence and it was not as unlikely a claim as it first seemed. The other gang, 'his side', was from Aston, and the court was told that they had been over in lower Highgate on another evening as well. Although Langford's address was now Charles Henry Street, he had recently moved from the Lichfield Road, where, a year before, as a schoolboy, he had been taken before the Aston Petty Sessions by an angry parent for striking two little boys who lived in the same court. So he was hardly the innocent lad that some people thought, and it was not surprising that he was still siding with the Aston sloggers now that he was living among the enemy.

George Langford was soon making himself at home in his new area. A few weeks after being patched up by the surgeons, he was this time on the wrong side of the law. Described as sixteen years old and a tinner, he was in a gang of five juvenile thieves up before the bench for breaking into a factory office with a jemmy and stealing some clothes and halfpenny postage stamps, although failing to open the safe. He and another had also stolen two pairs of boots from a pawnbroker's. He was sent to prison for six weeks. The boys left the dock laughing. A few months later, a George Langford of Emily Street, Highgate, again described as a sixteen-year-old tinner, was involved in stealing boots and galoshes from a shop with a smaller and far more efficient gang led by 'Barber' Ross, a sixteen-year-old whose role was to put a sharp elbow through shop windows and wait while the other two did the plundering. The *Post* reported that the three had 'caused something like a scare among the shopkeepers in the Moseley Street (police) division' by their successful smash-and-grab tactics in full daylight. This time Langford's penalty was four months behind bars and a spell in the Warwickshire Reformatory for Boys at Weston.

July 1889 also saw an unusual amount of fighting in the Islington area, off Broad Street. A gang led by a twenty-five-year-old brasscaster from the Newhall district attacked a smaller gang with buckled belts in Granville Street on a Monday evening, in revenge for the imprisonment of one of their mates. Only two were arrested in this act of reprisal, although P.C. Tidmarsh said in court that with some help he could have arrested a dozen others. Stipendiary Colmore told the police in such circumstances to call for reinforcements and warned the prisoner's suspected friends at the back of the court that if they identified themselves they would be severely dealt with.

The Worcestershire police at Balsall Heath not only had to deal with the Highgate Street gang but also face up to the Sparkbrook sloggers. Of these, the three Harper brothers of Highgate Road, all labourers and said to be 'court-entry loafers', were the most aggressive. In June 1889, John and Henry Harper were given six and three months respectively for being drunk and disorderly on a Saturday night and assaulting the police. Nine months later, all three were involved and it took three constables to arrest them, with great difficulty. The brothers resisted with kicks and stones, one of which cut through a policeman's helmet and wounded the back of his head. Their mates tore bricks out of a wall and broke them to use as missiles against their arrest, but in vain. At the Worcestershire Sessions, Willis Bund gave John, the oldest brother, eighteen months with hard labour and warned the rest of the gang of what they might get at his court. Such a sentence was a real deterrent.

In Digbeth, a long-standing feud was being fought out in Allison Street between the Leonard and Kilmartin brothers. They were both families of Irish extraction; the Kilmartins were gunworkers and the Leonards were in brass. John Kilmartin was attacked with buckled belts as he entered a pub on a Saturday night, in July 1889, by two of the Allison

Street slogging gang . Two months later, it was Thomas Kilmartin's turn
to be attacked by John and Matthew Leonard at the corner of Park Lane
and Allison Street. The cause of the row, as so often, was a previous court
case. Another John Leonard, or Lennard, nicknamed 'Cock', was also
prominent among the Allison Street mob. Superintendent Stephenson
described him as 'one of the worst characters they had to deal with in the
neighbourhood of Digbeth'. These three had no compunction about stabbing or beating up women who got in their way. Cock Lennard was
imprisoned for four months for assaulting Mary Shelley of Cheapside,
working off what the defence solicitor called 'an imaginary grievance
against the woman'.

Allison Street was described by a local landlord as being 'one of the
worst streets in the city'. Indeed Digbeth, more than ever since the destruction of much of central Birmingham, was a deprived and overcrowded
area. The condition of houses in Barn Street, near the Grand Union Canal
wharf, was analysed by the Medical Officer of Health at about this time.
Most of the 103 houses consisted of only three rooms, with no back
windows or doors and rudimentary sanitation, and the death rate was a
staggering forty-two per 1,000 – although still lower than in Park Street.
Life was cheap, and violent masculinity was at a premium.

The Gun Quarter's leading mob was now the Price Street gang. Their
claim to rule the roost was reinforced when they beat up Benjamin
Bridgwater, of the Gunmakers'Arms, Weaman Row, for giving evidence
to the police about the theft of goods from a local factory. One of the
leading Price Street fighters was a labourer from across the canal in Tower
Street, to the west of Summer Lane, who had many convictions for theft
and assault. Others were younger and less criminalized. The crew would
challenge anyone not in their group who ventured down the street. A
typical challenge was, 'Here's one of them,' or, 'What have you got to say?'
One man, in July 1890, would have no chance to respond to this last
question before his young challenger produced a brick from behind his
coat and struck him across the nose. In court, he could only think that
the attack was because he refused to have 'anything to do with them'.
Brookfields, to the west of the Jewellery Quarter and for a long time associated with prize fights, now also had a slogging gang, based around some
lads who lived close to each other in Ellen Street. They reportedly attacked
youths in other neighbourhoods with belts and sticks. Ashted, already
renamed Duddeston, similarly had a gang around Windsor Street, near
the cavalry barracks.

So by 1889 it was clear that slogging was once more a regular feature of Birmingham life, as reported by the newspapers. The impression is that times had changed since the gangs of the early 1870s had gone out for pitched battles of stone-throwing on Sunday afternoons. The battles of the late 1880s were fought at closer quarters. The gangs were also invading new territories, such as Nechells and Sparkbrook. People were moving out from the old centres of the town and slogging spread with them to the suburbs, where new identities and loyalties were being forged. Areas such as Islington, where slogging had been relatively unknown, were developing gangs apparently for the first time. There were few signs that the old tensions between the Irish and others played much of a part, perhaps because Birmingham was becoming more homogeneous even in the Digbeth area. This was partly from the fact that so many of the new generation had been born and bred in the city. Some boys of Irish descent were still proud to demonstrate their fighting skills, as was the occasional Welshman, while of the new minority groups, the Jews, in spite of attempting a low profile, were constantly in the news from the pogroms in Russia and the arrival of refugees in Britain. Many of these newcomers were said to be attracted to 'the hub of England' before moving to other towns, but they were, like the Italians, more the occasional victims of, rather than the regular participants in, slogging. One slogger did have an Italian name, a brass worker called John Taroni whose grandfather had arrived in the West Midlands from Lombardy. There were also at least two Irish-Americans. William Kennedy was born in the USA during the Civil War, but his Irish-born parents came to Birmingham soon afterwards and raised their family there. Kennedy was active with the Allison Street gang. The other was a much more criminal character called David Cherry, an American visitor to Balsall Heath and from there to most of the region's prisons. Such men were rarities among Birmingham's slogging fraternity.

THE RELOCATION of the Royal Small Arms factory from Sparkbrook to Enfield in Middlesex in 1888 was a big blow to the gun trade. However, the same year saw a boom in the Birmingham building trade. A general revival in trade then began, though it did not last beyond 1892. With the better times came a rash of strikes, as workers demanded higher pay and better conditions. The most famous were the matchgirls' and the dockers' strikes in London, although neither of these affected Birmingham directly. Locally, a brassworkers' strike was unsuccessful. Also in the midst of the revival of slogging gangs came a wave of school strikes. These were nation-wide and constituted a reaction to the first ten years of compulsory schooling. The strikes originated at Hawick in Scotland and spread to Greenock, where they may have been influenced by the great dock strike, and then to Glasgow and Aberdeen. They involved first board schools and then church schools too. The grievances varied. At Greenock, older scholars openly revolted on the grounds that school hours were too long and that they were being given too much homework. At Aberdeen, the boys demanded, among other things, free education, a major issue for parents that was only being gradually addressed by the Government. Another demand was for 'no strap'. The strike spread to London. A Clerkenwell magistrate complained condescendingly that 'no doubt they had been led away by reading in the newspapers things they didn't under-stand'. In Penrith, Cumberland, a Wesleyan schoolmaster who tried to drive his pupils back into school had two teeth knocked out.

In the Birmingham area, one of the first schools affected was the Smethwick Board School, where the children demanded the abolition of homework. But it was Ladywood where the strikes had locally most impact, starting at the Oozells Street North board schools, off Broad Street, in March 1890. The children said that the fees were too high and should be reduced by a halfpenny and their time in school reduced by two hours a day, with a half-holiday in the middle of the week and no use of the cane. They refused to go back in after break and threw missiles at the headmaster, a noted musician called Wiseman. This action was blamed by the press on 'the loungers of the district' goading the lads on. Then, armed with sticks, the strikers tried to turn out the children in Oozells Street School and next they began a march through Ladywood. At Nelson Street School, they gathered more children as they were coming out for dinner. By this stage, there were between six and seven hundred boys in the street. In spite of a warning that if they were not back in school by 2 p.m. they would be treated as truants, they continued to Ellen Street, by which time the police arrived.

The strikers moved on to the smaller St Mark's Church School, in King Edward's Road. It was the end of the dinner hour, so they followed the St Mark's children into the playground. Seeing them coming, the assistants shut the doors, so the strikers – simply 'idlers', not schoolboys, according to the press – threw stones and broke glass. When they reached the Helena Street branch of St Mark's School, the teachers reacted by closing the school for the afternoon. They moved on again to Steward

Street, off Spring Hill, where they were met by the police and ran in all directions, shouting. 'Technical and Foundry Road in the morning!' However, in the morning all was quiet and everyone in the Sandpits area was back at school when the school board visitors or truancy officers made their rounds. Taking stock, the masters wondered why the episode had started and who was behind it. It was assumed that the children had taken their cue from the striking coalminers.

The next day, about a hundred lads were seen marching about the neighbourhood of St George Street West, but they did not manage to get much support from schoolchildren in that area. In the district of Hope Street, several youths of over school age were reported as leading a 'juvenile mob' of three hundred. The *Post* commented that they 'had the appearance of regular truant-players, and were, for the most part, without shoes and stockings and very poorly dressed'. Their first stop was St Luke's Church School, where they pressed their faces against the windows and threw coal from a heap in the road, but they were chased off by the caretaker, armed with a Malacca cane. The mob moved on to Rea Street Schools, and then on to Highgate Park and Chandos Road Board School, where afternoon lessons had started. At Moseley Street police station, Superintendent Hervey armed some plainclothes men with canes and they chased the strikers around the park. Most dispersed. Back at St Luke's one ringleader told a *Mail* reporter, 'We don't want so much bloomin' school now the fine weather has come … We don't want so much coshin' (caning) just because we play the wag.' They didn't want homework either – but at that point the interview was cut short by the caretaker with his Malacca cane.

It was some cause of relief to the Birmingham authorities that the school strikes died away. There was less room for complacency about street conduct as a whole. By the spring of 1890, the influential *Mail* was in full panic mode. 'Mob law' had taken over in Birmingham, with rowdyism on the increase. Slogging gangs of between fifteen and thirty youths, ranging in age from seventeen to twenty-four years, were showing themselves in many quarters of the town. Some were confining themselves to shouting obscene language; others were harbouring ruffians whose aim was no more than to 'form a mutual protection league' – perhaps for hardened men like George Betts. They were infesting street corners and 'low' coffee-houses where, under the leadership of some rough – and Bowey Beard of the Digbeth gang (see Chapter 15) was cited as one such leader – they aired their grievances and decided who would be next to feel their strength and suffer accordingly. Word would be given out, according to the *Mail,* that 'So and So has got to go through', and the time of the attack and those to lead it would be decided upon.

It is not clear on what evidence the *Mail* based this account of the typical slogging gang's gatherings. Most of them were in fact half-educated lads and roughs assembling haphazardly in the street. The newspaper piece was no doubt designed to provoke action from the authorities, but there may have been some kernel of truth to the comments from a newspaper whose reporters, like the *Gazette*'s, penetrated the slum life of Birmingham. At least in terms of numbers in the gangs, leadership and patronage of certain refreshment or licensed houses, it was on firm ground.

CHAPTER 14

The Police in Trouble

THE BIRMINGHAM POLICE had many problems. Some drank, many were violent, all were exhausted by long shifts. There was a high turnover of personnel and a shortfall in numbers. Recruits were desperately sought. The risk of attack was considerable, especially in the 1870s. The violence shown to them, and the injuries they received, made service in Birmingham notorious. Slogging gangs constituted only one part of a wider threat of assaults by individuals or by groups. The danger of a constable going into any crowd alone was only partly overcome by working in pairs. Thugs would often wait until unpopular policemen were on their own before drawing them into a confrontation. The ratio of policemen to population was just over half what it was in Manchester and Liverpool. An increase in numbers, to five hundred and fifty in 1883 and seven hundred by 1897, did help reduce the danger to individuals, despite a parallel increase in population and the expansion of the city. By then exposure to all weathers and the likelihood of chronic bronchitis were said to be the worst dangers the constables faced.

Plain clothes were seen as the best form of self-defence, especially when making an arrest. It was clearly an effective form of disguise in many cases. P.C. Fletcher, who was involved in the Navigation Street arrests, arrested a tailor two years later after he had tugged three times at the plainclothesman's watch chain in an unwary attempt to steal his watch. But it did not always work. When an off-duty P.C. Daniels went into the Warwick Arms, in the Dudley Road, for a drink one afternoon while in civilian clothes, he was followed by some roughs, one of whom recognised him. 'That's the – who had me,' said the lout. All of them promptly set upon him and they only abandoned him after he had fallen semi-conscious outside in the street. There was no doubt that, as much as Brummies liked fighting each other, they liked fighting the police even more. The number of assaults on the police was always far higher than the number of slogging incidents. The *Post* urged Chief Superintendent Glossop to concentrate his men at 'threatened points' in a faster and more certain manner. One suggestion was for more action by mounted police.

Most of the police showed great bravery in the face of grave physical danger. It is not surprising that there were exceptions. One was P.C. Joseph Wragge, who was in Moseley Street in June 1873 when Thomas Wild, a timber merchant, came up to him, hauling behind him a nailcaster whom he had stopped from attacking a gentleman. Mr Wild handed the nail-caster to P.C. Wragge to be taken into custody. However he was not in custody for long, as his mates rescued him and the policeman ran away. Wragge admitted all this in court, where it was also revealed that he had asked Mr Wild for payment for attending as a witness.

The police faced great difficulties in obtaining information. There was a general reluctance to 'peach' or 'round' on neighbours. Those who did often had a grievance. Informers or 'coppers' often suffered from reprisals. Indeed the Bordesley Riot seems to have originated against someone who gave evidence at a police court. Retribution was often immediate. Informants were always in danger of reprisals from the mates of the convicted. John Simons was hit by a brick in his back in Jamaica Row one Saturday night in 1898 as he heard his assailant shout, 'Here's that – who got Jess Cox six months.'

Some felt real resentment against the police, for unexpected reasons. In the Allison Street area, for example, there was much ill-feeling for what were regarded as extortionate charges made by the bobby on the early beat for 'calling-up' or knocking on windows to wake people up for work. Baiting of policemen, or 'pinchers', was regarded by some as just one variant of the epidemics of ruffianism to which Victorian large towns were subject and only curable by repeated sharp punishment. An opposite, though much rarer, view was that it was the police themselves who encouraged slogging gangs by launching into groups of young people on the smallest pretext. A Mrs Smith of Aston, at the scene of a confronta-tion in Lichfield Road in 1874, complained that the policeman 'rioted amongst the young men in the violentest manner'. Levels of police brutality are not known, but these were rough-and-tumble times. Given the amount of violence suffered by the police, it is not surprising that sometimes they broke the law and used their staffs or truncheons in situ-ations where they were not acting in self-defence.

This went too far in the case of William John Whittaker, a sixteen-year-old iron foundry worker involved in some trouble in March 1891 that became known as the Beak Street slogging case. Whittaker died at the Queen's Hospital from two head wounds, one of them a depressed fracture of the skull. He had made a statement that he was merely coming home along another street, had followed some boys who were running away from a policeman, and that as he ran after them into Beak Street, which was off Lower Severn Street in central Birmingham, another policeman felled him with his staff. Superintendent Stephenson told the enquiry that various boys had been complained about for stone-throwing, breaking plate-glass windows and pelting people with mud. Three policemen had been put on duty. The boys, in their mid-teens, claimed to have been merely shouting and playing 'red dog', famous as a card game but here supposedly a running and catching game. Two of the boys identified P.C. 101 of 'A' Division, whose name was Thomas Watson, in the courtroom as the one they had seen striking a boy. Another boy said that A101 had hit him with a belt and told the court that 'every time they sees us, they runs us'.

'But policemen don't hit boys for playing, do they?' asked the coroner at the inquest.

'Yes, sir,' said John Lawley, a thirteen-year-old witness.

'So you ran away from them?'

'Yes.'

The coroner pronounced that policemen had no right to strike lads, especially when they were running away. The three constables denied hitting anyone. P.C. Watson told the coroner's inquest that he had been on duty at the tram terminus in John Bright Street, where there was a need to protect guards on late-evening trams from being slogged by local boys. He admitted he had chased boys earlier in the evening but said he had not used his staff or his belt. It seems possible that Watson had got wind of what was happening in nearby Beak Street and joined with two other constables who were already chasing the boys. P.C. Watson seems to have happened upon Whittaker, closed in on him and lashed out, probably with his belt or staff, to the back of the head. That was at any rate the conclusion of the coroner's jury. They returned a verdict of manslaughter by P.C. Watson. So the case went to the magistrates, but the policemen were admitting nothing. It was unclear whether the boy had been hit running up or down Beak Street, and it was Stipendiary Kynnersley's view that an assize jury would never be able to reach a guilty verdict on such conflicting evidence. So Watson was discharged.

Some constables clearly over-reacted under pressure, and police hostility probably encouraged the roughs to band together to take revenge, but police behaviour was far less important as a contributory factor to street violence than the intolerant public order code that they were supposed to enforce.

Attacks by older adults on the police were rare unless they were being arrested for drunkenness or had a child at risk. Then the policeman involved felt the full force of parental instincts. Men and women were equally protective. An angry father assaulted a constable for arresting his son, one of five boys 'chucking gravel' in a churchyard at Ashted. A few weeks earlier, at the corner of Thomas Street and Dale End, a group of twenty-five men causing an obstruction refused to disperse when told to do so by P.C. Jones. He arrested a young man called Allen, but Allen's father was not happy and struck Jones in the face and kicked him. Then the rest of the mob joined in. This was said to be the second assault endured by P.C. Jones in Thomas Street in a week. The constable turned his attention to the father, but he escaped in the crowd and was only recovered with the help of a second constable. He vigorously resisted, clutching Jones around the throat. The younger Allen was not charged, but his father was sentenced to two months' hard labour.

Sometimes the picture was unclear. P.C. Heritage arrested a fourteen-year-old for gambling in the street and was taking him to Moor Street police station one Saturday evening. When he got his prisoner to Brearley Street West, off Summer Lane, he found himself surrounded by a gang of youths and women, who all pelted him. Exhausted, he turned his back to the wall. According to his account, Rachel Gough, the boy's mother, then threw a stone which hit him in the mouth and cut through his cheek. He was hit in the eye by a brick from another quarter and had to go to hospital to have his injuries dressed. The defence counsel asserted that Mrs Gough had not struck him, but merely came close to ask him to loosen his grip on her boy, whom she said he was in the process of strangling. However the stipendiary saw no reason to disbelieve the constable and the mother was fined.

Family ties worked the other way as well. In December 1874, the two Giblin brothers, John and Thomas, aged sixteen and eleven, of Water Street, saw their father being taken through Livery Street for drunkenness by a P.C. Hill. With the help of other stone-throwing boys, they nearly freed their father two or three times. The policeman was so badly knocked about that he was off duty for three days, and the elder boy was sentenced to two months' hard labour. The Giblin boys would develop over time into two of Birmingham's most violent roughs; indeed in 1876 it was already stated before the Bench that there was 'scarcely a crime in the calendar of which the prisoner (John Giblin) had not been guilty'.

For P.C. Charles Price, there was the unusual humiliation of his own son turning into a leading rough. Charles Price junior was a glassblower by trade, although he often worked as a labourer. By 1891, when he was eighteen, he already had previous convictions and was described by a detective, speaking as a witness at the sessions, as the ringleader of a gang of young thieves. The following year he was sent down for six months for lunging out with a knife to stab a girl in a pub quarrel in Steelhouse Lane, and by 1895 he was reduced to trying to rob inmates of a Park Lane lodging house while they were asleep. Apart from his parentage, his story was all too common. Another policeman's son, John McDermott, was involved in two slogging incidents in the 1870s. The family lived in Cheapside and Bradford Street, where slogging was hard to avoid.

Among those singled out for street attacks were ex-policemen, against whom many held a grudge. An example was John Hession, attacked by a gang in Aston Manor in February 1900 when walking alone. He had been assaulted by them before, but this time he was rendered unconscious and his chief tormentor was sentenced to six months' imprisonment at Warwick Assizes. One ex-bobby, described as a 'wolf in sheep's clothing', became a nightwatchman. His name was linked to a number of burglaries and warehouse robberies in the Jewellery Quarter. When he was finally caught and sent to prison, it was said that that area would be much safer as a result. Another ex-policeman, who had perhaps found the work unbearable, sank to labouring and heavy drinking from being out of work. He became a wife-abuser and eventually cut his throat in the street.

By the end of the century, the police had learned to deal carefully with the roughs and to avoid antagonising them unnecessarily, especially in the badlands of Digbeth. One who had not was P.C. Connolly, who found a disturbance in the notorious Allison Street on a Monday night in 1898. He ordered the men to clear off, but one threw a brick at him, hitting him on the shoulder. He thought it was a man called Kennedy, although he saw another, O'Neil, heading for a heap of bricks, so he decided to go for help. He found two other policemen, and the three of them went looking for the two roughs at the house of a man named Kilmartin, one of the family previously fighting the Leonards. Kilmartin refused to open the door and something was thrown at the police from an upstairs window. P.C. Connolly broke open the door and the policemen were showered with coal and coal-dust. Three men were arrested including Kennedy and O'Neil. The magistrates' clerk was not impressed. He told Connolly publicly, 'You only wanted one (referring to Kennedy). You see you give the men a handle for doing this sort of thing. The worst thing that was done was that you had been struck on the shoulder with a brick and you could have summoned him for that any time.'

O'Neil and the third man were discharged. Kennedy had a previous conviction for assaulting P.C. Connolly and was given two months' hard labour. The stipendiary sighed, and his reported words were, 'This was the cause of the whole of the trouble.' Careful police handling of difficult situations was essential for relative peace in Birmingham's streets. It is hardly surprising that, with only rudimentary training and in the face of such extensive problems, judicious treatment was beyond the power of some policemen.

CHAPTER15

Gangs at Play

BEERHOUSES WERE OFTEN the headquarters of bands and gangs. Relations between the lads and the beerhouse masters were often strained. It is hardly surprising that landlords stood by sometimes and merely watched while the police tried to deal with any trouble. In autumn 1876, a landlord named James Ward was summonsed for failing to assist a policeman being assaulted by thirteen young men in the taproom of his inn, the Prince of Wales, Cliveland Street. Temperance advocates thought that a beer tax might help drive the sloggers out of such places, but this was wishful thinking. Coffee houses were also meeting places for the gangs. On a Saturday night in June 1889, 'the Square' gang, otherwise unrecorded, went to the house of Howard Cooper, a coffee house proprietor, in Ledsam Street, Ladywood, to take revenge on him for having refused them admittance. They rang his door bell, threw a lighted cigar in his face and gave him a black eye. One of the gang, a brassfounder from Summer Lane, then took off his belt and smashed the front window. The proprietor tried unwisely to arrest him and was promptly dealt a further blow on the head. The brassfounder went to prison for a month.

Theatres too attracted young people in large numbers. The historian Douglas Reid has shown them to have been places where customarily-organised groups of 'gallery boys' had rights, privileges and a degree of informal control, negotiating boundaries of behaviour with the management and the police. Pantomimes had become the rage by the early 1870s, with newspapers giving full details of the plots and the performances. Specially written for each occasion, their allusions to local places and issues were eagerly anticipated by the Birmingham audiences. High wages at this time meant that almost everyone could attend, and the two major theatres, the Royal and the Prince of Wales, were packed out. Both attracted rowdy elements. Often groups of young men in the gallery knocked each others' hats off inside the theatre and in the process disturbed or injured other members of the audience. Sometimes the shouting and fighting made it impossible to hear the voices of the actors, and so events in the gallery eclipsed those on stage. Police intervention only increased the sense of drama generated by the youthful 'gods', as they booed the police who waded in and cheered whoever had been arrested. The man arrested might call for help and the crowd might actively help him to resist.

Movement around a packed gallery was another problem. In February 1873, a thirteen-year-old boy fell from the top gallery of the Theatre Royal as he tried to clamber over the heads of spectators to reach his friends in the front row. As he neared the front, he rolled over the rail of the 'crescent' and fell forty feet into the pit below, fatally fracturing his skull. His father, a shoemaker from Windmill Street, said that he had been pushed by a woman, but the coroner's jury returned a verdict of accidental death.

A few weeks later, in the same theatre, there was another disturbance in the gods, or gallery, when two policemen tried to prevent roughs from selling places on the front row. At their court hearing, it was said that at first it seemed as if three men in the front were simply standing and calling to a friend at the back to come forward to join them. P.C. Russell, one of the two policemen on duty, told the men that there was no room for any more without crushing those who were already there. To this, one of the men, a toolmaker from Rea Street called Wilkes, replied that 'he would have his friend with him if he chose'. People complained at the disturbance, and P.C. Fletcher made his way over to help. The men were asked to sit down, but they refused in a threatening manner, turning up their sleeves and taking a fighting stance. Then a fight started, and one of the others, a labourer from Upper Trinity Street, Deritend, shouted to his mates to help him to throw the two bobbies into the pit. P.C. Russell fell down before he got to the railings, but heard the man call out, 'Land him one,' as about a dozen lads landed on top of him. P.C. Fletcher entered the fray, grabbing Wilkes' scarf – but that was cut with a knife – and then a waistcoat and shirt, but they also gave way. The two constables said that they were kicked about 'like footballs', and Fletcher only saved himself from going over into the pit by hooking his leg around the rail. Somehow they eventually took hold of three of the men and marched them to the police station. Wilkes was said to be a common disturber of the theatre and had been refused admittance for a long period. The men had been monopolising the front seats in the gallery and selling them. An independent witness confirmed that Wilkes had put up two fingers to indicate to someone at the back that a front seat could be had for tuppence. He had been going to the Royal for eleven years and had often seen money pass for front seats in this way. The three men were sent to prison for two months.

The case provoked various interesting letters to the *Post*. One suggested that concert hall audiences behaved better because, unlike the theatres, the halls did not admit 'low, dirty roughs'. Another asserted that members of the unofficial 'selling company' were in action the moment the gallery was open, so, no matter how early you got there, one of the self-appointed 'gods' would order you to pay tuppence to sit at the front or he would 'fill yer up'. This letter called on the theatre authorities to 'banish the black band from the gallery', adding cryptically, 'they are known'.[14] The Watch Committee was more cautious, merely recommending a third rail on the front of the gallery to protect the policemen on duty, while one alderman said, 'You cannot expect the proprietors to put up a cage as for wild beasts.' The practice of claiming the best seats by certain young men continued. One tried to push a policeman into the pit in 1875 when he had turned two youths out of their central seats in the gallery of the Prince of Wales.

Treatment of the performers was another issue. Things turned particularly bad in the spring of 1873, when the lads in the gods of the Prince of Wales targeted Elise Holt, starring in the pantomime *Twinkle, Twinkle, Little Star*. Billed as a 'celebrated burlesque actress from the Strand Theatre, London', she refused, unlike others, to pay the 'gallery brigands' for their applause, so she was hissed instead. One Saturday night she received huge cheering when she changed two lines of the pantomime to:

> It rests with you to say if I've done right
> In not paying the gallery boys to applaud me every night.

The hissing did not stop and at the end of an exceptionally long run a cabbage was thrown on stage.

---

14 There seems to be no link with the thieves of Harding Street, also called the Black Band or Gang.

Theatre staff had a blacklist and tried to keep out any people looking drunk or disorderly, but on Saturday nights anyone could slip through the crowd, and the entrance to the gallery was a place where roughs congregated and fights broke out. On Saturday, 4 July 1874, an actor called Toole, who played the part of the comic barrister in Albery's *Wig and Gown*, was making his farewell visit to the Prince of Wales Theatre. At about eleven o'clock, the usher or checktaker, Probert, saw a group of ten people standing at the bottom of the gallery steps near the entrance from King Edward's Place. One of them was called 'Blewy' or Richard Mole, a striker of Wellington Street, Icknield Square, a known yob who had previously been excluded from the theatre. Mole swore at him and demanded to know why he was not allowed in to see the show. The checktaker told him to complain to the managers, at which Mole rushed at him with an open clasp-knife and cut him in the thigh and the hand. Mole also grabbed the check-can and threw it at him. Probert fought back and took hold of Mole, who called on his companions to take off their belts and rescue him. He was later arrested and sent to the sessions. The jury did not believe the defence case that no knife had been used and that the wounds were an accident arising out of Mole merely throwing the check-can at Probert, and so he was sentenced to six months' imprisonment.

By 1889, in spite of improvements and rebuilding, overcrowding had again become serious in the pantomime season and was a problem for all Birmingham's theatres. Concert halls were even more popular than the theatre, with licences for drinking and dancing and sometimes hosting other entertainments such as boxing contests. The London Museum Concert Hall, at the top of Digbeth, was one of the biggest and rowdiest. Its licence meant that the audience could drink and smoke while they watched the show, and trouble arose when bottles and glasses were thrown. The police had moved in one Saturday night in December 1876 to eject two men who had caused a disturbance. One was arrested and taken to the station, the other followed on, hurling a bottle at the policeman and ending up in prison for a month. Later the Museum Concert Hall was reputed to be the headquarters of the Park Street gang. Out in the suburbs, the noisy and sometimes riotous behaviour of gangs emerging from the Balsall Heath Concert Hall in Sherbourne Road, especially on a Saturday night, caused indignation among residents.

It is still a matter of debate as to whether managements became more officious or the audience more difficult to handle at this time. There was a subtle relationship between the stars and their audiences, especially in the music halls, where the clientele was unsophisticated and audience participation common. Theatre and music hall performers could have their acts made or marred by the audience and there was always the possibility of blackmail. A music hall star in one such case was Jenny Hill. Born in poverty, the daughter of a London cabbie, Hill made her first appearance as a goose in an East End pantomime. She was indentured by her father to a Yorkshire publican for six years, getting up at dawn to clear the bars and singing to the customers from noon till closing-time. Her first appearance on the West End stage was at the London Pavilion, when the absence of one of the performers allowed her to go on as an extra turn, and her success led to her first long engagement. She became famous for song-and-dance routines and male impersonations, and was appearing at the Museum Concert Hall by 1865. Engagements at the other Birmingham halls soon followed and reviewers wrote favourably of her signature songs such as 'Bother the Men'. By 1874 she was topping the bill, and by 1880 was usually advertised, for her versatility and vim, as 'The Vital Spark'. Soon however there was competition in male impersonation from Vesta Tilley (Matilda Powles), who was fourteen years younger and who replaced Hill at the top of the bill of entertainers. Such was Hill's anger that she walked out on Day's Concert Hall in September 1882 and was not allowed to appear there again. Nevertheless Hill remained popular and found a new role at the Theatre Royal as the principal boy in pantomimes such as *Goody Two Shoes* and *Aladdin*. She roused the audience with stirring patriotic songs such as 'The Old Flag' as well as with the xenophobic 'England for the English' – a criticism of foreign immigrants taking English jobs – and her own hallmark style of songs about men. Success brought her considerable wealth and a big house at Streatham in South London. She prided herself on her generosity to those less fortunate, especially struggling artists. Like all entertainers she relied on her fans.

One such 'fan' was a disreputable young labourer, sometime iron moulder, from Hospital Street called Thomas Welch, who easily got into street fights. In 1883, he was sentenced to twelve months in prison, along with two others, for his part in a 'murderous affray' against a solitary polisher in Price Street, after the polisher had complained to one of them, who was married to his sister, about hitting her. Welch was then nineteen and already had nine previous convictions. Further appearances before the Bench followed for various misdemeanours – amounting to a page and a half in the record book – including drunken assaults on the police and taking part in the intimidation of a pearl-button maker who would not take part in a strike. By 1886, Welch was unemployed and living in Cheapside, relying on his parents for his upkeep.

In December 1886, it was Jenny Hill's last night after a fortnight's run at the Museum Concert Hall in Digbeth. Several friends were seeing her off and at 11.20 p.m. she finally left the theatre by the stage door in Park Street, where cabs were waiting for them. The *Post* reported that 'as usual there were several roughs and hangers-on lounging about, some of whom, it is stated, are in the habit of blackmailing the artists as they leave the hall.' Among them, Welch was seen making his way to Jenny Hill's side. Coming up to her he said, 'Don't you remember me? We met at the races.' She did not reply, but Welch persisted, and Mr Turnbull, her husband, urged her to get into the cab. On her wrist was a diamond bracelet and she was said to be wearing other jewellery worth several hundred pounds. He shouted, 'Mind your diamonds, Jenny.'

Welch, it was claimed, caught hold of her wrist as if to take the bracelet and was following her into her cab when two of her friends, including the Museum manager, pulled him back. The manager, Mr Hall, said, 'Come away, you scamp.' Welch turned round, snarling, 'I'll bang you,' and hit the manager in the face. Hall hit him back with a blow that knocked him over, but Welch got up, apparently unhurt, and went for him. In the scuffle, Welch lost his balance and hit his head against the hub of the cab wheel. The theatrical party then drove away in their cabs, while a constable picked up the unconscious Welch and took him to the hospital. Later the police got Hall out of bed and arrested him, although he was allowed home on bail when it was found that Welch was recovering.

In court, Welch, with his head swathed in hospital bandages, denied loitering about the Museum all evening and pestering people for drinks in the bar. He also denied the prosecution's suggestion that he belonged to a gang 'who frequented the Museum and molested the performers'. Welch refused to be intimidated. He did know Jenny Hill, but he denied speaking to her or trying to get in the cab with her. He also denied sparring at or striking Mr Hall. However one witness, who was standing at the stage door with about thirty others, confirmed that Welch had been very drunk, refused Hall's request to go away and had struck him in the face. The prosecution stuck to its claim that Welch was 'a member of a gang of roughs who habitually lounge around the

Museum', with the chief aim of extorting money from performers. For Welch, the defence case was also unflattering. Witnesses gave details of his actions that evening, including loitering, seeking for money for drink and asking for money off Jenny Hill from the step of her cab. The case ended with Hall giving Welch a sovereign as double compensation for his injuries and the stipendiary telling him not to loiter near the stage door in future.

This was not the last case of 'gallery boys' bothering the stars. The blackmailing of actresses reached the public's notice again early in 1889, when Miss Marie Loftus, star of the Prince of Wales's pantomime *Blue Beard* and well-loved for her signature song, 'I'm So Shy', complained to the police about being followed back to her lodgings. The next time she was followed home, her pursuer found other 'footlights favourites' in her landlady's front room, and as he began to demand money, a detective stepped out from behind a curtain and arrested him. The anonymous 'hulking fellow' was taken to Moor Street police station, but there let off with a caution.

Connections between street gangs and the music halls continued. The Aston sloggers who lived in or around Whitehouse Street were sometimes referred to as the Whitehouse Street gang. Their biggest thrill was to venture into other territory, especially Digbeth, with its London Museum Concert Hall. In February 1889, two members of the gang were coming out of that hall at 11 p.m. on a Saturday night when others came up and spoke to them. Whatever was said, they both took off their belts, ran down Digbeth and attacked a man. Two policemen who had followed them from the concert hall heard one, called Greening, shout, 'Whitehouse Gang for them. Let them have it.' The two bobbies made a grab for them and managed to get them, fighting and kicking, into a baker's shop, where Greening shouted to a crowd outside, 'Now lads, lay on, don't give over, we can lick these –.' The mob started throwing stones into the shop. A third bobby came up and heard another man shout, 'Now, Aston boys, we can give it these – .' Seven or eight men took off their belts and laid into the policemen. Five were arrested. The stipendiary magistrate called the affair 'a disgrace to a civilised city'.

THE NEXT gang incident at a music hall would lead to the death of a manager. The Digbeth gang comprised men from both Park Street and Digbeth, some of whom became notorious for their involvement in this high-profile murder case. The killing of the Canterbury Music Hall stage manager would be said to be the result of a confrontation between this gang, who had become used to free admission to the hall, and the management, which had suddenly stopped this privilege without any warning. According to the *Mail*, the members of the Digbeth gang held a meeting in March 1890 and planned a protest in the form of a serious disturbance in the hall on the following Saturday night.

That night, 22 March, the music hall was full to bursting with young people. A police superintendent looked in just before ten o'clock and saw nothing to indicate that anything untoward was afoot. Twenty minutes later, the show finished, the band played 'God Save The Queen' and the lights of the hall were lowered as a signal for the audience to leave. Suddenly a policeman standing near the doorway was struck on the head with a beer bottle and at once pandemomium broke out. Glass tumblers were thrown at the attendants from all over the hall. As if expecting trouble at some stage, the manager had a strong force of police at hand, and they bundled the young culprits down to the vaults on the ground floor, where fighting resumed. One policeman was cut on the ear by a tumbler and another was hit by a heavy pewter tankard thrown by one of the gang.

Such a limited amount of damage did not satisfy everyone and, when taken to extremes, the protest would end in a death. The perpetrator would be a prominent rough called William 'Bowey' Beard. He was said to be the leader of a Digbeth gang, but he was hardly a slogger in the stone-throwing sense and his gang credentials were less clear than his criminality. He had fallen foul of the police for shouting obscenities in the streets in 1884, and in 1887 had been given hard labour for assaulting and robbing his own father late one night outside their home in Emily Street, Highgate. In the company of several other youths, he had shouted, 'Here's the old 'un; let's give it him.' Together they had knocked down his father and Beard junior had held his parent on the ground while the others robbed him of about thirty shillings. His father told the court that this was the second time his son had attacked him. Beard, who worked as a brass finisher and later as a fish hawker, moved into lodgings in Park Street. He acquired the nickname 'Bowey', or bow-legged, perhaps as the result of an attack by another gang, led by an ironplate worker named Edward Dodd, alias 'Throttlem', who disfigured his face with a knife and threw a kettle of boiling water at him, which missed his head but went over his legs.

By 1890 Beard, now aged twenty-six, was a regular attender at the Canterbury Music Hall. He had become used to receiving free tickets, known as 'stiffs', perhaps to ensure that he and his mates, referred to by the *Daily News* as *claqueurs* or members of the audience who were paid to applaud, did not cause trouble. In the early afternoon of Wednesday, 2 April, he met the barman, Henry Schoenoick, of the Canterbury near the Park Street entrance.

Beard called out, 'Harry, have you got a stiff to give me?'

'No,' replied the barman.

Angered, Beard barged his way in, punching the barman and taking a couple of kicks at him. Later the barman saw Beard and Alfred Rutter, a twenty-three-year-old nailcaster, in the bar and told them to leave. Beard struck him in the face. At that moment Arthur Hyde, the theatrical manager, came in.

'Be quiet, chaps,' he pleaded.

In response, Rutter punched him in the face. The manager and the barman grabbed the two roughs and, after a two-minute struggle, managed to hustle them out into the street. Now Bowey's woman, Agnes Cullis, came on the scene. Aged nineteen, she was also a hawker when work was available. Described by the music hall charwoman as 'raving, with her hair down her back, looped with one hairpin', Cullis took hold of Hyde, pulled him against the wall and brutally scratched his face with a key, while Rutter picked up a brick and struck him behind the ear.

'Settle him,' Cullis shouted. 'If we don't do it now we'll do it tonight.'

She threatened to come back later with a knife to finish the job if the men had not done so already, and gave Hyde a second blow on the head with a brick to show she meant business. A crowd gathered, but nobody offered help. A local hairdresser saw other roughs holding Hyde, while Beard and Rutter punched him, but according to a man from a grocer's shop nearby, no-one else in the crowd joined in the attack. The barman was pulled out of harm's way back into the liquor vaults by his wife. Later he came back and found Hyde in the yard leading to Pearce's pie shop, on his own, bleeding profusely. He was taken to the Queen's Hospital, where a large clot of blood was removed from his brain. Then he was taken back to the vaults and eventually carried home. He died there two days later.

The barman knew Cullis and Beard well. He said Cullis was often in the liquor vaults begging, while Beard would also come round, selling collar studs. He had also seen Beard and Rutter singing at the corner of Park Street. Beard gave his occupation variously as 'hawker' or 'street singer and pavement artist', so his interest in the music hall might be seen as semi-professional. The barman said that there was no previous quarrel between them all.

Beard and Cullis could not be found. They had slipped out of Birmingham, in the company of a tramp called Gormley. Beard later explained that they had taken with them copies of a song about the 'Crewe tragedy', a recent murder case, and particularly poignant in that two brothers, aged sixteen and twenty, had been sentenced to death for the murder of their brutal and wastrel father as he returned home drunk one night near Crewe. The elder brother was hanged at Knutsford prison, denying to the end that he had ever taken an axe to his father.

Beard said later that he and Agnes Cullis were expecting to take up street-singing, a popular variation on hawking. They walked to Bromsgrove and then on to Worcester, sleeping in outhouses and fields. The police issued woodcut pictures of Beard, from photographs taken when he was previously in custody, to every Birmingham policeman and circulated them to other forces. Beard later told a detective that he learned of Hyde's death when he saw a *Post* news poster at Worcester. He and Cullis had then made their way back to Birmingham by side roads and were arrested in bed together at his sister's house in Bissell Street on 10 April. Cullis was a native of Wolverhampton who had married a Liverpool tramp called Dixon about eighteen months before, but had parted company with him and had since cohabited with Beard in lodgings in Park Street.

The music hall killing was followed by more trouble in the Digbeth area, described by the *Mail* as part of 'a reign of terror'. The landlord of a pub in the Bull Ring was severely beaten about the head when he insisted on payment for drinks. A grocer who had appealed to the police had his premises raided by the roughs. Hams were carried out of the shop and dropped in the gutter; and only by brandishing a large ham knife was he able to retrieve them. A hairdresser's assistant was fitting the outside window lamps when the stepladder he was standing on was pulled from under him. These were quite possibly attempts to terrorise the witnesses to Hyde's punishment. If so, they did not succeed. Alternatively, as Chief Constable Farndale claimed, they may have been coincidental and unconnected to the 'gang'.

In any case, at the assizes in August, Rutter, Beard and Cullis were charged with the wilful murder of Arthur Hyde. However the inquest verdict was manslaughter and they were found guilty on that charge. Mr Justice Hawkins sentenced Rutter and Beard to seven years' penal servitude and Cullis to five. As she heard the sentence, Cullis broke into a fit of hysterics and had to be carried out of the court.

The killing of the stage manager at the Canterbury Music Hall for refusing free admission, following a riot about the withdrawal of free passes, would give rise to a comment that the slogging gangs had been harassing the audiences and shopkeepers for at least six years. Ushers, or check-takers, were particularly at risk. In the April heatwave of 1893, two at the Queen's Theatre in Snow Hill were assaulted by a crowd of youths who were knocking hats off people as they left the theatre. A check-taker called Richard Danby came off worse. One of the youths pulled at his coat and tried to strike him with a belt, so Danby ran off into Slaney Street, followed by the whole gang. One of them stopped him and another stabbed him in the head, necessitating a skull operation and six weeks in hospital. Danby identified a seventeen-year-old from Highgate with a record of petty burglary, called William Clay, as the man who had stabbed him. His accomplice, Lane, was discovered to have passed a pocket-knife to a girl called Ada Berrow soon after the stabbing, saying, 'Take this, I have been in a bother.' Berrow tried to defend them both by saying that the knife she received had no bloodstains on it, but Clay was found guilty of unlawful wounding and narrowly escaped a sentence of penal servitude, while Lane was found guilty of common assault.

In April 1895, on a Saturday night, the police were finding it hard to take a notorious ruffian to the police station. Thomas Giblin, again, from Brearley Street off Summer Lane, was well known for his life-long record of assaults on the police and had only recently come out of prison. Over a dozen police were needed to withstand the throwing of Rowley rag stones by Giblin's companions. Then they were joined by a gang coming out of the Queen's Theatre and they all continued to stone the police who retreated inside the gates of the General Hospital where they had gone to have their wounds dressed. The police were frequently being called to the Queen's Theatre to sort out trouble, both outside and inside in the 'gods', there too the special territory of young men and women. Bottle-throwing was often the start of it. In May 1898 P.C. Smith was in the act of removing Frederick Kemp, aged seventeen, of no occupation or fixed abode, after being called in by a gallery keeper. As he resisted the policeman, Kemp shouted to the gallery, 'Don't let them take me', at which an eighteen-year-old polisher, said to be 'a quiet lad', threw a bottle at P.C. Smith creating a big cut on his left cheek, for which the stipendiary gave him three months in gaol. The crowded, raucous atmosphere of the theatre gallery attracted professional criminals as well as rowdies, as when two jewel thieves took refuge, after a robbery, in the Grand Theatre, Wolverhampton during *The Swiss Express* and were only arrested after a struggle with detectives in the interval.

FOOTBALL GROUNDS too were overcrowded and home to betting and violence, but they largely escaped association with gangs in this period. They were sited far from the centre of either Birmingham or Aston, yet one writer to the *Mail* referred to Saturday trams as crammed with 'footbrawlers' on their way back from a match. There was already much rivalry between the supporters of Aston Villa, formed in 1874, and winners of the F.A. Cup for the first time in 1887, and West Bromwich Albion, formed in 1878 and winners of the Cup the year after Villa. Both were founder members of the Football League. The Villa was regarded as the Birmingham team and the Albion as the Black Country's. Black Country Saturday shopping habits were said to have been seriously disrupted by the pull of a home game at West Bromwich, with wives meeting their menfolk after the match or even accompanying them to it. The Albion met Villa in that F.A. Cup final of 1887, but lost, and it was said that many Albion supporters would go without their Sunday dinners because of the earnings wagered and lost on the match. They met Villa again in the final in both 1892, when Albion won, and 1895, when Villa won. This neck-and-neck competition only increased the excitement and tension between the fans of the two teams, at a time when match attendances were beginning to grow. A crowd of over 42,000 watched the final of 1895 at the Crystal Palace in south London.

Rival gangs were not generally a feature of the late Victorians' support for football. Where violence broke out, it was more in the form of attacks on match officials, especially the referee, and players of visiting teams than on rival supporters. In 1884, some of the Aston crowd 'threw some sods of turf and packets of yellow ochre' at some of the Notts County players in a F.A. Cup semi-final between County and Blackburn Olympic held at Lower Grounds. The explanation was that this hostility was the result of the intense rivalry between Villa and County. At the Villa–Preston match of May 1885, attacks on the visiting players came at the end of the match, and the Preston men retaliated in what the *Gazette* called a 'free fight'. The roughs only left the field at the insistence of a small number of police.

It was not always Villa violence. In the cup-tie against Walsall in October of the same year, in reaction to a 0-5 defeat during which the play became rougher and rougher, the Walsall crowd invaded the pitch four minutes from the end and play was abandoned. Even after a long stay in the changing tent, the Villa team was pelted out of the Chuckery ground with stones, brickends and turf. When they went to play Everton in October 1888, the Villa players were greeted with verbal abuse and threats from 'young ragamuffins' in Liverpool. However, in November 1889, during a home match between Villa and Wolverhampton Wanderers, a key Wolves player, Booth, was hit by a piece of clinker thrown from the crowd. The culprit was alleged to have been a 'red-haired youth' urged on by a 'gang of men'. The club put up posters offering a £5 reward for infor-mation, as it was felt that the incident had somehow brought discredit on the Aston supporters.

Betting and bookmakers were felt by some critics to be a bigger problem than crowd behaviour. When the Albion unexpectedly beat the Villa 3-0 in the 1892 Cup Final, the last at the Oval, the Villa goalkeeper Jimmy Warner was accused of having 'sold' the match. He replied that he himself had placed money on a Villa victory, but he faced an angry crowd the next morning at his pub, the Old College, in Spring Hill. He needed police protection though he denied to a *Mail* reporter a rumour that his windows had been smashed.

The cup finals between Villa and the Albion in 1892 and 1895 produced intense interest but no outbreaks of violence. Football 'rowdyism' was often just that, drinking and disorderly behaviour leading to assault more often of the police than of the opposing supporters. Each of the local clubs claimed that its supporters were superior in social class and behaviour to the others. The secretary of West Bromwich Albion, T. Smith, was clearly biased when he wrote to the *Mail* in March 1886 complaining about the Albion's supporters being pelted with snowballs at Aston Lower Grounds – and criticising Walsall supporters as well – while claiming that the behaviour of the Albion's spectators at home was always 'exemplary'. In fact the Football League took action against the Albion in 1900, cautioning them for crowd disorderliness after half a dozen of what were described as the 'peaky fraternity' from Birmingham in the sixpenny stand spoiled the enjoyment of other spectators with their foul language

THE POLICE IN TROUBLE

and abuse, at a home game against Sunderland. However, sloggers and the later peaky blinders, like London's hooligans, were not much reported in a football context.

Lack of space exacerbated tensions among fans. At the Aston Villa-Preston cup-tie of January 1888, the unexpectedly large crowd and the sale of more tickets than for whom there was space available led to invasions of the pitch. The police, reinforced by two mounted hussars, managed eventually to clear the playing area so that the match could be finished. Overcrowding led to fighting between groups of rival fans at a match between Villa and their old enemy Notts County in October 1900. The 'free fight' at the Great Hall end and elsewhere among some of the 15,000 spectators was triggered by competition for shelter when wind and driving rain stopped play. Play was resumed after five minutes, which curtailed the fighting. It was reported that 'the spectators roared with laughter as an agile policeman lifted an intruder off the track bodily over the barrier', as the game restarted. In the same spirit, William McGregor of Aston Villa, writing in 1907, thought that football had 'undoubtedly brightened' the lives and habits of the 'lower classes' of Birmingham.

Meanwhile the growth in popularity of football made the issue of sports facilities for the public more pressing. The years 1886 to 1888 would be looked back on as the 'golden days' of Birmingham football, but they were really only the start. The game became a craze which gripped the whole town. Under the influence of George Kenrick, the school board began to teach football in the schools and from 1886 Aston Villa ran a charity cup for competing school teams. An attempt to stop football in the parks because it reduced grassy areas to 'wastes of sand' was abandoned. Yet the young still had nowhere much to play sport. This would change in the 1890s – with a public parks cricket association, for example – but was for a while overshadowed by the bursting forth of the late blooms of Victorian Birmingham's young street culture, the peaky blinders.

CHAPTER 16

The Peaky Blinders

IF THE SLOGGERS had by now long been infamous in Birmingham, the notoriety of their successors, the peaky blinders – a more generic term not confined to gangs – would extend well beyond the city. It is with them that the wider world first became aware of the sloggers' style: scarf around the neck, bell-bottom trousers and donkey fringe of hair brushed down in a curl over the foreheads culminating in a peak over one eye – which accounted for their name. That this style was shared by London hooligans and Manchester scuttlers shows one of the common features of the youth culture of these three great late-Victorian cities. However, unlike the Manchester and Salford scuttlers, who wore clogs, the Birmingham sloggers wore heavy metal-tipped boots. When they were on the march, there was not that ringing sound on northern cobbles but the heavy crunch over the Midland capital's roughly gravelled streets.

Their look was carefully stylized, as one F. Atkins recalled several decades later in the *Birmingham Weekly Post*:

> Their clothes consisted of trousers 22 inches round the bottom and 15 inches round the knee; some preferred moleskins or "cords". They wore a silk "daff"as they called it, twisted twice round their necks and tied at the ends. It was then called a "choker". Bowler hat with the brim made to fit the sides; the front of the brim came to a point almost like the spout of a jug. This was done by wetting the brim, warming it by the fire, then making it the shape required. This was worn on the side of the head to show the hair on the other side done in a "quiff".

> Another new fashion was for 'snakes' to clasp belts, rather than buckles. These were supposedly less harmful when wielded as weapons and this was suggested as a defence in slogging trials, but did not impress

the law or do much to reduce sentences. Whatever the type of fashion, it was noted that many of the young men who haunted the suburban streets were well-dressed. Perhaps this was one reason why 'peaky blinder' tended to replace the term 'rough'.

In spite of a general improvement in living standards over the previous twenty years, not all young men dressed stylishly, especially in poorer central areas. One verbal picture emerged in 1893 of fifteen-year-old Edward Hands, 'a sharp lad' known as 'Gallett'. He was a newsboy, making him 'well-acquainted with sporting fixtures' and whose fighting tendencies led to the manslaughter of an older youth. He was described for police purposes as 'having a scar under his left jaw and four tattoo dots on his right forearm, wearing a double-breasted dark reefer coat, much too large, a dirty pair of trousers which are ripped, old galoshes and a dirty light cap.' Many like Hands had been obliged by the Depression to leave skilled work for casual jobs which did not allow for much spending on clothes.

The first known reference to the peaky blinders was in relation to a violent gang in Bordesley. Adderley Street contained a branch of the Corporation gasworks, as well as iron and copper smelting works, and so was one of the most heavily polluted parts of Birmingham. Neighbouring Glover Street, Watery Lane and Garrison Lane all had reputations for gangs and Adderley Street was also close to the Coventry Road, the border between Bordesley and Small Heath. There was a tradition of highway robbery and assault in the area, especially of holidaymakers coming back from a day out in Yardley or Little Bromwich or of other travellers coming in from the east of the city.

One example of a holiday fight was on Easter Monday 1889, when two militiamen picked on a man from the other side of town who had been drinking in Arthur Street, Small Heath. They left him lying in the street unconscious with what turned out to be a compound depressed fracture of the skull. Luckily he was found by a constable who was on his way home. P.C. Wale called a cab and took the man to the Queen's Hospital. The two held responsible were identified by an eyewitness, but at the sessions the evidence against them was contradictory. The decisive accusation came when the police told the assistant barrister hearing the case that both were members of the Milk Street slogging gang. So they too were not close to 'base'. One was a nineteen-year-old filer from Barn Street who had many previous convictions. He left the dock to begin fifteen months' hard labour, with typical insolence. 'So long, Chicken,' he called out.

In March 1890, a young man from Arthur Street, named George Eastwood, crossed the Coventry Road and called at the Rainbow pub in Adderley Street, on a Saturday night. Aged twenty-one, he was the youngest of three unmarried brothers who lived with their parents. He was a total abstainer from alcohol, so, as usual, he ordered a bottle of ginger beer. He recognised a gang who came in as local men. They started making offensive remarks about his teetotal habits and about his drink, which was more usually available in fried fish shops and drunk by women or children.

'What do you drink that tack for?' asked the supposed captain of the gang, Thomas Mucklow.

'Mind your own business,' Eastwood replied.

When he asked the landlord whether he could not drink what he liked, someone tripped him up from behind. Knowing the evil reputation of the men concerned, Eastwood left the house, but they came out after him. They followed him down until he reached a lonely place where two bridges crossed the road.

'Now, boys, give it him hot,' shouted Mucklow.

They attacked with fists and belts. Eastwood fell and was kicked in the head and struck with buckles. He managed to gain his feet and, chased by the gang, ran as far as the back entrance of Allcock Street Board School. Remarkably, by scaling the wall, crossing the playground and climbing another wall, he got into Allcock Street, where he took refuge in a house. 'We'll kill him if we cop him!' the gang shouted outside. It was nearly midnight before he could be taken to hospital, where he was diagnosed with a fractured skull and bruises all over his legs and body. Subsequently he needed a trepanning operation and was kept in hospital for twenty-four days.

Superintendent Hervey ordered a search for the gang, but they had fled. Mucklow was the only one to be identified. Mucklow had always lived in Bordesley. Now twenty-five and married, but with no children, he had become a jobbing carter living and working with his father-in-law. They lived in Adderley Street. At the sessions he was supported by good character references, including one from a police detective. It was said that his companions were mostly to blame. However, assistant barrister T.S. Soden said that it would be almost impossible to find a worse case, inasmuch as the prisoner struck the prosecutor without provocation and incited other people to beat him with buckles. Mucklow was sentenced to nine months' hard labour. Arthur Street, where Eastwood lived, was shortly to be chosen as a centre for Primitive Methodists, who were all abstainers like him. It may be that this case had about it a touch of the kind of rough disapproval or retribution meted out to other evangelical Christians, such as the Salvationists, elsewhere in the city.

Arthur Street was not just the home of total abstainers. In 1893, a metal-roller from there and a number of other youths went roving into Washwood Heath on a Sunday evening and came across two local men, whom they surrounded with the familiar opening gambit, 'Is he one of them?' to which another replied, 'Yes.' One was stabbed with a knife and the metal-roller shot a man from Washwood Heath in the left eye with a catapult. The victim's eye was declared still in danger at the subsequent court hearing.

Mucklow's gang associates may have included another Adderley Street labourer called John Gavin, who was working up a long record of convictions for assault. He had been imprisoned for three months in September 1888, along with John Gallagher of Digbeth, for attacking a policeman and a man from Beak Street. A month after the attack on Eastwood, he was again being obstructive and violent in the street and assaulted a P.C. He was aged twenty-four. His excuse was that he was 'out of work and (had) got a drop of beer'. Ten years later, he was still striking total strangers and policemen in Adderley Street.

The Adderley Street gang was known as the 'peaky blinders' gang. Within five years, that name would become common currency in the press for groups of rowdies and indeed individuals who were ruffianly or violent. For the time being, however, the old terminology of slogging continued to prevail. One of the first individuals to be referred to as a peaky blinder, in 1895, was another metal roller from east of the city, this time Garrison Lane. His name was Lightfoot and he became notorious as much for his convictions for theft and assault as for his gang associations, which took the form of drunken melees in Cheapside and the Markets area. Lightfoot was a hardened rough rather than a slogger, and many of those later dubbed 'peaky' would not have the extensive criminal record that he had acquired (see again in Chapter 18).

The peaky's moll also had her own distinctive dress, with 'the same lavish display of pearl buttons, the well-developed fringe obscuring the whole of the forehead and descending nearly to her eyes and the characteristic gaudy-coloured silk handkerchief covering her throat,' according to the *Birmingham Weekly Post*. Peaky blinders were said to be as violent to their molls as they were to other boys. 'He'll pinch you and punch you every time he walks out with you, and if you speak to another chap he don't mind kicking you,' one girl declared. 'No, I shouldn't like him as well if he didn't knock me about a bit.'

Such rough treatment often led to injury. In one case, a lad from Hospital Street, aged fifteen but only four feet in height and 'attired after the fashion of the peaky blinder', was walking out together with a girl of the same age to a late hour each night. One night she refused to go with him, to which the boy answered, 'You've got to go.' He pulled a knife, stabbed her in the back and then walked away. When she realised what he had done he said he had not meant to, but still walked off. Fortunately her mother took her to the hospital to have the wound stitched and she recovered. In court, the mother said that the boy had frequently beat her daughter with a stick.

An even worse case resulted in the tragic death of eighteen-year-old Emily Pimm, in what was known as the Summer Lane Kicking Case. Her killer, a metal polisher of the same age called James Harper, was lucky to get only six years' penal servitude at Birmingham Assizes from Mr Justice Mathew, who declared himself unwilling to take away from such a young man the prospect of ever being free again. In November 1898, wearing army boots with metal tips on heels and toes, he had kicked her and stamped on her face in revenge for her breaking a jug over his head in an earlier exchange of blows. Another twenty-two-year-old described as being 'of the "peaky" type' had split up from his twenty-one-year-old girlfriend after a two-year relationship during which she had become pregnant by him. The two happened to meet in Cox Street in November 1898. When she spoke to him, he responded with a violent kick to her abdomen. Then he followed her up the street and kicked her again. They parted and she spent the night in great pain and had a miscarriage. A warrant was issued for him and he was sentenced to two months' hard labour.

Another extreme case involved Harry Holdcroft, alias Cooke, a seventeen-year-old ironcaster of Great Russell Street, Hockley, who had done four years in a reformatory and frequently fired off his pistol even though he claimed that it was a plaything used for shooting rats. When he shot dead his ex-sweetheart, Maud Mansell, a fourteen-year-old who worked at Jacobs, gilt jewellers, the big question was whether or not it was an accident, as he claimed. They had fallen out and she had started to keep company with another young ironworker. On the day before the incident, Holdcroft had started firing his pistol at the Mansells' house and had been warned by Maud's mother that he would break the windows if he carried on. The next day, a Saturday, he shot again at the house and then, muttering threats, fired down the entry where a number of young men and women were gathered. One shot grazed the new boyfriend; another hit Maud in the head. She died the following day. Holdcroft was sent to the assizes on a charge of wilful murder. A cabman gave evidence that the bullet had rebounded, although a detective had found no sign of it in the entry. The jury found criminal negligence and manslaughter, but recommended mercy on account of his age. Mr Justice Wills sentenced Holdcroft to nine months' hard labour.

Reference has already been made to the panic of 1890, when the *Mail* proclaimed a state of mob law arising from a death outside the Canterbury Music Hall, between Digbeth and Park Street. Stabbing cases were high and assaults on policemen were reaching a new peak, higher than at any time since 1877-8. There were now slogging gangs in the suburbs as well as ruffianism in the city streets. Park Street was still a dangerous place for outsiders. Only the previous year, a Park Street gang was carrying out a series of highway robberies. In one case an architect who had been drinking heavily was found unconscious on the footpath with his pockets rifled and no watch or money, unable to explain how he had got into the locality. On another occasion, an elderly man from Hockley who had worked for the Post Office for fifty-two years was on his way to a house in Fazeley Street and found himself followed by eight or nine of 'the most ruffianly fellows I ever saw in my life', one of whom carried a piece of jagged granite. At the corner of Park Street, one snatched at his watch and wrenched it from its steel chain.

THE KILLING of Arthur Hyde had caused uproar in Digbeth and the district was slow to quieten down. A policeman interrupted a violent exchange between an unemployed engine smith and his girl, after a bout of very heavy midday drinking. The smith wrestled the policeman onto the ground and started kicking him. Two Digbeth men rushed to the policeman's rescue and one grabbed his whistle to summon help, but instead of more police the sound of the whistle brought a number of Park Street lads onto the scene. They set upon the policeman and his would-be rescuers, so that the latter made a dash for the safety of Moor Street police station. It took several more police to get the smith to the station and into a cell, kicking and biting all the while. In April 1890, the lads from Great

Barr Street were coming in to fight the Milk Street gang with belts and stones. The Milk Street mob was led by a thirty-year-old barge boatman called Bloxwich, or 'Block'. In one such battle, in Coventry Street, one man wielded a pickaxe and another fired a pistol. Block himself went to prison for three months for throwing a half-brick at the policeman who was about to grab the pickaxe.

Meanwhile the *Mail* indulged in a major panic about the dangers from the gangs, such as of Whitehouse Street, where 'inoffensive persons' were likely to be attacked at night on waste ground, as well as Park Street and Summer Lane. One admirer of Birmingham in 1890 described the new city as 'super-civilised', a comment which many people found absurd.

The *Mail* tried to find an answer. It was loath to blame the Birmingham police force. Instead it felt that the recent spate of rowdyism must be connected to the revival in trade, by which youths could gain 'odd coppers for carrying a bag or singing a song', presumably like Bowey Beard. Why was it that when all cities had some streets which were unsafe after dark, in Birmingham what the Watch Committee had always called 'rowdyism' could assert itself in busy streets even in the middle of the day? Only in Birmingham too was it felt that such behaviour was so wide-spread – elsewhere it was more confined to certain districts. Yet cities like Manchester, Liverpool or London in fact had similar problems, and worse records of heavy drinking and prostitution. (A slight pause might be noticed at times of greatest hardship, such as the severe winter of 1890-1 when distress, although not as bad as five years before, still affected all kinds of outdoor labour especially the building trade, and in St George's, brassworkers, jewellers and gunmakers as well.)

Birmingham, like the other cities, had many faces, and many of its citizens were reluctant to be dragooned into civilised uniformity. Perhaps it was that in Birmingham everyone with money, and supposedly civilised habits, headed south to Edgbaston or Moseley, leaving the other points of the compass to more traditional 'Brummies' who preferred a good scrap to a game of croquet. Also remarkable, perhaps, was the extent to which the young street-fighters travelled readily across town from Aston to Balsall Heath, and out of town from Winson Green to Perry Barr and from Deritend to Moseley.

Many parts of Birmingham suffered from the activities not just of youth gangs but of older thugs aged between twenty-five to thirty-five, men like Bowey Beard and Throttlem Dodd. They were happy to fight in gangs, in smaller groups or even solo when against the police. Such men often built up fearsome reputations. They had followings and acquired nicknames, such as 'Bluey' Byers, with his pugilistic name and his thirty-nine convictions for drunk and disorderly by the age of thirty-two. 'Gunner' Pimm, who was always ready for a slog in Aston, had still not fulfilled his ambition of becoming a soldier of the Queen. He was continually in and out of prison, for offences such as assaulting the landlord and landlady of the Prince of Wales pub in Great Francis Street, and, with other men, smashing all their jugs and glasses.

Pimm described himself as a labourer or tube drawer. He lived for a time in Cato Street North, Bloomsbury, but, like many of his kind, was always on the move. He was one of those almost pathological fighters, who in cold weather, could turn easily from leading a group in snowballing passers-by, to throwing bricks at them if they took it badly. When buying a piece of meat at a butcher's in Coleshill Street, he disputed the price and ended up throwing meat at the hapless butcher. Then he tried to throw a two-pound weight at him and failed, so he picked up a knife instead and threatened to stab him. His wife Jane was of the same ilk, attacking the detective who came to arrest her husband with stones and fists. Sam Timmins had described Pimm as 'one of the most violent and dangerous characters ever before the court'. Charles Jobson, alias 'Staggam', a tinner of Balsall Heath, had a similar reputation for unprovoked assault and led a gang of young thieves.

THE SEVERITY of exemplary sentences passed by the recorder, J.S. Dugdale, at the Birmingham Quarter Sessions in April 1890, were said at last to have left a profound impression. An eighteen-year-old labourer called Everall was given five years' penal servitude as the leader of a slogging gang who – in Mr Dugdale's words – had apparently 'made up their minds to murder' George Onions, of Farm Street, the previous November. Onions had seen Everall attack another man and had taken his side. Everall threatened him with a knife and heavily-buckled belt and then went off to find the rest of his gang. One of them used a cellar-window chain as a weapon. They found Onions in Summer Lane.

'There he is lads; knock him down; kill him!' shouted Everall.

Another called out, 'Don't let's leave him alive.'

They gave up only when someone blew a whistle. Apparently one of the gang had a grudge against Onions for kicking his dog. The unfortunate Onions suffered a fractured skull and was in hospital for eleven weeks. Everall unsuccessfully tried to bribe a witness with a sovereign and a suit of clothes to say he had acted in self-defence. His friend with the chain was sentenced to twelve months' hard labour.

In another case, a nineteen-year-old was given five years for wounding two men in a riot in Deritend. The grand jury endorsed the recorder's action and urged him to ask for the magistrates to 'inflict more severe punishment in the cases daily brought before them'. According to the *Mail* that same month, in one gang fight in Bordesley Street, a man had received as many as thirteen wounds to his head from a buckled belt. The favourite weapon of the gangs was now said to be the cosh, a short, heavy stick which could be concealed up the sleeve. This, like the belt, was in fact a traditional weapon.

The Watch Committee was of course anxious to pour cold water on all the excitement. It emphasised that the Birmingham police were far less likely to be assaulted when arresting for drunkenness than in other British cities. More controversially, Chief Constable Farndale, who had risen from pounding the beat to become first Leicester's and then Birmingham's top police officer, believed that events in Digbeth following the death of Mr Hyde had been exaggerated, and that although two groups had quarrelled, they were not organised slogging gangs. In fact, he claimed, there had been 'no evidence of slogging gangs in the city for a very long time and the superintendent reported that for years they had been decreasing in numbers and power'. Three of the cases mentioned in the press had all occurred outside the city, namely in Aston, Perry Barr and Balsall Heath.

This view was debatable, to say the least. Perhaps the term 'slogging gang' had been used rather too loosely by the press; however, to most of those reading the Chief Constable's words, the distinction between old and new gangs must have seemed a semantic quibble. Aston and Balsall Heath might be outside his jurisdiction, with their own police forces, but they were integral parts of the Birmingham conurbation as far as most people were concerned. If the gangs of Digbeth were no longer youths throwing stones at each other but hardened louts beating each other up and picking on individuals, again the distinction was lost on most Birmingham ratepayers. Farndale had admitted that the Milk Street disturbances were of the old type, with 'a quarrel between two opposing bodies', and seven extra constables had been deployed there.

The police seemed to be brushing slogging under the carpet, as they had in 1874 when the police and Watch Committee had proclaimed that rowdyism was at an end. The *Post* thought that the Chief Constable's assurances were 'comforting … but not so easy to reconcile with popular report and with the notorious conduct of large bodies of roughs'. Even if the number and power of 'such organisations' were on the wane, it was not credible to think them 'altogether extinct'. The *Mail* felt that Farndale was being both complacent and splitting hairs. If the dastardly killing of Mr Hyde and the assaults on shopkeepers were not slogging, what were they? Clearly the slogger was 'something more than a mythical presence in our midst'. However the press did not want to go so far as to accuse the police of losing control of the city or to print anything which might push the police into going on strike for more pay, as was threatened in London then (and again in the summer of 1990).

The police responded to the concern about violence in Digbeth by redrawing the boundaries of its divisions. For a long time, prisoners from Digbeth had to be taken to Moseley Street police station, headquarters of E division. From now on, A division, with its police station at Moor Street, would be extended to take in Allison Street, Meriden Street and part of Bordesley Street. Six men would be transferred from E to A division. The reorganisation showed that Allison Street needed more efficient policing and in future miscreants would be dragged off – more easily – to Moor Street. The change met with general approval and the view that it was long overdue. Yet the borough's outskirts remained a problem, as was clear from a complaint from Lennox Street on the Aston border that the bobby on his beat appeared only once in any evening for two minutes, during which time the gangs of rough boys and girls, who made the neighbourhood unbearable for shopkeepers and others, disappeared into Aston only to reappear when he had gone.

Heavy sentences at the assizes were already having an effect. The Butterworth brothers formed the nucleus of the Highgate Street gang, with Henry, a brasscaster of Highgate Terrace, as their leader. By 1886, he had a record for being drunk and disorderly and assaulting the police. On August Bank Holiday Monday of that year, he was turned out of the Fighting Cocks Inn for brawling by a policeman. He returned to resume his quarrel and the policeman had to be called back thirty minutes later. Butterworth threw a glass bottle at him, which hit his helmet and smashed against the doorpost. He was sent to prison for three months and was described by Superintendent Tyler as one of the most violent men in the neighbourhood, although his brother was sentenced for twice as long for another assault on a police officer.

The brothers had regular confrontations with the police after too much to drink. It took a sergeant, a constable and a member of the public to get Butterworth and a mate into custody in Longmore Street, Balsall Heath, in 1888, while others tried to rescue them. Butterworth received four months' hard labour for assault and an extra fourteen days for being drunk and disorderly. In 1890 he was sentenced to six months for assaulting a policeman, again in Longmore Street. In the process of his arrest, P.C. Lyons tried twice to drag Butterworth inside a butcher's shop. On the second attempt, the butcher, called Swadkins, stood in his shop-door with a meat cleaver to keep Butterworth's mates at bay.

A few weeks later, the police caught up with Henry Butterworth's brother Arthur, a grinder, who had moved to Waterworks Road, Aston. P.C. Lyons had interrupted a fight with buckled belts and loaded catgut and had been hit on the head with one such piece of gut with a lead weight attached to it. In court, Arthur did not deny hitting the constable, but declared that he had, since then, 'become a member of the Gospel Temperance Society' and was 'striving hard to redeem his past life'. Perhaps because of this, his sentence was only six weeks. A third brother, Alfred, got three weeks for throwing a lump of coal at P.C. Lyons. The following year, three of the gang were sent to the assizes for highway robbery with violence in Highgate Street. Henry, now described as a labourer, was again involved, although he called himself 'Richard' at the preliminary police court hearing. This time he received five years' penal servitude from Baron Coleridge, Lord Chief Justice of England, and went down to the cells in tears.

It is not surprising that some lads either were deterred by these sentences or got slogging fatigue. One was William Davis of Hospital Street, off Summer Lane, who was beaten up by his ex-mates for not wanting to go with them to slog the Bagot Street boys. At the police court he had to explain himself.

Mr Rowlands, magistrates' clerk: 'What were you to go together for?'

Davis: 'I don't know.'

Rowlands: 'What band do you belong to?'

Davis: 'The band of friendship. I was a member of the Cross Street gang.'

Rowlands: 'What did he want you to do to the Bagot Street lot?'

Davis: 'Slog them, I suppose.'

Rowlands: 'And didn't you want to do so?'

Davis: 'Yes, I had enough of it.'

Old Cross Street was in the Gosta Green area and perhaps Davis had lived there previously. For this disloyalty, one of his companions hit him on the side of the head and another on the back of the head with a buckled belt. His wounds bled profusely. Later, the two were sent to prison for two and three weeks each.

The spring of 1891 saw two cases of assault against deserting members of the Charles Henry Street gang. In the first, a youth was hit by a flying ginger beer bottle and a buckled belt, leading to two months jail for his attacker. In the second, one John Riley, who also no longer joined in with the others – perhaps after a stab wound received in 'play' – met another nineteen-year-old who was still in the gang. Riley was confronted by this 'ganger' (a journalist's term) as to why he had sent one of their number to prison, and his 'peaching' was deemed sufficient for him to receive a sudden blow on the nose, which knocked him over, and then a kicking to the head and chest in front of his mother. His assailant was fined ten shillings. Yet none of these incidents seem to have discouraged others from the call to slog.

For example a new leader emerged momentarily in Wainwright Street, Aston, in 1891, a seventeen-year-old called Charles Bond. Bond had started work young as a galvanizer, but gave his occupation to the police as a boatman. He was identified as a leader of a dozen lads in that street by a local woman, who criticized them for their drinking and bad language. He took his gang to Duddeston and received a month's hard labour for leading them in wounding a man by pelting him with ginger beer bottles.

There was now growing competition for gang activities from cricket and football: in one case at Handsworth Police Court in 1891 a farmer protested against gangs of youths coming out from Birmingham to play football on his field without permission. Yet slogging continued. To the west, in the Bath Row/St Thomas's area, was seen the classic pattern of battles between town centre and suburban youth. Bromsgrove Street was the heart of the town centre gang, whose foes were drawn from suburban roads towards Edgbaston. When two boys, aged twelve and fifteen, from the town centre were arrested, the *Mail* reported, 'The prisoners form part of the rank and file of an army of young lads who band together to sustain the reputation of rowdies in Bromsgrove Street, Bow Street and Irving Street. The enemy is drawn from Bellbarn Road and Lee Bank Road. The conflicting parties meet in the streets and fight with sticks and stones.' The two prisoners were caught one evening in April 1891 'while reconnoitering the hostile force in Bellbarn Road' in possession of an Indian club and a stick. The Bench decided to adjourn the case for a month and see how they behaved themselves. To the east, Garrison Lane was still an irresistible venue for sloggers, and one brickworks manager was fined a shilling for boxing the ears of some stone-throwers on his property. New villains emerged, such as the four aptly-named Bashford brothers from Thomas Street, Sparkbrook, who were implicated in stone-throwing in King's Heath, as well as theft.

In August 1892, a gang of five swooped on two young men and two young women sitting on a doorstep in Rea Street. A Cheapside girl, Ada Berrow, later gave evidence at the sessions that a young brasscaster had asked one of her companions – who included George Cosier of Barford Street (see next chapter) – whether he had been in a 'slug' the previous night. He denied it, but the gang attacked them and a brick knocked Berrow unconscious. She spent three weeks with a fractured skull in the Queen's Hospital, where she contracted scarlet fever and had to be transferred to the Fever Hospital and then to the Convalescent Home. In sentencing the brick-thrower to six months' imprisonment, Recorder Dugdale drily remarked that slogging gangs would never be put down until there was a 'flogging gang', to which several jurymen added, 'Hear, hear.'

To the north, on the border with Aston the Corporation responded to a local petition by turning part of the Old Peck, increasingly encroached on by builders, into an asphalted recreation ground in 1892. However the area continued to be unsafe at night for lone young men, and slogging encounters continued alongside the Aston part of the Hockley Brook, described by one correspondent in the *Post,* fearful of a new outbreak of cholera, as a stinking 'fever river' full, at different times, of 'dead dogs, cats, fish and even young pigs'.

Bordesley Green was becoming as dangerous as Bordesley and Small Heath. At the August Bank Holiday in 1890 about forty boys were reported fighting with buckles, 'in pairs', in Little Green Lane. On Christmas night in 1892, two men drinking in the Black Horse, in Green Lane, Bordesley Green, were set upon after leaving by three youths, who lived close by and probably regarded them as intruders. One used a belt, another a knife and the third his boot. Later it took four officers to drag them from a house where they were assembled with twenty other roughs. On one of the group, an eighteen-year-old labourer from Greenway Street, was found a buckled belt and catapult. The belt had no fewer than sixteen heavy brass ornaments on it, highlighting the peaky fashion for ornamented weaponry, while the catapult had forty-eight pieces of elastic on either side. There was easy access to firearms, sometimes with fatal results. A sixteen-year-old fatally shot his eleven-year-old brother with a revolver at home in Witton Lane, Aston. The weapon had been bought for six shillings from a thirteen-year-old boy who had stolen it from the warehouse of Messrs Webley, where he worked.

Older streetfighters continued their own version of slogging. The Simpson brothers, having shifted their activities further west when they moved from Aston to New John Street, Birmingham, soon became another element in what were dubbed the 'Summer Lane disturbances'. They were especially dangerous with buckled belts. John once applied for bail for his brothers James and Charles, only to strike the constable when he was refused and get himself locked up. All three appeared in court the next day with their heads swathed in bloodstained bandages, claiming that they had been assaulted by the constables without provocation. When they were told to remove the bandages in court, they revealed no injuries. James had already done fifteen months for assaulting the police and now went down for six months more for having smashed up a pub in New Summer Street on Whit Monday 1891. The Simpsons did not mind fighting amongst themselves either. One Saturday night three of them, including George's wife Eliza, had a general family punch-up outside the court where George lived, after which Alfred went in, attacked his sister-in-law and took a hammer to her window frame. She admitted in court that she had given Alfred 'one kick just to keep him a bit quiet'. The police regarded Alfred as 'one of the worst ruffians in the city'.

Attacking policemen in the Suffolk Street area was the speciality of men like the thirty-five-year-old John Gilhooley, who was getting too old for serious streetfighting but had developed an almost pathological addiction to assaulting constables. In his teens, in the mid-1870s, this watchmaker from Howard Place, in the Markets area, had collected three sentences for assaulting policemen, culminating in breaking a policeman's jaw and biting another's hand, leading to seven years' penal servitude and five years' police supervision. In 1884, highway robbery and an assault on the police had led to another five years' penal servitude and thirty lashes with the cat. In 1891, he tried to rile a policeman outside the Wheatsheaf in Severn Street at closing time, was arrested for foul language and then released on the pleadings of his mates. However he could not resist going further and, when re-arrested for drunkenness and refusing to go home, he started fighting in what achieved notoriety as 'the Beak Street Slogging Case'. Perhaps in revenge for the death of young William Whittaker, and when two days after the policeman implicated had been discharged of manslaughter, Gilhooley attacked P.C. Thompson near the very spot where Whittaker had received his fatal blow. He struck the constable in the face with a beer glass, and then the crowd threw stones, one of which fractured the policeman's skull. Gilhooley denied shouting, 'Let him have it lads,' but the authorities were not going to let him off lightly, and he got the maximum sentence of six months' hard labour.

Gilhooley was not a name that the police relished. An equally violent and uncontrolled character was James Gilhooley, a porter and labourer of Great Barr Street. He too was a record-holder for assaulting the police and for the bad language he used even in court. He was so often drunk that it was probably true that he could not remember his individual acts of brutality, whether kicking a barman in the stomach for refusing him any more drink or kicking police on the way to the station. By 1895, at the age of thirty-two, he had been in custody over seventy-five times.

The Farmer brothers had similar records for assault. James, or Jemmy, Farmer, alias Joyce, was said to be Birmingham's most notorious rough and a terror to the police authorities. He was undiscrimating as to whom he punched, whether it was a pub landlady, the policeman who arrested him or the warder who took him to his cell. He often threatened that he would be hung for murdering either a 'copper' or a 'screw' and had the same visceral loathing of the police as the Gilhooleys. He burned with a sense of injustice that the police always picked on him and seemed to hate each officer he crossed more than the one before. While many thought that the cat-o'-nine-tails was the answer, this man was proof against it. He had been lashed so often in prison, it was said, as to appear impervious to pain. In June 1890, having been read his sentence of two months for assaulting the landlady of a pub in Inge Street and of P.C. Price, who had made the arrest, the *Post* reported how in court 'he leaped out of the dock and alighted on the table. He made a kick at the witness (P.C. Price) and then hit him twice in the face. He kicked out right and left, but several officers closed with him and after Superintendent Stephenson had removed his boots, he was got back into the dock, where he made use of the most disgusting and offensive language to the justices.'

In the week that followed he wrote a long letter of apology to the stipendiary magistrate, but claimed that great injustice had been done him and blamed P.C. Price for following him about and manufacturing evidence against him. When he appeared in court to receive an extra sentence for his previous behaviour, he was handcuffed and carefully guarded and his heavy boots had been replaced by a pair of slippers. His was such an impossible case that the veteran alderman Henry Manton and the prison governor Admiral Tinklar arranged for him to be sent to Queensland, Australia, in 1891 to make a new start. He went, but by the following year he was back in Birmingham, breaking shop windows, assaulting policemen and showing all his old paranoia. By the time he died in Winson Green Asylum, at the age of thirty-four in 1897, he had been convicted over thirty times and spent over eleven years of his life in prison.

Compared to the spotlight on colourful behaviour of individual recidivists like Farmer, traditional slogging matches now received little publicity. Yet they carried on in areas such as the Gun Quarter and Duddeston. Duddeston was a social mix of iron workers, glassblowers, gasworkers and railway 'servants', with St Matthew's District having a rough reputation. Here, inter-school slogging was taken seriously. In November 1892, a nineteen-year-old brassfounder became infuriated by schoolboy sloggers constantly breaking windows at the manufactory in Lupin Street where he worked. One day he decided he had had enough. He rushed into the street and grabbed a schoolboy called Thomas Giblin, who was at the head of about 250 boys from St Matthew's Church Schools as they met in Lupin Street for the start of a dinner-hour slog with about 200 from Loxton Street Board Schools. Giblin, from Bloomsbury, was taken before the magistrates and admitted carrying the stones, but maintained that 'the other side began it'. He was fined half a crown.

If the numbers reported are correct, this was nearly half the children at the smaller St Matthew's turning out to do battle with about one fifth of the children at the mighty Loxton Street. The two schools, at either ends of Lupin Street, exemplified some of the differences between church and board schools. The much older and less well-equipped St Matthew's was a penny a week more expensive for older children, complained of stinking ashpits directly outside its windows and had been used for local Conservative meetings. Loxton Street, on the other hand, was a product of the second wave of board schools in the 1880s, prided itself on its new buildings and its bigger playground and provided a meeting place for the local Liberals. It was at the cutting edge, finding notable success and winning trophies in the new adult-organised competitions between schools in football, drill and athletics, sponsored by the Birmingham Athletic Association. By contrast that lunchtime slog, albeit aborted by senior intervention, was an example of how Birmingham's inter-school rivalry was more traditionally conducted and what many boys still preferred.

Duddeston was not subdued by one half-crown fine or a football competition. Weekly pitched battles, especially on Sunday evenings, in Heneage Street – parallel with Lupin Street – produced turnouts of about a hundred lads in the summer of 1893. In June, a nineteen-year-old labourer and a fifteen-year-old wireworker, both from neighbouring Adams Street, were fined. This street was the address of Alfred Simpson and had a reputation for assaults on school board visitors and constables. It was close to Dartmouth Street, famous for its fighters who still made excursions, along with pickpockets, into neighbouring Aston. One of the bigger factories in the street was a firm of edge-tool makers, constantly being fined for emissions of dense black smoke.

In August, as many as five hundred engaged in the nightly combat between the Cliveland Street gang and the Weaman Street gang – just outside and inside the Gun Quarter respectively. On one of these evenings, two passers-by in Shadwell Street sustained head injuries and some windows were broken in St Chad's Cathedral, which was once again in the firing line, as in the late 1860s. However, again where it was a case of stones rather than belts, fines were the preferred sanction. In the Gun Quarter, only two boys of thirteen and fourteen were arrested and they were merely cautioned and fined a token half-crown each.

These were in contrast with two more pathological fighters in the same area, in their twenties, one of whom, James Herrick, had spent some time in a lunatic asylum and was supposedly looked after by his sister. He was often in the company of a 'madman' – as the press styled him – called Michael Surr, a labourer who lived in Hospital Street. Surr was quarrelsome when drunk and himself the victim of a stab wound and blows with poker and shovel. He hated the police and was always stirring up a mob when an arrest was made. He was continually being sent to prison for assaulting constables, and the press recorded his forty-seventh appearance in that same year of 1893.

Even when a three-year-old child was killed in a pram by a flying stone from an eighteen-year-old labourer in Allison Street, the stone-throwing in that street continued, as did cases of 'ruffianism' against the police across the city. The older roughs took it as a challenge. One hardened twenty-eight-year-old who was given a total of four months for attacking a detective and a constable outside a pub in Chapel Street called out as he left the dock, 'I'll assault yer when I get out, see if I don't.' Individual policemen continued to be the victims of gang violence, all over Birmingham. Two policemen were battered by two men in Bishop Ryder's District with poker and brick in a typical attempt at rescue. There was a similar battle in neighbouring Lawrence Street between drunk and disorderly roughs with brick-ends and policemen with staves. One constable who interfered with a slogging gang in Bordesley Green was lucky merely to be kicked and have his lamp smashed.

CHAPTER 17

The Knife

KNIVES OFTEN TOOK gangs further than they intended, causing serious injury, even death, in encounters that otherwise would have resulted in nothing more than a few bumps and bruises. So it was worrying when the city's most popular newspaper reported in 1890 that gang leaders were now appointing members to act as 'chiviers' to wield the knife in a row. The chivier, according to this report, had instructions to stab enemies in the back, but not fatally if possible. How far could this be believed? For one thing, stabbings in the back were rarer than stabbings in the head, but they were becoming more frequent. In 1891, a reckless eighteen-year-old wireworker from Bishop Ryder's received the exemplary sentence of five years for stabbing a man from St Matthew's and another from Bloomsbury in two incidents five months apart. Recorder Dugdale, in his charge to the grand jury before the trial, expressed himself astonished that 'in a city like Birmingham there could be gangs of youths going about armed with knives'. The following September, a policeman managed to survive twelve stab wounds, ten of them in the back, while trying to arrest one of three young men for using obscene language in Loveday Street. Whether the *Mail*'s claim about the chivier was fanciful news copy or not, the use of the knife continued to have deadly implications, as the next big gang killing showed.

John Metcalfe, a labourer aged twenty, was stabbed by John Thomas Cherry, an eighteen-year-old nailmaker, outside the London Museum Concert Hall two days before the Christmas of 1893. The quarrel was said to be one between the Barford Street and Park Street gangs, with Cherry representing Barford Street and Metcalfe, Park Street. Metcalfe and his friends were heavily outnumbered, and he died almost at once. The prosecution based its case on the words of William Fallon, a brickie's labourer from the Islington area. At fifteen he was the youngest of those involved in the concert hall fight and turned Queen's evidence. (His family background seems to have been typical of the worst parts of downtown Birmingham: his uncle kept a brothel and he had acted as a pimp.) According to Fallon, the origin of the affray was that a certain William Bond, an eighteen-year-old brassfitter of Benacre Street, was aggrieved about being the only one of a group, including Fallon, who was convicted for the theft of some material and had demanded money from his associates, presumably to pay his fine. Bond's nickname, 'Major', was a jokey reference to the authoritarian former Chief Constable and was not inappropriate, as one of the same gang referred to him as one of its 'commanding officers'. Bond and Fallon were apparently in opposing gangs – Park Street and Barford Street – although it seems that they had both been involved in the robbery for which Bond had taken the rap. In any case they had met in the street in the September after the crime, quarrelled, and Fallon had stabbed at Bond. The resulting wound was slight and Bond brought no charge against Fallon for this, but he harboured a grudge and decided to teach him a lesson as he came out of the Museum Concert Hall on Saturday, 23 December.

Members of both gangs went to the hall that night. Bond went with 'Diddy' Palmer of the Park Street, while Fallon and Cherry were among a number of the Barford Street, and most remained until closing time. Somehow Fallon got wind that something was going to be done against him by Bond or his juniors, so he left the hall in the comparatively safe company of two girls. As he did so, a number of men, including Metcalfe, rushed at him from an entry and knocked him down. Fallon quickly got up and took off his buckled belt ready to defend himself. A general affray broke out, but it was Metcalfe, not Fallon, who had the hardest time. One of Fallon's Barford Street allies, Hubert Cash, a seventeen-year-old brasscaster of Garrison Lane, rushed at Metcalfe and knocked him against a coffeehouse door. Metcalfe managed to catch hold of the brass rod on the door, but was kicked by Cash and fell to the ground. At that moment, George Cosier, a nineteen-year-old carter from Barford Street, and Cherry, the nailmaker from Balsall Heath, rushed over. Cherry was seen by another witness to pull out a knife and make an upward stab. The knife reached into Metcalfe's gullet, as the surgeon later confirmed, and two policemen, even with ambulance training, could not save his life.

Cherry was seen coming away with Cosier, with a knife in his hand. Going down Digbeth, he met the rival gang leader, Bond, who seems to have missed the fight and who called out in the dark, 'Is that Cherry?' In answer, Cherry stabbed at him twice in the face before running off.

The next day, Cherry was talking calmly to another lad in the street about Metcalfe's death, which he had seen reported in a Sunday newspaper. Cherry pulled out his knife and remarked strangely, 'I did chivvy a man last night, but I didn't think this knife could have done it.' He later said the same to Fallon, who advised him to give himself up and then made his own statement to an inspector. Bond denied being a member of the Park Street gang, but said that Metcalfe had been and that the gang went to the Museum every evening, as he did himself. Bond had been originally arrested for the murder, but had told the police that Cherry of the Barford Street gang had done it. Bond admitted that he had a quarrel with Fallon of the Barford Street boys, whom he referred to as 'the Tykes' (presumably as dogs rather than Yorkshiremen), and had gone to the concert hall to see him. However he denied calling out the Park Street gang to thrash him.

Bond's denial of being one of the Park Street gang was undermined by his evidence at the Assizes, under cross-examination, that he was 'one of the officers'. With very few lieutenants, he was certainly greatly outnumbered that night at the concert hall. If we judge by the addresses the boys gave to the police, which were dispersed through a large part of the conurbation, these two gangs seem at this juncture to have been the personal followings of Bond and Cosier rather than territorial groups. Bond did not live in or near Park Street, but far away, off the Bristol Road, and George Cosier was the only one of his gang to live in Barford Street. There were five Cosier brothers, of whom three at least had convictions for street-fighting. George was the second brother after Reuben and, like him, had started work as a brasscaster and then taken an unskilled job, perhaps when jobs became scarce again after 1892. Reuben Cosier had previously led the Barford Street boys against Patrick Joyce and his Park Street gang, so it was not surprising for any enemies of George Cosier's crowd, including Bond, to associate themselves with Park Street.

Cherry claimed that he was drunk that night and could not recall what he did. Unfortunately for him an independent witness who had been at the music hall identified him as the man who had stabbed Metcalfe. When Cherry was arrested, he was carrying a brown hafted knife with a damaged blade, but witnesses who had seen the murder weapon said it had a white handle and a good blade, three-and-a-half inches long and sharp enough to cause the fatal wound. The prosecution claimed Cherry had switched the knives before his arrest. Another witness, called William 'Diddy' Palmer, who eventually admitted to being in the Park Street gang, said that he had gone with Metcalfe to the concert hall with the intention of seeking out Fallon. On Major Bond's instructions, Palmer had stood sentry on the street corner to watch out for any of the others and to call up any of his lot who were passing. Meanwhile Bond and Metcalfe also took up positions elsewhere in the street, but close to the door.

Under cross-examination Palmer told how when Fallon had emerged from the concert hall he was immediately set upon and knocked down by Metcalfe. A general fight had ensued, during which Cherry administered the fatal blow. The defence had few witnesses to call, but his schoolmaster and a barber who had employed Cherry for three years both gave him good character references as a 'quiet, well-behaved lad'. Cherry, who had been calm and apparently unaffected by the proceedings until that moment, found these accolades too much and broke down and sobbed, burying his head in his hands. The defence counsel argued that the prosecution had been remorseless, on wholly unreliable evidence.

In summing up, the judge, Baron Pollock, who was well-used to dealing with violent cases among the scuttlers of Manchester, said that Metcalfe's death would have been 'a disgrace to any place' and that it was remarkable that 'proceedings of such extraordinary barbarity should take place in a country that was supposed to be civilised and educated and above most other countries on the face of the earth'. He did not believe that there had been a conspiracy of witnesses to take the prisoner's life.

The jury found Cherry guilty of manslaughter and the next day Baron Pollock passed sentence. He showed leniency on the grounds that 'a boy at the prisoner's time of life, in the heat of the moment, using a knife, which was an ordinary instrument for him to carry with him, might not from his knowledge of the human body have expected the terrible results that followed' and so only sentenced him to five years' penal servitude. Once again a judge, well used to handing out tough sentences to the young, was using leniency when violence tipped over into manslaughter in fights on the streets of Birmingham. His sentence was clearly much better than John Cherry had expected, and the *Post* reporter described how suddenly he regained his composure and, with a smile, 'turned round, looked up at the gallery and laughed, and with a wave of his hand, tripped gaily from the dock'. The newspaper editors were not impressed. The *Gazette* commented sarcastically that 'Well might Cherry chuckle. It was an excellent joke'. The same newspaper was concerned also about that 'organisation' called the 'Tykes', but those fears were likely to have been exaggerated as it was never mentioned again.

Six weeks later, Fallon was challenged in the street by a Park Street gang member called Collett, the previous recipient of sentences for assault, receipt of stolen goods and being ejected from the Prince of Wales Theatre, who had just been released from Winson Green after a six-month stay. Collett had missed the Museum fracas but was persuaded by his mates that either way, Fallon was to blame for everything that had happened – both Metcalfe's death and Cherry's imprisonment. Collett, with his record, and claiming to be a friend of Cherry, was just the man to teach Fallon a lesson.

Fallon went to the detectives' office and told them that Collett had come up to him and grabbed him saying, 'You're the one as went against Cherry, warn't yer?' Collett then caught hold of the handkerchief round his neck and struck him in the eye, drawing blood. At a subsequent hearing, Collett gave his version of events: that the two had a seven-round fight lasting ten minutes, at the end of which Fallon refused to give Collett 'best man' – or concede victory – and went to the police. Fallon denied this and claimed that Collett's black eye was from falling on a kerbstone. Collett was remanded to be able to call witnesses, although not allowed bail, but the second hearing did not go much better for him, even though Fallon had to admit that there had been a fight rather than just an assault. Fallon continued to be a derided figure and a target for bottle-throwing in the music hall. It seems that his act of going twice to the police was a more serious crime in the eyes of his peers than being in the wrong gang.

As a footnote to this story, it appears that Collett of the Barford, who was eighteen, and a member of the Park called William 'Mac' Sheridan, aged seventeen, were both involved at different times in violence in the south-eastern suburbs. Collett, who in the census of 1891 lived in Cheapside but a few months later gave his address as Devon Street, Duddeston, had in October of that year been involved in a pub brawl at the Gypsy's Tent, Cherrywood Lane, Bordesley Green and was sentenced to twelve months' hard labour at the Birmingham Assizes for wounding. Sheridan was one of several from both gangs who came from the outer suburbs, in his case the village of Greet, south of Small Heath. In the October before the Digbeth tragedy, Sheridan had been arrested for obstruction in Percy Road and for brandishing a twelve-inch knife over his head. Four months later, he was arrested and fined again for obstruction. Gang links betweeen the centre of Birmingham and its suburbs worried the authorities and fed demands for the extension of the city's jurisdiction.

WILLIAM SHERIDAN brandished his knife out of bravado and probably learned a lesson from the trial of Cherry. Others who subsequently would be described as 'of the peaky type' were more reckless. One was Edward Gallagher. He lived with his brother John, who would kill a man in a fight in Ryder Street, close to the Gun Quarter. John was three years older and was described by the police as a very bad character when the two of them were arrested for assaulting three constables in Staniforth Street on a Saturday night in October 1889. Edward, aged eighteen, clearly joined in the fighting that his drunken, violent brother had started. Edward was fined twenty shillings, compared to the sentence of four months' hard labour for John.

In October 1892, Edward was taken to the General Hospital early one Sunday morning with minor knife cuts on his head and neck, after fighting with another man. At first he readily gave the man's name, but later would not or could not swear to who had stabbed him. It appeared that they had been in a fight in York Street with sticks and belts and none of the combatants would give evidence against each other. However 'several well-known roughs' were involved, according to the *Post*, and a case was taken to the sessions against a nineteen-year-old labourer called Thomas Hawkins for the malicious wounding of Edward Gallagher in Canal Street on that Sunday morning. The prosecution alleged that Hawkins had stabbed Gallagher and then thrown down the knife and run away. The defence case was that the stabbing had been done by a sailor who was with Hawkins at the time. It was also maintained that the fight was caused by Gallagher and his friends, who were part of a slogging gang and were attempting to levy blackmail on Hawkins. One witness said that Gallagher was already bleeding before he met Hawkins and that he was stabbed by neither the sailor nor the accused. Hawkins' sweetheart, Mary Ann Connolly, also denied he had stabbed Gallagher, so the prosecution case collapsed and Hawkins was acquitted.

It was rare for Gallagher to be on the receiving end, and it was not long before he was back in the dock for being drunk and disorderly and for laying into two people on a Saturday night with a poker, sending them to hospital. On this occasion he went to prison for a month. Even more serious was a charge made against him in April 1894, by which time he was described as a hawker, living once more in a court off Staniforth Street. Again it was a Saturday night, but this time the victims of his drunken violence were two policemen. Nor was it in a fair fight; he meant to do damage. He crept up behind them with a heavy hammer and brought it down on P.C. Hoben's head, smashing the policeman's helmet. In court, Gallagher pleaded for leniency, saying that he had been in prison for twelve months for burglary, which was true but he made it sound as if he had just been released, which was not the case. The philanthropic Staniforth Street Society was going to help him, and when he came out of prison he would ask them to help him get to America. This was the sort of story that magistrates were used to hearing and from Gallagher's mouth it was especially rich. The magistrate responded sharply that Gallagher should thank his lucky stars that he was not in the dock on a more serious charge: he might have killed the constable. His sentence was six months in prison.

A much older man who also readily resorted to the knife was Tommy, brother of John Giblin. By the age of sixteen, in 1882, he was a streetfighter of no fixed address, and took on an Irish lad called Thomas Flynn in an impromptu barefist bout within a ring of fifty youths and girls in Water Street. A year later, he was central to a stabbing affray in Summer Lane and was sent to prison for ten years. When he came out on a ticket-of-leave, he was sent back again for trying to climb over the counter to stab the landlord of the Angel in Hospital Street for refusing him drink. Giblin was in and out of the tramp ward at the workhouse and by the age of thirty was regarded as one of the most violent men in the city. He was an intermittent menace to his neighbours, but could sound quite reasonable when sober and was a master of injured innocence. Perhaps this enabled him, in April 1895, once more fresh from prison, to gather support as a kind of street hero in Cecil Street, where he now lived. When drunk as usual on a Saturday night, he provided the familiar spectacle of resisting arrest by three officers, while his companions pelted them with loose stones. The excited crowd rose in size to nearly three hundred as a dozen more constables arrived in order to escort him and the three officers to the gates of the General Hospital, where they were still being stoned, and finally inside to safety and the treatment of the wounds of all four. The next day's court appearance was reckoned as Giblin's twenty-fifth conviction for assault and wounding.

Irish family feuds often attracted publicity. One of the Kelly brothers readily used a knife in the feud with another family, the Joyces, following a Saturday night incident at the Plough and Harrow, in March 1895. William Kelly, the potman there, had turned Patrick Joyce out of the pub. The next day, the two sets of brothers met each other, in one version in a chance passing in Birchall Street off Cheapside, in another version in one of a series of regular encounters by the brothers in a gully near Lombard Street. Thomas Kelly, a twenty-eight-year-old stoker, came up to twenty-two-year-old Patrick Joyce and challenged him with: 'Are you as good a man now as you were last night?'

'Yes, I am,' replied Joyce.

The pair proceeded to fight. Edward Joyce stood by to see fair play, but was soon intervening to help his younger brother when William Kelly took a stick to strike Patrick. Then Thomas Kelly pulled a knife and, in the struggle, stabbed Edward Joyce in the head and back. Meanwhile Patrick had started hitting Thomas Kelly with a brick, but in turn he was knocked out by William Kelly's stick. Thomas Kelly was identified by the police as a returned convict who had failed to report himself. Edward Joyce was taken to the Queen's Hospital in a dangerous condition, but recovered; Thomas Kelly was found to have thirteen previous convictions and was sent at the Birmingham Sessions to twelve months' hard labour.

Sometimes knives were used with calculated effect. One such case was when William Latham, a young employee of a firm of ginger-beer manufacturers, was talking to a girl late one night in August 1895, at the corner of Barton Street and Park Lane, in Aston. They were approached by three eighteen-year-olds, one of whom asked Latham if he was a member of the Park Lane gang. He denied it, but one of the youths, Samuel Preece, said he was and hit him with a pair of buckles. He tried to get away but was followed, and Samuel Greer, eighteen, from Vicarage Road, stabbed him in the chest while the other two held him and kicked him when he fell to the ground. He was unconscious when he was taken to hospital and spent six weeks there recovering from his injuries, which included a pierced lung. A witness at the Warwickshire Assizes in December said that he had lent Greer the knife 'to cut an apple' earlier that evening; he had seen Latham running down Barton Street, but had not seen what followed. Greer had later handed him back his knife. In the earlier police court hearing, it was established that the three came from north Aston and that Greer had been attacked by one of the Park Lane gang six months' previously. This might seem a long time to nurse a grievance, but this may have been the first opportunity for taking a safe form of vengeance on an individual outside a group. At the assizes, the police witness said that Greer had confessed to stabbing Latham and had a buckled belt in his pocket. The other two had made statements that they had only struck Latham with their fists. However a buckled belt had been found in the house of one of them, and also the knife which had been hidden.

The sergeant also presented evidence that the three were hard-working youths, but unfortunately they belonged to the Lichfield Road gang, who were engaged in a feud with the Park Lane gang, to which they supposed Latham belonged. The case was heard by the formidable Mr Justice Day, a passionate believer in the flogging of garrotters and the scourge of youth gangs in Liverpool and Manchester. He declared that he 'would break up the Lichfield Road arrangement for some time'. The next day he passed sentence, proclaiming that 'they were a gang of ruffians who infested the suburbs of Birmingham' and that he 'was determined to stamp this sort of thing out as he had done in another great city' – referring to Liverpool, where he had dealt with the notorious High Rip and other gangs at many assizes between 1883 and 1893 and where he was known as 'Judgement' Day. He gave Greer ten years' penal servitude and his mates two years' hard labour each.

The ever-present danger of attack in certain quarters provoked an arms race in which young men were almost obliged to carry weapons for self-defence. Joseph Gould, an eighteen-year-old printer from Vicarage Road, Aston, told the sessions that one night in September 1893 he had been followed about by a number of boys, so the next night he had taken a chopper with him for protection. He was with friends when they were approached by a lad from Gosta Green, who came across the road to ask one of them if he would go to a show. Gould asked the lad if he knew a certain Jenkins and when the lad said he did, Gould produced the chopper from behind his back and struck him a blow on the back of the neck, felling him. As the lad got up, partially stunned, another of the lads said 'Give him another.' Fortunately Gould refrained. His victim had to be attended to by Dr Joseph Sampson Gamgee, the renowned resident surgeon at the General Hospital, for a wound in his neck. Gould's unconvincing explanation was, 'If I didn't down him, they would me.' He was sent to prison for a month's hard labour.

There was an advantage in getting your retaliation in first. The Recorder deplored 'the practice prevalent in Birmingham for gangs of boys going about at night and attacking one another or other people'. A group arrested for starting a fight in William Street, Islington, with two youths on a Saturday evening in 1894, excused themselves to the police, by saying, 'If we hadn't put them through it they would have put us through it.' Honour was at stake and conflict was not to be avoided. In fact this was a rare example of a reported case before the magistrates where the prosecutors and victims, who had been struck to the ground and kicked, but not seriously injured, did not want to press charges and arrangements for compensation were made.

One letter-writer to the *Post* was sure that sentences of two to five years' penal servitude for members of the 'buckled belt fraternity' would soon solve the problem, but such sentences were way beyond the powers of the magistrates. A slogging gang with support from Smethwick and Handsworth, using the old name Forty Thieves, was causing trouble in the local pubs. The landlord and barman of the Grove Inn, Handsworth, were struck in the face with a heavily buckled belt after asking a Smethwick ironworker to leave. On another occasion, the gang roamed along Dudley Road towards Smethwick on a Saturday night before Christmas, 1894. When they came across a young man from Cape Hill, one of them laid into him with his belt. He later claimed it was self-defence, but a magistrate called the attack unprovoked and 'very cowardly', and gave him one month in prison without the option of a fine, to protect the public and to make an example of him.

The victim was often uncertain about what had led to the attack. When William Cook received an unprovoked blow in the face from the buckled belt of a seventeen-year-old in Digbeth one Sunday in September 1893, he could only reason that the gang thought that he had informed against one of them for stealing money. Another lad was stabbed in St Vincent Street, Ladywood, allegedly because he had given evidence at a police court in a metal-stealing case. Two of a gang from the Brookfields area attacked and wounded a brassworker in Icknield Port Road and then turned on a man who had gone to help him. The defence claimed that the two were playing football that afternoon, one with the Soho Villa Club, but the magistrate said that they were black-guards who deserved the cat, and the secretary of the club later denied any connection.

One Sunday night, Alfred Brampton, a respectable young brass filer who had recently moved to Aston from St Bartholomew's, was talking to 'his young woman' in Chester Street, on the border between Aston, Nechells and Duddeston, when three other women passed and called up a gang, two of whom came from Adams Street, St Matthew's. They swarmed round Brampton and began to attack him with sticks and buckles. In court the prisoners' excuses were not taken seriously by the magistrates who were annoyed at the way they asked for a remand and talked to their friends present in the courtroom.

Tit-for-tat slogging fights were a frequent occurrence. A coal dealer's family became a gang target in revenge for a court action, but overdid their retaliation. Twenty-year-old Charles Hodgetts lived with his older brother Frank at their parents' house in Moorsom Street, the sloggers' paradise off Newtown Row. The prosecution case at the sessions was that these two, one armed with a chopper, the other with a poker, had gone up to a hawker of the same age called Joseph Flanagan in Moorsom Street late on Christmas Eve 1894. Frank had called out, 'Here is Corney,' and struck him on the head with the chopper. Flanagan had run for shelter to the house of a witness called Gibson. While he was bathing his wounded head in water, the Hodgetts brothers had burst open the door and attacked him again with poker and chopper. In the struggle he had nearly lost the tips of three fingers and had been taken unconscious to the hospital. Under cross-examination, Gibson admitted that previously he had thrown a brick at the Hodgetts' door, but denied belonging to a slogging gang in the neighbourhood.

The prisoners' father, John Hodgetts, a coal haulier, told the court that bricks had been frequently thrown at his door ever since his son Charles had prosecuted a man who had stolen his horse and cart. On Christmas Eve, about a dozen members of a slogging gang, including Flanagan, had gathered in front of his house and thrown bricks at the door. John Hodgetts went to the door and remonstrated with the roughs, who replied, 'We don't want you. It's your son, Charley; we mean to knock his top in.' After this, the two brothers armed themselves in self-defence and headed out into the street, where Frank was hit on the nose with the buckle end of a belt. Flanagan had got what he deserved, said Mr Hodgetts. In the end Frank Hodgetts was sentenced to four months and Charles to three months with hard labour.

Older people might be attacked for interfering in gang activities, as when a tailor called Peter Nyland intervened to prevent the ill-treatment of a boy in Highgate Street on Christmas Day 1893. He then went back up the street followed by a brassworker with a knife and a gardener with a buckled belt. The brassworker was heard to say, 'Let's chivey him and put his light out.' Both struck Nyland, and as he put up his hand to protect his face, the blade of the knife passed clean through one of the fingers in his right hand and into his lip. A third man ran up and knocked him down with a jar. The jury at the sessions was not impressed by the alibis of the men concerned, and the brassworker got three years' penal servitude. Their victim, the tailor, could no longer work at his trade. The magistrates were concerned to protect the wider public not only for 'having a go' against the sloggers, but also in coming forward to give evidence. It was announced that any gang members who threatened witnesses could expect especially severe punishment, although in fact the sentencing power of magistrates was strictly limited.

Young men in areas like Digbeth seemed addicted to fighting. Any knot of men standing around in the street had always to be on the defence against attacks by other groups. Sometimes the fines were small if the police thought it was just a 'general melee', as in Barn Street in April 1895. No one had been seriously hurt and none had resisted arrest. Six men were arrested and were only fined ten shillings and costs or sentenced to seven days in prison.

Thugs like the Simpson brothers continued to be a menace across the whole of north Birmingham. In 1895, the police were called to a pub at the corner of Dartmouth and Chester Streets, an area notorious for its street fighting and a meeting point between St Stephen's, St Mary's and Nechells districts. Three of the brothers were drinking there and again trying to intimidate the landlord. When a P.C. Scadden arrived, William Pettifer, landlord of the Grand Junction Inn, accused two of the Simpsons of stealing and breaking his watch. Scadden told them that they were under arrest, and asked them to go quietly with him to the station, but then in came John, the oldest, and struck him in the mouth. The four of them then closed in on the constable, knocked him down and kicked him. He managed to struggle into the street where the attack was resumed and one of them bit his hand. In the end only two of the brothers went to prison, this time John and Joseph. All of them were peakies before their time.

CHAPTER 18

Honours Even?

BY 1895, THE most successful public figure in Aston was Edward Ansell. Aged forty-six and one of the leading members of Birmingham's foremost brewing company, which controlled an increasing numbers of pubs and was set to swallow up many of its smaller rivals, he was an alderman, a leading Unionist and member of the Warwickshire County Council. As 'Mr Big' in Aston, he provided land for public baths in Victoria Road, supported technical education, physical training, swimming and athletics. He was also a former cricketer and so was an obvious choice as the guest of honour at the Aston Police Cricket and Recreation Club dinner at the Queen's Hotel public house in Victoria Road. His was the first and most important speech, proposing, 'Success to the Cricket and Recreation Club.' The club, Ansell thought, provided all that was essential to success in cricket, namely 'regular and continued practice and a good wicket'; it was just a pity that it had lost several of its best batsmen and bowlers in recent years. However the recreation room, established by Superintendent Walker in 1885, was a credit not only to the police but also to the district, and he congratulated the club on raising 'a handsome sum' of money at its last concert.

Warming to his theme, the great man congratulated the district police for an 'extraordinary decrease in crime' in the past thirteen years. 'Many of the residents recollected the time when Aston bore a some-what unenviable reputation,' he said, 'when the district was the home of the rough and the rowdy, when the notorious slogging gang which infested the Ten Arches and Rocky Lane created a veritable reign of terror and rendered the thoroughfares unsafe for respectable citizens.' Ansell attributed the change in that 'disgraceful state of affairs' to the determination of Superintendent H.A. Walker, who had come to Aston thirteen years before. He also praised the fearlessness of the police and the severity of the actions of the magistrates, and considered crime of a serious character to have become 'non-existent in Aston'. The prize-giving followed, including a prize donated by Ansell himself, and four more toasts were drunk, with proposals and thanks to match and solos sung in between by bobbies from the police choir. Yet many will have felt that Ansell's tribute, and the general air of police self-congratulation, were premature.

February 1895 was again a time of great distress in the area with 'hundreds and hundreds of half-starved creatures' besieging the offices of the Charity Organisation Society rather than submit to 'the brow-beating of the cast iron Poor Law', according to the *Clarion*, a new socialist newspaper. As the year drew on, there were some signs of economic recovery. Improving conditions were being reported in the jewellery and bedstead trades, even if the heavier metal industries still showed high levels of unemployment and the prospects for railway-carriage making were regarded as 'dull'. In April came news that a 'couple of gangs assembled in Cheapside to adjust certain differences'. Two policemen asked them to leave. One twenty-year-old from Allison Street refused and was arrested. The crowd hounded the officers all the way to the police station. The prisoner had no police record, but was given six months by the magistrate as a warning that 'assaults on police officers and gang fights would not be allowed'.

What had happened to the peaky blinders? Far from remaining a distinct gang associated with Bordesley or Small Heath – juvenile terrors from there were dubbed 'small heathens' – the phrase had become dormant only to re-emerge as a favoured journalistic term for any big group of youths creating a disturbance. The first of such groups to be so described was the twenty or so people who had to be turned out of the Stag and Pheasant on the corner of Pershore and Bromsgrove Streets in the modern Markets area, by two constables, on a Saturday night in October 1895. For one of the gang, a labourer of Cheapside, this turned out to be his nineteenth conviction, once again for assault. For good or ill, he represented a long tradition. James Cuson, now twenty-eight, was of Irish stock and had lived as a child at Court No. 44, the Gullet, close to the spot where John Kirkham was killed.

'Peaky' became a term for a rough or criminal thief or drunken youth or loafer as well as a group. So the word was applied to Henry Lightfoot (see page 219), originally from Garrison Lane, but of no fixed abode by the age of twenty-two, who was drunk and striking men with a stick in a beerhouse in the Markets area one Saturday night in 1895. He hit the landlord and his wife as he went out and was reported as striking out at anyone he passed. When he met Detective Tingle in Bromsgrove Street, he shouted, 'You're a jack. Hop off.' And he hit him on the head. The detective returned the punch, knocking Lightfoot into the horseway. Then a mate of Lightfoot's hit Tingle. Lightfoot was eventually arrested and sentenced to six months in prison. He had had many prison sentences already for burglary and assault including of the police, notably at Hay Mills and Small Heath, outside the city, and the magistrates considered him to be 'evidently a "peaky blinder" of a dangerous type'.

In a much less violent context, the phrase was used to describe two youths for selling to little boys flutes and whistles which they had stolen by breaking a shop window in Spring Hill. Peaky blinder rapidly became a generic name for all rowdy juveniles using obscene language or causing damage. Identification was made easier, as Mr Justice Wills endorsed in 1897, by including any 'ill-favoured youth with a great patch of hair plastered down in a broad band upon his forehead'. Chief Constable Farndale, in his annual report for 1897, saw the peaky as a moral coward who 'cares nothing for the pain he causes others to suffer, but strongly resents any pain or inconvenience inflicted upon himself'. By the late 1890s it was easy to condemn a young person by referring to him or, more rarely her, as a member of the peaky blinder order, class or type. However, it had not become interchangeable with 'slogger'.[15]

BY THE spring of 1896, trade was picking up in earnest. It was the beginning of the last great boom of the nineteenth century, to be followed by the long Edwardian Depression, which would end only three years before the start of the Great War. It was also the year of the great bicycle boom, with Coventry leading the way but Birmingham not far behind. Men and boys who had found the trades of brassfounding, gunmaking or locksmithing overcrowded, depressed or unexciting, eagerly joined the ranks of those making cycles. Bobbies on bicycles provided inviting targets for boys with catapults and glass balls from ginger beer bottles. Soon the offence of 'scorching', or cycling at the shocking speed of twelve

---

15 It was perhaps more akin to modern usage of the word 'chav' than to 'hooligan'.

miles per hour, became a new reason why youths were hauled before the magistrates. Surprisingly the Bench was also concerned about the policemen on bicycles who needed to scorch after the scorchers to have any chance of catching them.

Birmingham specialised in the supply of cycle parts such as lamps and tyres: Joseph Lucas's workforce at Great King Street more than doubled in the 1890s and Dunlop brought his pneumatic tyre to Aston Cross. The rubber boom was such that people were wondering whether rubber-shod horses and rubber-paved streets would arrive next. However, the McKinley tariff of 1890 made the U.S. market hard to enter, and Britain's policy of free trade allowed American and German goods to compete freely with Birmingham-made goods and often at a lower price. Such conditions meant that even the bicycle boom was over by 1898. Likewise the gun trade enjoyed a brief revival but then it too was hit by high American tariffs. Birmingham had to turn to unreliable markets, such as Africa, and selling to the Afridi tribesmen fighting the British on the North-West Frontier between the Indian Empire and Afghanistan. These weapons tended to get confiscated on their way out by the British or Persian goverments, and so were never paid for. It was hardly surprising that few young men were being apprenticed any more in the gun trade.

With thirty additional police, the Birmingham force, boasted by its Watch Committee to be second to none for 'discipline, honour and appearance', was ready for anything. This included putting down football in the street, regardless of what the *Mail* called the 'prevailing football mania'. However, the Chief Constable ruefully reported in 1898 that 'however perfect may be the government of our city, it is too much to expect that we shall ever be altogether free from crime'. This realism was just as well, as, in the next two years, the enlarged authority faced a record number of assaults on police officers.

At the same time, a revision of the by-laws clamped down even further on the range of street activities. There were to be no games, no noise, no jostling, no larking, no bad language, no shouting and no singing. Nothing here was new, but the fact that all this was forbidden once more emphasised that the street was even more an area of close official regulation and would continue to be a battleground between the free spirits and the police. All music in the streets was to be subject to the pleasure of the adjacent householders who had the right to ask any musician or singer to fall silent. This seemed to spell the end to the hurdy-gurdy man, the Highland piper and countless other types of street music. The expected clamp-down on street music worried some people. The *Mail* called clause two of the new by-laws, covering street sounds, the 'comprehensive repression of the musical person'. The new supplementary code was issued on New Year's Day 1897, and it was wondered if this would be the last time that the dawn of the New Year would be ushered in by the traditional chorus of steam whistles or 'bulls' from Birmingham's workshops. In practice, although there were efforts to reduce the period of time when bulls were sounded, it was hard to abolish them altogether as an integral part of every working day. Other street sounds would also carry on. After the battering received by the Birmingham police in Queen Victoria's reign, they were going to get better at turning a blind eye.

May 1896 had seen new rules for the treatment of juvenile offenders in prison. Any offender under sixteen would in future serve his or her term in accommodation set apart from adult prisoners and should be ensured school instruction and be seated in chapel away from adults, and if possible out of their sight. These juveniles should not have to sleep on a plank bed, should have physical drill rather than the walking exercise of adults and should be allowed extra visits 'to improve their moral welfare and future career'.

Two members of the Ten Arches gang were given two months – after a long list of previous convictions – for assaulting two constables who interrupted a belt fight in Grosvenor Road, Aston, on Christmas night 1896. Both claimed that the police, one of whom was in plain clothes, had unnecessarily interfered. Rowlands, the magistrate's clerk, replied, 'You say the police are far too active, but we hear it complained that they are not active enough.' To this Hayes, one of the gang, remarked, 'I don't know about that, but you can read the *Mail* any time and see if they're not too active.' His father was called. He had seen P.C. Wale hit his son, with a blow which 'fairly knocked him out'. Inspector Clarke then said that both were members of the Ten Arches and this was regarded as conclusive.

An encounter between two slogging gangs in Ladywood in April 1897 was prevented by the arrival of the police. The *Mail* reported that as they fled, the sloggers dropped 'among other weapons of warfare, a sword bayonet, a whip, two heavy handcart handles and an ironbar loaded with lead'. This perhaps showed the *Mail's* readers that the authorities had more than street music to contend with. The police forestalled another fight on the following evening in Owen Street by a number of peakies and about twenty girls, most of them armed with sticks. The eighteeen-year-old boy arrested kicked and bit P.C. Nicholls, and at the station was found to be carrying a number of stones weighing nearly half-a-pound apiece. He was sent to prison for a month's hard labour.

Heath Street, between Spring Hill and Cape Hill, Smethwick, resounded with slogging, in the traditional way, between two gangs of boys, numbering fifty in all, in August 1897. One eighteen-year-old labourer from Windmill Lane, Cape Hill, struck a postman delivering letters with a stone and also the recipient. He was chased by P.C. Cumming and threw away his stick as he ran. It was found to have on it two heavy iron nuts. When searched, he was also found to be carrying a strong catapult. In the same month, in the Bishop Ryder's District, a labourer who had been drinking heavily at the Barley Mow, Ryder Street, arrived home one Saturday night in a bad state, saying that he had been injured by 'the Green lot' – a reference to a gang from either nearby Gosta Green or more distant Bordesley Green. He died the next afternoon from internal haemorrhage. The affair was reported as a case of kicking to death, surrounded by mystery.

THERE HAS been heated debate as to whether Britain has ever known really organised gangs as defined in the classic model of Chicago sociologist Frederic Thrasher, where gang cohesion was promoted by criminal acts and by constant clashes with other gangs in the purportedly anarchic conditions of urban America. Evidence of organisation is difficult to come by. In Birmingham, youths were reluctant to admit in court to being members or captains of a gang, although prosecutors were keen to use such accusations to arouse the wrath of the magistrates, compound the offence and achieve a maximum sentence. Victorian journalists and policemen were fond of using the word gang but often just meant a group. Evidence of organisation is bound to be rare where criminal intent, or protection or narcotics rackets, are absent. The issue is often one of commitment and criminality rather than organisation.

In Manchester, the young street gangs known as scuttlers admitted to holding hardship funds for those who had gone to prison. In London, a police court hearing revealed that a Southwark gang called the Hooligan Boys was supposedly organised enough to pay a secretary twopence a week towards settling fines imposed on members for assaults on the police. Gang members were fined twopence if found at a turnout without a belt or stick. Such precise rules and finances rarely came to light and their veracity is uncertain.

Nevertheless, there was some evidence in Birmingham of *ad hoc* collections for those who were about to leave or who had just left prison, and an Aston magistrate declared in 1888 that 'one reason why the Aston roughs were always sent to prison was that if a fine was inflicted, the other roughs managed to collect the money and pay the fine'. It is easy to forget the clubbability of Victorians and that, in the days before the welfare state, all medical help had to be paid for and there were no social benefits. Charity, dependence and the Poor Law were frowned upon. Even in prison, you paid for your subsistence by hard labour. Free schooling took time to establish and even then there were many hidden costs. In the 1890s, there were still no free school meals.

An odd example of fund-raising by and for the Birmingham gangs was that for a George Glasby, a nineteen-year-old who at one court appearance called himself a seaman – unusual in the Midland capital and perhaps just a joke. At earlier hearings, he gave no occupation at all, although he was described as a jeweller in the 1891 census at the address he was still using four years later in Branston Street, Hockley. He became known as 'Gallett' Glasby, supposedly in recognition of a kind of chieftainship: the title or nickname 'Gallett' was accorded to several street fighters, including Edward Hands (see above). Glasby had a record of shop-breaking and assault, leading to several prison sentences. On Whit Monday in 1895, a labourer called Williams produced an appeal that he had written for him on sugar paper:

> For Gallett Glasby,
> Kind friends this his for Gallitt, he as a bit of trouble and I should be very glad if you would put a copper towards burying his child. We would not ask, only he is out of work, all coppers thankfully received. Don't forget him, pals.

A policeman came upon this in Tower Street, as well as a list with six names on it and subscriptions ranging from twopence to sixpence. It was claimed in court that Glasby and Williams, delighted by their success, started 'buckle-belting people right and left'. Next on the scene was a policeman, who they also assaulted. They were said to belong to a slogging gang and went to prison for two months and one month respectively. It was never clear whether Glasby's child really existed or whether the two were just 'getting help for the holidays'.

Later that year, just before Christmas, Glasby was out again and this time was denied admission to the Queen's Theatre, Snow Hill, by the check-takers for his threatening language – perhaps not surprisingly after the stabbing of the usher, Richard Danby, earlier in the year. When he refused two policemen's request to go home and swore at them, Glasby was arrested. He was so violent that it took three constables to drag him to the station; one of them fell and broke his wrist.

Glasby was said to be the gallett, or chief, and Williams was his lieutenant. The police were always keen to label those whom they had arrested as the 'captain' of a slogging band. This may have originated in the early 1870s, when they had often been criticised by the Bench for arresting only juveniles, who were not believed to be the real movers behind street disturbances. It leaves us with the difficulty of whether to believe the police or not. No-one was keen to admit to being a captain in court in case it meant a higher sentence.

More signs of organisation came in the form of meeting places. Many gangs had their regular dens, which got very little publicity but occasionally came to light in court proceedings. These might be in beerhouses or coffee shops run by sympathetic landlords. Thomas Bayliss ran an unobtrusive coffee house in Aston which was located by a police sergeant tracking a 'furtive' youth one Sunday evening in April 1897. The sergeant found eighteen youths at three tables playing shove ha'penny. The sergeant and a constable then forced their way down in to the cellar, where seventeen more youths were gambling. They vanished through a hole in the wall when the two policemen went upstairs again to get more help, but when the two pretended to go away the youths emerged in batches of four from an outhouse where they had been hiding. The *Mail* described the scene as like 'a leaf torn from a penny dreadful or Jack Sheppard type of literature' and the landlord was fined in court. *Jack Sheppard*, the story of the infamous thief, prison-breaker and popular hero hanged at Tyburn in 1724 at the age of twenty-two, may have been condemned as juvenile literature, but it had been playing to packed houses as a comic burlesque, with a pretty actress taking the part of Jack, like a pantomime lead, at Birmingham's theatres and elsewhere for some years.

The power of the gang still lay heavily over the licensees of local pubs and beerhouses. Landlords benefited from their custom and their heavy drinking, but sometimes this went too far. There was a point at which the landlord would say 'no more' and this was often the trigger of trouble. If the man being served took the refusal badly, the landlord or his wife would send at once for the police. They did not always have time. When the landlady of the Thatched Cottage pub in Lee Bank Road, Edgbaston, put outside two brass workers on a Saturday night in July 1888, one of them went to the door and whistled. Within a few minutes, over a dozen youths had assembled, armed with drawn knives and buckles, and besieged the house. 'Come on chaps, knife 'em,' shouted one of the brass workers. The landlady's family stood no chance, but eventually the police took control and the two who started it were sent to prison for three months each. On a similar occasion, the publican of the Welcome beer-house in Dean Street was assaulted by an entire gang.

THE GREAT national challenge of the 1890s – to reform the gang members and so destroy the gangs – was thrown down by the adult establishment, from newspaper editors to bishops. The challenge was taken up with enthusiasm in cities like Birmingham and Manchester. In July 1889, in Lawrence Street, near Gosta Green, 'the very heart of that wretched and crime-ridden district' as one promoter called it, the Kyrle Society had already opened one of the first boys' clubs in Birmingham for concerts and entertainments free from the taint of alcohol. Other such 'quixotic' efforts, as the *Mail* called them, were associated with widely-publicised individuals. Just as the reform of the Manchester scuttler became the life work of Alex Devine, journalist, police court missionary and pioneer of the boys' club movement, in Birmingham the name most associated with trying to take youth off the streets was Arnold Pinchard.

Arnold Theophilus Biddulph Pinchard was a High Church Anglican priest from Somerset, whose first curacy was at downtown Holy Trinity, Bordesley, in 1885. Later he served the English and Argentine communities as vicar of a southern district of Buenos Aires. In 1896, he returned to Birmingham and became vicar of the working-class parish of St Jude's, in Tonk Street. He was interested in the stage, and in due course would be associated with Barry Jackson in the formation of the Pilgrim Players, which led to the founding of the Birmingham Repertory Theatre Company in 1911 and the opening of the first purpose-built repertory theatre in Station Street in 1913. From his arrival at St Jude's, Pinchard's mission was to tame the peaky blinder. He would first elevate the peaky to the top of the new city's agenda, and in doing so he popularised the term, which was soon on everyone's lips, and one young man would tell the police that he was 'one of Arnold Pinchard's peaky blinders'.

Pinchard's first move was to transform part of the Mission Hall in Inge Street. There he opened a club for young men, with a subscription of a penny a week, payable in advance. The club was intended for 'budding peaky blinders' and street-corner loafers aged eighteen to twenty. Games of draughts and an old piano were the first pieces of equipment, but more important were two pairs of boxing gloves with which the young men could work off their high spirits. The club was open every evening, including Sundays after evensong, with the assistance of a curate, a Church Army captain and a lay helper. The new vicar also had plans to start a Church Lads' Brigade for boys under eighteen, who were already members of some other parish organisation. They would be formed into a corps, kept under military discipline, drilled and taught gymnastics.

Pinchard's approach was daring and unconventional. Within a few months, he was campaigning for a girls' recreation room and bedrooms for girls of the lower classes turned out of home at night and 'thrown open to temptation'. A great self-publicist, he soon emerged as a controversial character. Anglo-Catholics had had a rough ride in Birmingham, especially in the 1860s when the Pollock brothers were founding their Leopold Street mission and then St Alban the Martyr just at the time when the tide of Murphyite Protestantism was at its height. Pinchard did not face that degree of opposition, but it soon turned out that he was a socialist as well, which put off a number of potential middle class supporters.

However, had the Baptists beaten the Anglicans to it? Word came that three young ladies in the Hockley district were already providing games of cricket in the summer and football in the winter for a class of twenty or so peaky blinders. No doubt there were peakies and peakies. The *Mail* commented that 'there are some terrible young termagants among the female rowdies who stand quite as much in need of civilising influence as the roughs of the other sex'. By such action, it was hoped, the term 'peaky blinder' would be eradicated from the lexicon of youth.

Even Chief Constable Farndale, who had sent plain clothes men to Pinchard's new club, was impressed by the effects on the district and thought it 'a step in the right direction'. Within two months of starting, he was able to hold a boxing competition, although there were no ropes, so the boxers fell into the laps of the front-row spectators. The boys fought in ordinary dress, namely flannel shirts, corduroy trousers, belts and heavy boots, for a first prize of a suit of clothes and a second prize of a pair of boots. The winner, called Copestick, was described as having 'a peaky fringe shown to best advantage'.

Next up were the Congregationalists, whose Sunday evening services in Steelhouse Lane had been attended for over three years by loafers and gamblers. Over the same period, their Youths' Social Club, connected with their Homes Mission in Dartmouth Street, had also aimed at Christianising 'that class of youth styled "peakies"'. They used the same combination of board games, gymnastics and Bible class on week nights, all without charge.

These impressive efforts to deal with inadequate leisure facilities for the city's young did not entirely overcome any tendencies of rough youth to behave mischievously towards the churches. The Salvation Army continued to attract the rowdiest elements, although with less frequency. A more traditional escapade was instanced when three youths in bell-bottomed trousers and fringes of hair brushed down over their foreheads climbed on the roof of St Catherine's Roman Catholic Church in Horse Fair during Sunday morning Mass and interrupted the homily by clattering about. One of the congregation went to fetch the police, and soon afer two constables got onto the roof to bring the three lads down. The sight of the five on the church roof attracted a large crowd who stayed until they had all climbed down safely. The boys were sent to prison for a month.

Heavy sentences were the other means of dealing with ruffianism. Four youths from Lawley Street, aged between eighteen and twenty-one and said to be 'perfect terrors to the city', were given the maximum sentence of six months' hard labour for savagely kicking a police constable in Vauxhall Road, Duddeston, in February 1897. The sentences elicited an immediate response. As they left the dock, they 'showered imprecations and threats on the officers' and loud shrieks were heard from some women at the back. One woman was carried out in a fainting condition by what a reporter described as 'a small crowd of hysterical females'.

Birmingham, which had been hailed as the the best-governed city in the country, regarded these 'street pests' as a blot on its civic reputation, especially on the eve of the Queen's Diamond Jubilee. One newspaper editor also decried other 'spurious' slurs which damaged the city's name, including 'smokiness, (bad) manners (and) morals, brutality, crime, sham jewellery and commercial trickery in general'. Stabbings also were thought too common. There was a fear that such a range of smears endangered the city's trade, especially as a shopping centre for a large area of the West Midlands.

The final climax of rowdiness came in 1897, not long after the Diamond

Jubilee. Birmingham, like the other major cities, often saw assaults against policemen enforcing the by-laws of Victorian Britain, which interfered so much with working class life, particularly in the street. The response to this violence was never to modify the by-laws or their enforcement, but always to try to toughen sentences. This could not be done without changes in the law, yet successive Home Secretaries were not particularly impressed by the scale of street violence, even when directly approached, as by a deputation of Manchester and Salford magistrates seeking more powers against scuttling in 1890. So the police had to soldier on as the working class enemy number one and the target for every drunken or angry rough.

The injuries from assault in street and home were often horrific, both to civilians and police. Some policemen died as a result of their injuries; others died before their time. Just as the killing of P.C. Lines had been the great scandal of 1875, so the death of another officer became the *cause célèbre* of 1897. The news broke on 19 July that P.C . Snipe of 'C' Division had been killed in a row the previous evening in Bridge Street West, off Summer Lane. The district had a reputation for violence against the police and a police substation had been set up in that very street. In some ways there was nothing exceptional about the tragedy. Throwing stones or bricks at policemen was common. Sometimes the unfortunate policeman was felled by a missile, but rarely did the injury prove fatal. George Snipe was twenty-nine years of age. He had already had a jaw broken by a piece of wood while on duty in the streets, three years before. He was the most unfortunate of many unlucky victims of a clash between two cultures, 'civilised' and 'street'.

Snipe was on duty in uniform in Hockley Hill on the evening of Sunday, 18 July 1897, when there was a confrontation with a group of youths. As they moved towards Bridge Street West, Snipe arrested a man called Colrain. He resisted violently and Snipe needed the help of P.C. Mead to move him along. At the corner of Well Street, a large crowd gathered and stones and bricks began to fly. One thrown at short range hit Snipe and knocked him out. Mead took over the prisoner and Snipe was taken to the General Hospital, where he died four hours later.

Four men were initially arrested, three of them as part of the original disturbance. Eyewitness Polly Mullins, aged eighteen, told the coroner that she saw a man later identified as James Franklin, a nineteen-year-old file cutter from Wilton Street, Lozells, standing at the back of the crowd with the lethal brick in his hand and saw him throw it at Snipe. It hit him on his left temple. She caught hold of Snipe and screamed for help.

Snipe did not speak and bled very much. Mullins cried out at Franklin, 'Oh you scamp, you have killed him.' Then she picked up Snipe's helmet and ran with it towards the police station. She said that Franklin had followed her, cornered her in an entry and snatched it off her. He then threw it on the ground and jumped on it. He later gave it to the police, saying that he had picked it up. A couple who lived in Bridge Street West said they had also seen Franklin jumping on the helmet. In the meantime, P.C. Snipe had collapsed and been taken away. Franklin denied killing him.

The coroner's inquest lasted six and a half hours, and a whole range of evidence was heard. At the end, even though two men had asserted that the man they had seen throwing the brick from three yards' range was not Franklin, a private enquiry agent called Slide corroborated Mullins' story. The jury was of the unanimous opinion that it was Franklin who had thrown the brick that caused the policeman's death and coroner Isaac Bradley pronounced a verdict of murder.

Snipe's funeral, at the Warstone Lane Church of England cemetery, not far from where he had lived, was intended to impress. Over two hundred policemen lined the route and fell in behind the cortege as it passed. The *Post* reported: 'Truly was it remarked that if the procession instead of passing through these crowds of law-abiding jewellery workers and mechanics had gone through the rough district where the officer met his death, the lesson might have been deep and lasting.' A collection was made, with maximum press publicity, for Snipe's widow and baby. At the same time, Franklin's friends mobilised quickly, with a house-to-house collection to pay for his defence. At a demonstration in the Bull Ring on his behalf, a young man came forward to say that he had seen the blow struck and knew the man concerned. The culprit was not Franklin, and he had left Birmingham that morning. Later the young man gave his story to the police. Already the case against Franklin was weakening, but evidence, as always, came at a price. One prosecution witness sought police protection after being kicked in the back and told to 'Cop that.'

By the beginning of August, four men had been charged before the magistrates with assault. They were older than Franklin, ranging in age from twenty-three to thirty-four. Two, including the one with the most violent history, were labourers. They were remanded by Stipendiary Colmore on a charge of assaulting the police in the execution of their duty, while Franklin was charged with wilful murder. Colmore had been one of the lawyers involved in the Navigation Street case twenty-two years before, and he specifically avoided committing the four others for anything more than assault, unlike in 1875, when all those arrested from the comparable affray had been sent automatically to the assizes for wilful murder.

The police were also looking for a sixth man named 'Cloggy' Price, or Williams, who had disappeared since the crime. At a hearing of the police court, he was described as the man at the scene who was dressed 'in a light suit, was wearing a plaid cap on his head and a muffler round his neck' and afterwards ran away down Well Street. By contrast, Franklin's girlfriend insisted that her man was dressed that night in a black coat and vest and blue trousers. A Lozells hackney carriage driver, named Harper, gave evidence that he saw Williams pick a brick out of the gutter, run towards Snipe and throw it. He said he had only come forward because Franklin's neck was in danger. Other witnesses agreed that Franklin had not thrown the brick. Nevertheless the case went for trial at the assizes with Franklin still answerable to a capital charge. The prosecution lawyer, McCardie, asked for police protection for his witnesses, some of whom had been threatened. At a special police court hearing for the other four defendants, it was decided that their offence of obstructing the police in the execution of their duty was nothing more than might be expected in an ordinary Saturday night brawl, so they were committed to the sessions rather than the assizes and granted bail in return for substantial sureties.

The city buzzed with talk of the forthcoming trial of Franklin. It even coined a new verb: one drunk and disorderly young woman from Farm Street threatened to 'snipe' Sergeant Deakin as he arrested her, and struck him on the ear. In October 1897, the other four appeared before Mr Recorder Dugdale – now celebrating twenty-five years of his recordership – at the Birmingham Quarter Sessions, charged with unlawful assault on P.C.s Snipe and Mead. The court heard that the four had been asked by the police to move on from Hockley Hill. They had done so, although Snipe had taken Colrain into custody opposite St Saviour's Church for bad language. Colrain had fought back and Snipe had used his staff, which enraged the crowd of over seven hundred, according to one estimate, who followed on behind and attacked the policeman. When they reached the corner of Well Street, near the Star public house, someone threw the brick which sent Snipe unconscious to the ground. It was alleged that Colrain kicked Snipe in the head as he lay there and also kicked P.C. Mead's head and neck while he was bending over Snipe.

Snipe's *post mortem* examination had shown that the brick had caught him on the left temple and caused a triple compound fracture. The recorder told the four that it was fortunate for them that that they had no complicity with the man who threw the fatal brick. Their sentence was a warning to them and others. Colrain was sent down for eighteen months' hard labour, the other three for nine months'.

A month later, James Franklin was tried for murder at the Birmingham Assizes. The trial attracted enormous interest and the newspapers reported that the sitting accommodation in the court had been 'snapped up by fashionably-attired ladies'. Franklin was described as 'bullet-headed, with a slight moustache darkening his upper lip and generally thick-set' and so looking 'at least three years older' than his official age of nineteen. The key prosecution witness was again Polly Mullins, the only one of the onlookers to swear that Franklin had thrown the lethal brick. She had been at Snipe's side as he fell 'into her arms on being struck'. Her testimony 'drew a smile of contemptuous incredulity from Franklin in the dock'. On cross-examination, she denied any knowledge of the presence of a man known as 'Cloggy' in the disturbance. Her claim that Franklin was a yard in front of the rest of the crowd was challenged by the defence lawyer, who maintained that before the coroner, she had said that Franklin was at the back.

Harper once again gave evidence that the man responsible was in fact Cloggy Williams. But it was a James 'Chicken' Jones who gave the fullest explanation of what had taken place that day. He had been in the Tramway Stores tavern in Hunter's Lane with Colrain, Cloggy Williams and others. Williams said that a P.C. Holdsworth was outside and that he intended to get his own back, as Holdsworth had previously got him two months in prison. They 'had been drinking all day and were fighting all evening', Jones related. They went out and saw the policeman, thought to be Holdsworth. Cloggy threw the brick. A girl then pulled him away and he and Cloggy walked off along Bridge Street together. He said to Cloggy, 'You have done something now.' Cloggy replied, 'It has not hurt him.' The next afternoon, said Jones, he was setting out to visit his married sister in Bolton, and Cloggy insisted on going with him. At Stafford, he bought a copy of the *Post* and saw that P.C. Snipe was dead. Cloggy accompanied Jones to Bolton and then disappeared. Jones's sister confirmed this in court. It transpired that afterwards she had written to the police, which had led to her brother coming forward. After this convincing story, the prosecution case was no longer thought to have any credibility. Franklin was acquitted, to a loud burst of applause from the gallery, which quickly emptied when Mr Justice Wills angrily ordered the police to bring before him anyone who had taken part.

Birmingham waited for the appearance of the supposed real culprit, Cloggy Williams, a glass beveller by trade who lived at the back of Edward Street, off the Parade. A description and picture were published of him and over 5,000 copies were circulated, but he was nowhere to be found. In fact he was working as a cattle drover, constantly moving around the country in charge of livestock. In January 1898, he finally tramped from Gloucester back to Birmingham to visit his mother, perhaps because he had run out of money. The approaches to her house must have been under surveillance, for he had only just arrived and was heading along Clement Street at about midnight when he was pounced on by a detective sergeant and taken to Kenion Street police station. He was charged but pleaded not guilty. At his first committal, he tried to assume an air of nonchalance as he leaned on the rail and stared round at the court. Later he said that if he had known the policeman was Snipe he would not have thrown the brick for 'a thousand pounds'. He had thought it was a constable called Holdsworth, who had recently left the force. Holdsworth bore a strong general likeness in build, height and complexion to Snipe. Williams, aged twenty, was said to have been an industrious employee for O.C. Hawkes of Bromsgrove Street, but this no longer counted for anything.

George 'Cloggy' Williams was tried at the Birmingham Assizes of March 1898 by the Lord Chief Justice, Lord Russell of Killowen. He was found guilty of manslaughter and sentenced to penal servitude for life. The *Mail* concluded that the members of the Birmingham crowd might not be willing to help the police, but they did not want to see the wrong man punished.

CHAPTER 19

Peace at Last?

THE KILLING of P.C. Snipe was the climax of what the *Mail* called an 'epidemic of ruffianism'. The case caused uproar, and on 26 July 1897 an 'indignation' meeting was held at Smith Street Board School. This was close to the scene of the crime and where, one dinnertime four years before, the headmaster had been assaulted with a buckled belt by a sixteen-year-old as he led other intruders into the playground. One councillor accused the magistrates who lived 'in quiet and peaceful Edgbaston' of being out of touch with 'the habits of the peaky blinder' and being unable to understand 'what peaceable working people suffered at their hands'. Magistrates, he said, were too hard on constables who used their staffs. As the law was interpreted in Birmingham, a constable had to endure being 'half-killed' before he could use it in self-defence, whereas in fact his 'first duty should be to have a good grip on his staff'. The meeting, organised by the Liberal Unionists, or Chamberlainites, of St George's Ward, demanded the lash for ruffians. This was met with a roar of approval that 'seemed to shake the roof', according to the *Mail*. The chairman lamented that 'the reforming influence of philanthropic, educational and religious agencies was lost apparently upon the morally submerged class, popularly known as the peaky blinder – the class that toil not, neither do they spin – whose occupation seemed to be to prove a constant menace to the well-being of peaceable law-abiding people'. An exhibition of peaky weapons picked up in Farm Street included a short, thick piece of wood with thorns sticking out of the lead-headed end and spring-fastened on the other end or handle to ensure a 'firm hold on the wrist'.

Members of the Watch Committee were in agreement. Both the Lord Mayor and Chief Constable Farndale wanted the introduction of flogging to deal with street violence, but the Garotting Act only allowed use of the cat if assault was accompanied by robbery. The Chief Constable said he could do nothing more with the existing strength of the force. The punishment of offenders was too light and flogging was the only way to deal with them. The committee chairman blamed 'plenty of work' for the increase in drunkenness, on the grounds that it gave workers the money to spend on alcohol.

Stipendiary Colmore's supposed weakness in sentencing had come in for criticism before, and while he was away on holiday that August, a meeting was held of the Birmingham justices of the peace to remind them of their powers and guidelines. The chairman, Arthur Chamberlain, Joseph's younger brother, felt that there had been too much leniency by the Bench. He knew that 'the lamb in the dock was different from the lion in the street' and pointed out that far too many recent assaults on Birmingham policemen had been punished by fines. Magistrates had the power to imprison for up to six months in such cases and needed to use it. He reminded them that there should never be a question of fines for assaults on women or the police. One magistrate chimed in with a story of how Charles Henry Street had become so notorious for peaky blinders, especially in Saturday night rows, that six months previously four or five of its shops were untenanted. Now, thanks to some prison sentences, as opposed to fruitless fines, from a 'particularly stringent' member of the Bench, the shops were all tenanted and doing very well.

Statistics showed there had been over one hundred and fifty cases of assault on the police in the previous three months of 1897, but only in about a third of the cases had offenders been imprisoned without the option of a fine. The longest prison sentences had been only four months for assaults on police in D and E divisions and three months in A and C. Longer custodial sentences seemed necessary to many at a time when the criminal law was moving in a more liberal direction. However, in the hot summer of 1897 public debate ranged from the need for compulsory military service, as in Germany, to the inadequacies of a board school education, especially in matters of religion and morals. A letter to the *Post* drew attention to twenty or so street children, 'blossoms of the board school', seen 'fighting for places to scramble up the statue of the late Sir Josiah Mason' in Chamberlain Square. One view was that the public should be armed, another that the police should be armed with garden water syringes.

The three years from 1897 to 1899 saw a much higher number of convictions for police assault than the average, and by 1900 the

Birmingham force had a total of nine officers disabled through assault. In one case, however, policemen were found guilty of unjustified violence towards civilians, which exacerbated an already inflammatory situation. Within the Birmingham police area, Digbeth and Highgate were still the most violent places, and youths in their teens were still the most likely to be involved, with buckled belts and sometimes knives or hammers. The police had to be deployed in force. Five constables had to be sent to Barford Street in June 1900 to repress disorder and arrest two brothers who were at the centre of the mayhem.

The old complaints of Birmingham roughs causing trouble in the surrounding suburbs and villages resurfaced. On the warm Bank Holiday Monday of August 1897 the Cock and Magpie Inn, Warley, near Quinton, became the scene of two clashes between young men and the police on the same day. Four men in their twenties from Stour Street, Birmingham (near Spring Hill) were arrested by the Smethwick force for creating a disturbance at the first inn, then assaulting the landlord of the Beech Tree Inn and finally resisting police arrest in Beech Lanes. The police took the unusual step of getting the Cock and Magpie's licence withdrawn on the grounds that it was a frequent resort of peaky blinders and their 'molls'. Mitchells the brewers appealed on the grounds that the pub was just outside the city's three-mile limit and so was ideal for *bona fide* travellers needing refreshment while out on a Sunday ramble. They argued that the residents were well-accustomed to parties in omnibuses and brakes going along the Hagley Road to the inn on Sundays and returning in high spirits, even if the customers had become less 'aristo-cratic' and were currently 'bell-bottomed and buckle-belted swains'.

One of the features of the boom in the years 1896 to 1899 was the increased frequency of accidents and assaults involving firearms. One of the witnesses in the Snipe case was shot at, though no link was found between the shooting and the trials. Revolvers could be bought from the pawnbroker and were not just carried by those inflamed by sensational literature or by a visit to Buffalo Bill's circus, as the authorities had once tended to think. In his introductory remarks at the assizes of autumn 1897, Mr Justice Wills deprecated not only the gangs but also the cheap-ness of firearms. A revolver could be purchased for as little as a shilling and sixpence. No wonder that a fifteen-year-old was accused of shooting his young lady of sixteen in the leg with such a weapon. The judge recom-mended that children under fifteen who carried revolvers and cartridges should be whipped rather than sent to prison. Toy pistols were also popular and easily available, causing a spate of accidents. One fourteen-year-old boy died in agony from lockjaw after being shot in the backside with a toy revolver during some dinnertime larking at a works in Sheep Street, near Gosta Green.

Mr Recorder Dugdale, in his charge to the Birmingham Grand Jury early in 1898, complimented the skill of Birmingham doctors who had saved two persons' lives. He referred to pistol-carrying and shooting as offences almost as bad as knives among the gangs. In his view, other large towns did not have such a bad state of affairs. Dugdale may have been thinking of two seventeen-year-olds who went to hospital, both with toy pistol bullets in the thigh. One had been shot at in Suffolk Street after a threat from a gang of youths at the World's Fair at Bingley Hall, the city's premier exhibition space, a few evenings beforehand. Their wounds were dressed in the Queen's Hospital, but they were not regarded as serious, and in neither case was the bullet extracted. However it was pointed out that these pistols, although they could be bought without a licence, could penetrate a three-quarter-inch plank at short range and so could easily be fatal. When a policeman in Harborne was nearly hit by the pistol of a youth, the weapon was impounded and the boy fined fifteen shillings with costs.

One thirteen-year-old girl had a bullet in her stomach fired by one of a gang in Rea Street, who insulted her and shot at her as she came out of the court where she lived. Occasionally, the peakies were on the receiving end. In July 1900, a nightwatchman, called Bebbington, was charged with maliciously shooting a peaky called Stack in Bow Street, off Horse Fair. Stack's story was that, as they passed the watchman's house between 11 p.m. and midnight in April, the door flew open and out rushed Bebbington, firing a revolver and hitting Stack in the arm. The defence case was rather different. There had been a great disturbance in the street that night, the Bebbingtons' door had been kicked open and the father had gone out to investigate and had been knocked down unconscious. Bebbington himself had then rushed out, found the young men round his father and drawn his revolver to shoot into the air to call the attention of the police. The weapon had gone off accidentally. Bebbington explained that he owned such a weapon because he was a watchman at premises where there had recently been a burglary. The sergeant who made the arrest said that Stack and his friends belonged to the Bow Street gang of peaky blinders who went about insulting people and kicking up rows. His views were supported by several defence witnesses. The judge asked the jury whether they did not think that Bebbington's story was the more likely of the two. The jury agreed and Bebbington was discharged.

By 1900, the possession of a loaded revolver at the scene of a crime was regarded as incriminating in itself and carried heavy penalties. One young man caught for stealing lead was found also to have a loaded revolver and his sentence escalated to five years' penal servitude. Henry Blakemore, a nineteen-year-old labourer, was arrested for burglary and the policeman found a loaded six-chamber revolver on him, so the magistrate gave him thirteen months. As he was taken down to the cells he called out, 'I'll shoot him when I come out. I'll shoot him as sure as I'm going down these steps.' From the public gallery a woman's voice came loud and clear, 'Cheer up! You do it!'

THE CITY centre was losing population. The future lay with the suburbs. City centre churches and schools saw dwindling numbers of parishioners and pupils, while there was a growing need in outlying areas such as Sparkhill, Saltley and parts of Edgbaston. Some of the slum courts in the centre were being improved; others were just written off as needing demolition. When the roof and back wall of a lodging house, over a century old, collapsed in St Mary's Row, nineteen lodgers were in one room. One man was killed and seven were injured. The coroner recommended that such places should be inspected externally as well as internally. Somehow the courts were not so 'alien' once they became host to cheap Saturday concerts. By the summer of 1899, forty open-air concerts were planned in the poorer parts of the city. However the neglect and the poverty continued to be stark. The Bull Ring Mission took three thousand 'street robins' from the alleys, courts and slums of the city to Sutton Park by train, providing them with a summer treat of breakfast and dinner as well as games and Punch and Judy shows. At Christmas there was a treat for five thousand planned at Bingley Hall.

The importance of the wider area was seen in terms of gangs as well. At New Year, 1900, there was said to be a great increase in fighting on the streets of Oldbury. According to the police, a large number of peakies had formed themselves into the 'Black Gang' and paraded the streets. Street theft by peakies – no longer called highway robbery – was still a problem, and in Bordesley Green the shopkeepers said they were in fear of gangs of thieves living in the neighbourhood whom they were too frightened to prosecute.

Yet Brummies could also laugh at their peaky blinders. Although the *Post* newspaper regretted topical and local allusions in Christmas panto-mimes, audiences enjoyed them hugely. In 1895, *Goody Two Shoes* was put on at the Prince of Wales Theatre in Broad Street, in a tradition of pantomime going back to 1862. The *Post's* arts critic was disappointed to find the 'dainty story of Goody Clearrill, the mistress of the village school and chosen Queen of the May and her noble lover the Duke of Mistymorn interrupted by allusions to the stolen Football Cup, the Iron and Steel Institute, the ill-treated Mason statue, inspectors of school, "peaky blinders" and much more to the same effect.' However, it was added that the author of the show, Mr Anderton, after a long series of successful pantomimes, 'probably understands to a nicety the requirements of his patrons' and that the show could expect a long and successful run.

The term 'peaky blinder' had caught the national imagination. Its arrival in the 1890s had coincided with the scientific discoveries of Pasteur and the Curies. One Manchester newspaper thought that the modern doctor, like the Fat Boy in *Pickwick*, 'do like to make our flesh creep':

Almost every day they find a new kind of bacillus and unchain the ferocious brute to chew up their fellow humans. You can scarcely walk a yard without meeting a gang of peaky blinder microbes ready to commit assault and battery.

The emergence of 'hooliganism' in London after 1894 led rapidly to comparisons between the capital and Birmingham. No longer were educationists glibly claiming to have solved the problem of juvenile gangs, as they had done in the 1870s. The Dean of St Paul's Cathedral naturally wondered whether ruffians from both cities were more likely to be the product of board schools than church schools. The Government School Inspector for Birmingham blamed the so-called five-year system, by which the brightest pupils could leave school after five years' attendance, for the formation of 'the peaky blinder brigade'. The chairman of the School Attendance Committee echoed this view.

'Under the law of the land,' he complained, 'boys had been leaving school before they were old enough to enter the factories and in the interval they graduated in crime at the street-corners.' In this way did the twentieth century launch its debates on the 'boy labour problem'. In Birmingham there was an increasing tendency to use the phrase 'the peaky blinder class' when referring to young criminals of every description. The problem was now seen as one of individuals or a whole socio-economic group rather than of gangs.

The Birmingham police had gained a major advantage from the extension of the borough boundaries in 1891. Before this time, they had been hampered in their work by the existence of half a dozen other police authorities all around the outside of the town: Birmingham gained Balsall Heath, Saltley, Ward End and Harborne, but Quinton remained separate until 1909, and Aston, Handsworth, Erdington, Yardley and Northfield until 1911. With the major extension of the borough's frontiers, effective telephone communication could at last be established between the outskirts and the police headquarters. The suburbs could no longer be used as a safe haven for slogging gangs or a launch-pad for criminal operations in the town centre, and valuable time was saved in detectives no longer having to give evidence or obtain search warrants for the suburbs at the county towns of Warwick, Worcester or Stafford. Prison vans now took prisoners from outside the old borough to Winson Green rather than them having to be led handcuffed through the streets as before. There could be better control of suburban drinking, especially on Sundays, and uniform standards could now be applied to central and suburban cab proprietors. The *Mail* was optimistic about the future of the suburbs: 'Into all these corners of the earth, Birmingham will send its army of detectives, police, School Board officers and health inspectors, and cleanliness, order and tranquillity will prevail.'

There was a sense of the end of an era when Chief Constable Farndale resigned in 1899 from ill-health after being in post since 1882; Superintendent Walker had resigned for similar reasons at Aston in 1898. Farndale received a full pension of £600 per annum while Walker received a gold watch and a purse of gold from the Aston magistrates. At the Aston force, he had trained four hundred constables, eight superintendents, eleven inspectors and twenty-one sergeants in his eighteen years in charge of the division. Dr Griffiths added a word of thanks as an old resident of Aston for Mr Walker's apparent repression of the slogging gangs. Another old man, Alderman White, looking back on fifty years in Birmingham, thought, optimistically, that there had been 'a wonderful improvement in the manners of the people'. The Birmingham Fair, on the Old Peck, had contracted in size and had become dominated by one large proprietor who leased smaller pitches to the other showmen. Yet the crowd was still considerable, with a showman's estimate of 50,000 spectators one Saturday night in June 1898. Slogging on the site was treated like a distant memory.

The *Post* was more pessimistic about the degree of progress which had occurred, concluding that 'during the past decade the refining influences of civilisation have failed to make any deep impression on certain classes of the community'. Its new editor subscribed to the old 'epidemic' view of ruffianism, suggesting that violent street behaviour came and went like outbreaks of measles or cholera, requiring special measures for their extinction, rather like diseases. At one time, he argued, slogging gangs made certain districts intolerable; at another, 'the baiting of policemen is indulged in until repeated sharp punishment brings about a temporary cessation'. However the editor was not naïve enough, even at the dawn of a new century, to think that all Birmingham's problems of law and order were solved, or that 'the exuberant vitality of the hobble-de-hoy' could ever be entirely stifled. At least, he thought, for the time being, slogging was a thing of the past. This might be so, but the playing of pitch and toss in the streets, to which slogging was often linked, was as popular as ever and described still as an 'obligatory amusement'.

Extreme nationalism, called jingoism after a popular music hall song of the 1870s, seemed suddenly to sweep the city as the popular press concentrated everyone's attention on the events of the South African War. Youthful energies were poured into marching, singing and flag-waving, especially as the news dramatically turned from impending disaster to apparently heroic victory in the course of 1900. Pro-Boers, like the author Silas Hocking, came bravely to Birmingham and faced a hard time from the crowd. At Hocking's lecture on 'John Bull in His Best Clothes' at Soho Hill Congregational Church, there were several rows of young men sat at the back of the gallery to protest at whatever he said. Hocking tried to be humorous and non-political, but from the gallery came 'ill-timed interruptions, idiotic exclamations, stamping, laughter and applause'. Afterwards a gang of young men marched up and down Soho Hill waving a flag and singing 'Rule Britannia'.

In May, at the news of the relief of Mafeking, where Baden-Powell's garrison had vigorously withstood a Boer siege for two hundred and seventeen days, Birmingham went into carnival mood. There were improvised processions of people accompanied by every kind of tin trumpet, hooter and concertina. Young men hijacked a cab and drew it through the streets and regarded it as open season for kissing girls. In Aston there were 'gangs of youths and maidens singing and cheering' and the *Mail* reported public houses as having to deal with 'a tremendous rush of custom in the last half-hour before closing time'. When bonfires were lit in the streets – the first in living memory – to burn Kruger, the Boer leader in effigy, the police did not seem to mind. In St George's Street, an Italian street-harmonium player called Dominico Powell was attacked by a woman who had been told that he was Kruger and had come from South Africa.

The city's jingoism was still unabated when the outspoken Liberal MP David Lloyd George came again to speak in Birmingham. He had received a rowdy reception on the Old Peck in 1890, but this time it was not just the drink lobby that he had angered. He had become the most prominent challenger to Joseph Chamberlain, now at the pinnacle of his political career as Colonial Secretary. Lloyd George virtually accused the Chamberlain family, integral to Birmingham business as well as to its representation in Parliament, of being war profiteers. In view of what were regarded as calumnies against the city's premier dynasty, Lloyd George was unwise to agree to address a meeting at the Town Hall on 18 December 1901.

The meeting predictably triggered a riotous demonstration in the old tradition of Aston Lower Grounds, on a monumental scale. A crowd stormed the platform and broke up the meeting. One person died, twenty-eight civilians were injured and ninety-seven policemen reported hurt. The Town Hall was extensively damaged and Lloyd George, famously, had to be smuggled out of the city in a helmet and cape, disguised as a policeman. Once again the two sides hotly denied responsibility. Unionists blamed the Liberals for enflaming Birmingham opinion by holding the meeting in the first place. Liberals replied that their motives had been misrepresented in the local press and that fake tickets for the meeting had been circulated as well as a forged telegram giving details of Lloyd George's whereabouts. Sandwich-board men, they said, had been going round all day before the meeting, calling on people to assemble at the Town Hall to defend the King, the Government and Mr Chamberlain and to denounce the 'Brum Boers'.

The young man killed was Harold Ernest Curtin, who was standing in the crowd which had stayed outside the Town Hall while the meeting was being abandoned inside. Stones were thrown which broke street lamps and some of the hall windows, revolvers were fired and some tried to find out if Lloyd George was still inside by breaking down a door using a scaffolding pole. As the lights went out in the hall, and a snowstorm gathered strength outside, penny crackers were heard to go off. Then there was a warning shout from the crowd. The police had had enough. They drew their truncheons and proceeded to charge the mob, which fled before them out of Victoria Square, down Colmore Row and as far as Snow Hill. Curtin got separated from his friends, was caught by a baton near the Bluecoat School and fell to the ground, perhaps hitting his head on a kerbstone as he did so. He died in the General Hospital with a fractured skull. Doctors were in disagreement as to whether a ragged wound behind his right ear could have been caused by a fall on the kerb or not. The verdict of the coroner's jury was manslaughter, but no one had taken the policeman's number, and in spite of a Watch Committee inquiry the incident left a trail of bitterness.

It proved Birmingham was still capable of a grand political turnout, if no longer for a two-sided battle of 1884 proportions. But what of slogging? The *Mail*, perhaps overwhelmed by the heat of the summer of 1900, perhaps also a little drunk on jingoism and ignoring the numbers of those still attacked with buckled belts in the city centre, concluded that whereas some time before, slogging gangs had been rampant all over the city, it was now only in Garrison Lane – home of the brickies – where 'anything like a reign of terror' still obtained. One letter to the *Mail* in July 1900 claimed that 'Park Street at its worst was a paradise in comparison'. In the Garrison Lane area there was a gang of lads robbing people and carts in the streets and bricks were being thrown at people passing on foot down the Lane from Small Heath, while on Sundays youths broke into the brickyards, damaged machinery and pushed carts, barrows, ladders and tables down the sandholes.

Yet even in this area, football was increasingly popular. The game was still outlawed in the street, but it had been taken up by the schools, encouraged by George Kenrick's important gift of playing fields on the Pershore Road near Pebble Mill in 1893. By the late 1890s, a cul-de-sac off Garrison Lane was used for training purposes by the Tilton Road Board School team, twice a week after afternoon school, in spite of complaints from other footpath users. This was a new school opened with over a thousand places in 1891. Football was banned in the school playground, but the teaching staff subscribed from their own pockets to hire a field two miles away in the Yardley Road. One year the team won the Schools' League Challenge Shield and in another reached the final of the Aston Villa Cup competition. In the future, all schools would look to the provision of equipment and playing fields, not just Indian clubs and dumbbells for gymnastics. Already, successful local footballers had their portraits drawn for the newspapers and were the new youth heroes. Tilton Road, as Kelynge Street, had been the home of Henry Lightfoot, the primordial peaky; soon it would become the home not only of a successful board school football team, but also of Birmingham (later City) Football Club.

In spite of eventual victory in the South African War, the jingo euphoria would die away and the people of Birmingham would face the Edwardian Depression, although the steady increase in the success of the Jewellery Quarter would continue up to the First World War and the city would not fall out of love with the Chamberlains. The west window in the Great Hall of the new Victoria Courts in Corporation Street showed fifteen of Birmingham's most famous crafts. Was there less tension and rivalry between them, now that mechanization and the spread of bigger factories were undermining some of their independence and status? Would gang fighting also die away? Like coining, it had become a subject to be represented on the Birmingham stage. However this was not necessarily a sign that gang fighting was a thing of the past, as London hooliganism had been fed by the London music halls. In 1900 a play called *The Rich and Poor of London* was shown at the Queen's Theatre, Snow Hill. One of its chief attractions was the fight with revolvers and bludgeons between 'members of the Hooligan gang'.

The word 'gang' is hard to pin down and difficult to define. Both the word and the phenomenon have been influenced by fashion. Some would say that they have been the creations of fashion and of journalists; the word was certainly used more often to imply a group rather than some kind of organisation. The term which had been used to describe every conceivable group of people in the early 1870s had gone out of fashion by the late 1890s. The *Mail* hardly used 'gang' in the years 1896 to 1899, although 'ruffianism' seemed to take its place. At the height of the fashion for gangs in the early 1870s and again in the late 1880s, youths were anxious to be identified as members of 'a gang'. Every gang in Birmingham sought the accolade of recognition as '*the* slogging gang'. Policemen and reporters were eager to follow on – or, as some would say, lead. At one point, by emphasising gang membership or leadership, policemen as witnesses often seemed to be trying to obtain the harshest sentence available for those they had captured at such personal cost, from magistrates who were sometimes difficult to convince. As the years passed, however, the press spotlight turned away from rough youth engaged in turf wars and exhibitions of toughness, and such activities were denied the oxygen of publicity. Sports news was already proving a more popular and less controversial way of reporting the exploits of local youth and, no doubt, of selling newspapers. At the same time, 'slogging' was increasingly limited to use as a sporting term to describe coarse forms of boxing or batting in cricket.

There had been many sorts of street gangs in Victorian Birmingham. They had ranged from gangs of schoolboys in their dinner-time, to gangs of young men of the same occupation or area such as the Gun Quarter, through gangs that celebrated a particular street such as Charles Henry Street, to the more amorphous gangs of Aston and Bordesley. The Aston slogging gang had various incarnations based on different parts of Aston and showed a surprising willingness to include fighters from St Stephen's and Duddeston who might have been expected to have been their mortal enemies. Streets of deprivation or martial renown, such as Park Street or Allison Street, would still be able to muster gangs in quantity. City centre roughs continued to catch the headlines for terrible deeds. Yet it was towards the suburbs that sloggers had been driven and behind them marched the slow but relentless boots of the Birmingham bobby.

Slogging represented an era of Birmingham's history that was passing away by 1900, although many of the elements which had contributed to it would continue. An area like Garrison Lane, a long way from any police station, would still be the scene of 'pandemonium' most evenings in summer 1901, and some old traditions continued to flourish: the *Mail* noted that pitch and toss was as popular as ever, while stone-throwing too would endure.[16] The new century demanded a new vocabulary, and 'hooliganism' was, for a while, in vogue. But the sheer scale and intensity of the sloggers' pitched battles would rarely be

---

16 The monumental sculptor, John Protheroe recalls the expectant glee of watching boys when he restored the outstretched right palm and fingers to the mutilated public marble statue of Thomas Attwood in the 1960s. 'We'll soon 'ave those fingers off', remarked one of them. The statue, again badly mutilated, is now in store.

repeated. And within a decade or so, the dark shadow of a far greater conflict loomed over Europe. The toughness and rowdiness exhibited by the sloggers had been at one time compared by the *Post* to the beer-guzzling and duelling of German university fighting clubs. In 1914, the heirs of the two traditions would be tested on the field of battle in the bloodiest of circumstances, and the old days of street fights would fade even from memory.

In understanding the defeat of the sloggers, punishment and police organisation must be set alongside schooling and youth provision. Whether a decline in publicity from the local press played a part is less clear. At least they seemed to see things differently. Ruffianism, always a popular term for street violence by groups or individuals, was no longer seen as a problem of gangs. 'Peaky' behaviour, too, was increasingly seen as individual rather than collective. For youths, gang confrontation, especially between those in their late teens, may have become less fashionable. There would be other spectacles than local drunks resisting arrest. Other forms of leisure activity, such as football, brought more lasting satisfaction and much less risk. Toughness would no longer be measured by groups brawling and throwing stones at each other; fighting could find other outlets, such as boxing. Gang criminality would take new forms, such as organised intimidation and crime on racecourses.

The focus on law and order with a new chief constable, the long-serving and later knighted Charles Haughton Rafter, an increasing police force and a spreading number of police stations would aim to instil the city with a greater sense of order on the streets. Youth was higher up the agenda of the ruling classes than ever before and would continue to receive an increasing amount of attention, not least in the Edwardian Children's Act and the introduction of juvenile courts. The agencies for dealing with youth were basic but were growing and no longer overwhelmed. It would not all be plain sailing – the Kyrle Society found difficulties with its annual summer camps – but such developments would put a squeeze on gang culture.

In due course, Birmingham would happily choose to forget its slogging tradition altogether. The view of the Chamberlainite consensus was that the new city had been cleaned up physically and morally and already faced a great future as the hub not only of England but of the whole Empire. From that perspective, the violence of the past should only be remembered with a shudder or a joke. Only the evocative term 'peaky blinder' would continue to resonate. The progressive enlargement of the city would increase the difference between territories, but also increase the distance between them. Turf loyalty would find a wide range of alternative forms of expression. Social homogeneity had already snuffed out most elements of ethnic violence. Yet personal followings would continue to be important, and groups with the power to bully and create mayhem would continue to emerge, while issues of masculinity, adolescent peer pressure and group competition would continue to be problematic. Gangs had flourished in Victorian Birmingham – and would, in time, return.

Acknowledgements

MY INTEREST IN street gangs was first aroused on an M.Ed. course at the Youth Studies Centre of the University of Manchester in 1977-80, and I am ever grateful to its director, Chris Murray.

This book has emerged from eight years of part-time and eighteen months of full-time research into the Birmingham sloggers and other gangs. I need to thank my ex-colleagues and especially Jason Smith for selflessly covering my house, Rees Court, at Bedstone College, Shropshire, while I was doing some of the research on occasional Wednesday evenings.

I have relied from the start on the services of Birmingham Central Library's excellent local history section and archives. More recently I have depended on the Special Collections at the Elsevier Reading Room, John Rylands Library, Deansgate, Manchester, part of Manchester University, as well as the Cambridge University Library, where Thomson Gale's Nineteenth Century British Library Newspapers Online has been an invaluable resource and has allowed progress to accelerate and links to be made which manually would have taken a lifetime. When working at home, the Birmingham History Forum online has always helped me regain my bearings. The Ancestry Library edition of the censuses, by courtesy of the National Archives, accessed through Manchester Central and Bury Libraries, has helped to identify some of the characters more clearly.

One side of my family was once all Brummy or Handsworth, but sadly nearly all of them have now passed on. So I am particularly grateful to John and Pat Protheroe, also with Brum in their blood, for some correction and confirmation. Dilip Desai has kept me open-mouthed while describing his early experiences in Nechells. Alan and Linda Hughes, Greg Anderson, Adrian Dixon, Jonathan Parsons, Martin Hopkinson, Don Robinson, Ken Smith, Les Johnson, John Bisson, Ken Brown, Mike Winstanley and others have helped and encouraged in various ways.

On the academic side, Andrew Davies of Liverpool University, with whom I have a common interest in scuttlers, has given friendly advice, and he alerted me to his article on James Harper and Emily Pimm. Carl Chinn of Birmingham University has shown typical generosity with his material. Dave Cross of the West Midlands Police Museum has kindly provided photographs. I owe a debt too to the late Barbara Weinberger of Warwick University for her work on the gangs of Birmingham in the early 1870s, although some of our conclusions are very different.

Peter Walsh has been a most patient and helpful publisher and editor, with an instinct for the relevant and a great source of sound advice and judicious wording.

Finally I am very grateful to all members of my family, especially my wife, Maryse, for her help with checking the text, assisting with the maps and being always an encouraging presence.

As they all say, the faults are mine, which is as ever true.

Locations of Gangs/Street Groups

1872

'The Slogging Gang': Cheapside, St Martin's; Gun Quarter, St Mary's;
  Livery Street, St Paul's
Sheep Street, Bishop Ryder's, St Mary's
Hall Street, Jewellery Quarter, St Paul's
Bordesley

1873

Aston (Clifford Street, Lozells)

1874

Suffolk Street, Market Hall/Bow Street, St Thomas'
Park Street, St Bartholomew's
Milk Street, St Bartholomew's
Loveday Street/Price Street, St Mary's
Allison Street, St Bartholomew's
Barn Street, St Bartholomew's

1876

Glory Hole, Hope Street, St Martin's

1877

Spring Hill, All Saints'
Cape Hill, Smethwick

1883

Ten Arches, Aston

1886

Wainwright Street, Aston
Charles Arthur Street and Nechells Green
Parade, Sand Pits, St Paul's

1887

Farm Street, St George's

1888

Highgate Street, Deritend
Great Barr Street, St Bartholomew's
Nova Scotia Street, St Bartholomew's
Park Street, St Bartholomew's

1889

Whitehouse Street, Aston
Milk Street, St Bartholomew's
Charles Henry Street, Deritend
Sparkbrook, Bordesley
The Square, Ladywood
Allison Street, St Bartholomew's
Price Street, Gun Quarter, St Mary's

1890

Peaky blinders, Adderley Street, Bordesley

1893

Cliveland Street, St Mary's
Weaman Street, Gun Quarter, St Mary's
Park Street, St Bartholomew's
Barford Street, St Martin's

1894

Spring Hill, All Saints'
Cape Hill, Smethwick
Adams Street, St Matthew's, Nechells
Moorsom Street, St Stephen's

1895

Great Barr Street, St Bartholomew's
Lichfield Road, Aston
Park Lane, Aston

1896

Ten Arches, Aston

1900

Bow Street, St Thomas'
Garrison Lane, St Bartholomew's

Other streets referred to are Navigation Street, Farm Street, Summer Lane, Lee Bank Road and Bromsgrove Street, and other areas include Duddeston, Brookfields, Hockley, Lozells, Islington and Bordesley Green.

Notes

Introduction

Briggs, Bird, Barnsby, Cherry

Chapter 1: The Midland Metropolis

Bird, Cherry, Brigggs, Timmins, Reid on decline of St Monday, P.
Morris;
newspaper refs: BDM 30/5/92, 28/1/99, BDG 23/9/73;
forgers Hull Packet & Advertiser 5/9/09; Booth: Jackson's Oxford Journal
    4/4/12, Morning Chronicle 4/8/12, BDP Notes & Queries 31/5/71,
    Derby Mercury 13/8/12, B.Gazette 10/8/12, J's OJ 5/3/08 & 16/4/08,
    Ipswich Journal 22/8/12, Gentlemen's Magazine Apl 1812; Griffiths:
    BDP 1/8/62; 13/4/59; 31/10/62, 6 & 15/11/62, 29/10/62,12/1/63,
    The Times 7&12/1/63;
coiners BDP 16/9/72; Hull Packet 15/6/13 & 31/8/13; Glasgow Herald
    19/2/49; Daily News 30/10/51; BDP 24/1/60; 10 & 13/5/84; BDM
    12/2/90.

Chapter 2: The Fighting Tradition

McConville, Flinn, Chinn, Showell, Tyrrell, Behagg;
newspaper refs: election roughs BDP 25/7/67; Irish incidents 3/8/60,
    8/7/62, 7/11/70, BDM 13/6/71; Murphy: BDP 17&18/6/67, 21,23
    &25/11/67; ethnic groups BDM 5/1/97; BDP 9/2/92; BDM12/11/89,
    BDP 18/4/64;
prize-fighting 27/5/84, B.Journal 3/9/31, 30/11/31; Brettle BDM
    10/4/72; Highand BDP 8/10/81; Greenfield internet and BDG
    11/7/95; Ireland etc BDP 24/2/77; BDM 17/9/87; 11/7/84 from
    G.H.Osborne newscuttings B.Central Library Internet; street fights

BDP 25/8/68, 26/12/94; 12/6/67, BDG 27/10/75; BDP 9/10/95; 29/12/74; Shustoke 22/10/72,1/3/73; pubs BDM 16/5/71; 10/1/77; Swan Pool BDP 3,4&28/2/68; children BDM 5/5/71; BDP 4/6/66; BDG 23/1/74.

Chapter 3: The Sloggers' Environment

Barnsby, Showell, Timmins, Skipp, Thorne, Cherry, Flinn, Developing Birmingham, Mannions, Chinn on Streets, P&P, Bird;

newspaper refs: reapers BDM 28/8/72; trades: 10/8/75, BDP 20&21/12/75; BDM 18/7/96; 17/4/88; Icknield school 12/12/96; dilapidation 8/6/75; BWeekly Post 23/10/69, BDM 3/5/71, 28/12/72; Pritchett BDG 10/6/73; BDP 31/5/64, 21&27/10/64; 15/8/62, BWP 11/6/70; BDP 21/6/59, 15/1/63; 9/9/59, 15/8/60, 17/6/73; child prostitution BDP13/1/93; BDM19/2/73, BDP 28/10/79; 29/4/63; Langford BDM 3/10/89, BDP 21/3/59, St Bartholomew's 9/12/63, 14/4/64, 28/9/66; BDM 16/6/75; Bishop Ryder's 12/11/74; BDP 6/9/81, BDM 8/7/89; soup kitchens BDP 7/1/91; Ladywood 30/10/73; Aston 30/7/66, 9/2/71; brickyards BDM 6/9/72, 23/9/89; Smethwick 19/6/72.

Chapter 4 Youth Gangs

Briggs, Barnsby, Tyrrell, Chinn on betting;

newspaper refs: juvenile justice BJournal 7/6/45, BDP 7/1/74, 14/5/74, 4/4/77,11/9/69, trams BDM 21/9/86, 25/6/88, 23/1/90; Park Street BDP17/11/74; Cannon Hill 23/9/74, 11/9/74; Sullivan18/12//74; New Street BDM 13/5/72, 3/6/89, BDP18/10/80; Bearwood BDM 11/8/90, Gravelly Hill 31/3/96, 27/3/1900; fast fellows BDP 14/11/60, 4/10/62; bonfire night 10/11/76;

juvenile crime 30/5/59, 9/8/59; 31/8/93; 1/7/74; 22/10/74; 3/4/69; 23/1/74, 'regulators' BDM 6/11/96; Mails 21/1/74; rape BDP 28/2/72; crime rate 28/7/76; 12/2/73; betting 3/7/84, 8/3/59; pubs BDM1/2/75,BDP15&16/3/75,21/4/75,4/6/75;street corner16/4/77, 25/2/79; Gold 28/6/79; Russell 7 &9/8/79.

Chapter 5: The Origins of Slogging

Showell, Dent, Chinn on Irish, P.Davis;

newspaper refs: BDP 18/4/64, 26/2/76; BDM19/6/79, BDP 7/6/93; bailiffs BDM 25/11/71, police 22/7/69, 22/6/74; boatmen BDP16/7/77, 25/10/77; fatality 26/3/92;

Benacre BDM 30/4/70; definition BDG 23/9/73;

post-Murphy riots BDP 7&18/6/69, BDM 16-19/3/72; early slogging BDP 19/7/71,15/5/74, 27/12/73, 17/11/71; BDM 8/4/72; BDP 1 & 3/4/73; BDM, BDG &BDP 9 & 10/4/72; Melson BDG 11/4/72; Morris BDP 29/1/68, BDM 29/4/72, BDP31/4/72; 2/9/70, BDM14/10/70, BDP 13/4/70, BDM 27/2/72, 28/7/73, Lozells 15/5/72, Watery Lane BDP18/11/70, BDM1/6/72, licensing 20/8/72, Park Street BDP 17/9/72.

Chapter 6: The First Peak

Gillis, Chinn, Whates;

newspaper refs: BDP 1 & 11/4/73, BDM 24/3/73, 30/4/73; 1& 3/4/73; BDP 23/3/71, 15/5/73, 7/3/74; BDM 7/5/73; Cook BDP 18/6/73, BDM 1/7/73; 24/6/73, 2& 17/7/73, BDP 7/8/73; BDM 20 & 22/9/73, BDG 23/9/73, BDM1/10/73; BDP 26/9/73, 16 & 18/10/73; BDM 7/1/74; BDP 11/9/73, 18/11/73, BDM 19/11/73; BDP26/8/73, 17/7/73, 8/4/74; Kirkham BDM 18/2/74, BDG 9/7/74; BDP 9/5/74, 25/2/79; 6/8/74; Milk BDG 21/4/74, weapons BDP 27/11/67; Roach Manchester Times 1&8/7/71, BDP 18/7/71, 12/9/74; 15/1/74; BDM 13/3/74; Gosta Green BDP 3/8/82; Crook BDG 24/4/74; BDM 28/4/74, 7/7/74, BDG 3/7/74.

Chapter 7: The Bordesley Riot

Chinn on Irish;

newspaper refs:BDP, BDM & BDG 14&23/9/74, 15/7/74, 31/7/74; 25/8/74, 7&8/9/74; BDP 22/4/75, 18/9/74, 19/12/74; BDM 26/9/74; 9/10/74; 22/9/74; 6& 20/10/74; 3/11/74; Sparkbrook BDP 3/12/74; Allison 9/1/75.

Chapter 8: Death in Navigation Street

Reilly, Showell, Weinberger;

newspaper refs: Bayliss BDP 7/1/74, 28/2/74, 14/3/74; beats12/7/76; Lines 7-13/7/75; 30/3/75, 13/1/86; 28/7/75; 26/2/77, 12/6/78; BDM 30/3/75.

Chapter 9: Other Gang Crime

Pearson, Reilly;

newspaper refs: sharpers BDP 16/12/93; 1/2/93; 11&17/65; poachers 22/8/60, 19/1/74;

burglars 20/12/75,11/5/58; 28/6/62, Manchester Guardian 14/6/62, BDP 30/6/62, 1/7/62, 12&13/8/62, 29/9/62;

garrotters 26/12/62; 10/2/59; 22/3/58; 17& 23/3/59; 21/6/59; 29/12/70,12/5/75, 3/9/75,20/7/75; BDM 3/7/73, 1/8/89, 16/11/77; 17/4/72; BDP 20/12/75, 30/11/87,3/4/89,22/11/89; BDM 21/12/97; BDP 29/6/94.

Chapter 10: The Great Depression

Barnsby, Cherry, Bunce, Chinn on housing, Weinberger, Reilly, Ward;

newspaper refs: BDP 13/11/75; BDM18/11/74; 6/11/83; 4/12/74, 25/1/75, BDG 23/3/75, BDM 24/6/75, 23/10/75; 11/4/76, 11&12/7/76, 29/7/76; 27/2/77; BDP 15/10/77, 25/2/79, 6/8/79; 14/5/78; 24/2/80; election roughs 1/4/80, Reynolds News 1/7/83, BDP 7/11/84, 2-6/3/85; 6/7/80,18/8/81; 28/2/82,12/4/82.

Chapter 11: The Castle Bromwich Disturbance

Barnsby;

newspaper refs: BDM 20/12/87, 2 & 12/6/88; 31/3/84; 12/5/85, waifs BDG 9/4/88, 23/9/85, 5/5/86, Castle Bromwich BDM,BDP&BDG 15-16, 22-27/3/86, 25/5/86; bayonets BDM 15/3/86; slogging King Edward's BAC 10/12/87;

S.Army BDM 5/4/87,16/3/88, BDP 30/4/88; Old Peck 7/5/90, 8/1/91, 26/3/90; 30/9/89.

Chapter 12: The Aston Sloggers

Ward;

newspaper refs: enquiry BDP 21/12/88; Dan BDP 6&28/6 & 4/7/82; Whateley 18/2/85; collection BAC 28/8/86; BDM15/6/98; Ten Arches BDP 17/5/83; Park Road BDM 20-21/7/86; Rocky Lane 17/8/86, BDP 18/8/86; 11/12/86; BAC 2/10/86, AT 29/6/89, BAC 9/10/86, 4/12/86; Read BDM 17/6/87, 8/7/87, BDP 1/8/87, BDM

24/4/88, 12/6/88; Emery 22/8/88; Husselbee BDP 5/6/89; Frith BDM 21/12/88; Hands14/6/89; Greening 25/2/89, BDP 15/3/94; Casey 20/3/89, 18/10/87; Deveridge 20/6/88, 10/11/91; Simpsons 27/6/93, 21/4/92, Guy 31/7/89, Betts BDM 27/1/88, 31/8/88, 3/10/88, BDP 24/10/90; Moorsom 9/7/91; Lloyd George 23/6/90; Hartley 9/3/91.

Chapter 13: Mob Law

Chinn;

newspaper refs: Joyce BDG 23/11/86, BDP 6/3/91; petition BDM 20/5/87; 27/6/87; 22/10/87; Farm 15/11/87; strike 17/4/88; Highgate 27/1/88; Cox BDP 2/12/89; fashion BDM 9/5/87; Nova Scotia 4&5/5/88, BDP 11/9/89; Milk 7/5/88; Mail 5/5/88; 11/7/88; Oxford 31/10/88, Cosier 13/6/89, 11/11/93; Legge 27/2/89; Granville BDM 30/7/89; Harper BDP 15/6/89, 17/3/90; Allison BDM 10/9/89, 2/10/89, 20/5/99; Price BDP 14/7/85, 18/1/89, 29/7/90; Taroni 9/6/92; Cherry 19/6/1900;

school strikes BDM 17/10/89, 27-29/3/90, 11/4/90

Chapter 14: Police in Trouble

Reilly;

newspaper refs: BDP 4/8/74; 6/4/77; Daniels 31/8/87; Wragge 25/6/73; Cox BDM 7/11/98; 'calling up' BDP 3/5/76; Smith 20/8/74; Beak 24&27/3/91, 7 & 18/4/91; Jones 24/6/73; Heritage 1/4/74; Hill BDM 23/12/74, Price BDP 18/2/95; Hession 10/3/1900; Others 14/4/93, 28/6/90; Connolly BDM 8/11/98.

Chapter 15: Gangs at Play

D.Reid, Dunning etc, Brown and Brittle;

internet resources for Jenny Hill, Vesta Tilley, Birmingham Zulus;

newspaper refs: theatre: Ward BDP 28/10/76; Moseley 2/11/92; Cooper BDM 10/6/89; theatre 10/11/71, BDP 13/9/71; 20/2/73; Wilkes 5, 6,10&12/3/73;6/7/75; Holt 25/3/73, 11/4/73; Probert BDM 6/7/74, BDP 27/10/74; 2/12/76; Hill 30/10/93, 27/9/82, 24/12/87; Welch 25/12/86; blackmail 24–29/2/80, 29/1/89; Whitehouse BDM 25/2/89; Hyde BDP 9,17&18/4/90, 6&11/8/90; Danby 9/5/93, 7/7/93; Giblin BDM 15/4/95; Kemp 3/5/98; Wolverhampton BDG 25/8/99;

football: BDM 7/11/98, BDG 11/5/85, BDP 19/10/85, BDM 10/10/88, 25/11/89, 21/3/92, 22/4/95, 21/3/98, 18/3/86, 26/11/1900, 13/10/1900, 18/3/92.

Chapter 16: The Peaky Blinders

Newspaper refs: Style BDP 15/10/90; B Weekly Post, 3/4/1936, Hands BDP 13/9/93; Small Heath 26/4/89; Eastwood BDM 24/3/90, BDP 29/5/90; Washwood 18/3/93; Gavin BDM 3/9/88; Lightfoot BDP 3/12/95; molls BDM 19/11/98,12/1/99, 16/12/98, 29/11/98; Mansell 9/2/91, 13/3/91; Park 14/3/89; Digbeth 11&12/4/90; Pimm BDP 4/8/91, 24/11/91, 26/1/86; Onions BDM 18/11/89; 21/1/90, 16/4/90; Watch 22& 23/4/90; 8/7/90; police divisions 26/4/90, Butterworth BDP 2/9/86; 28/1/88,12/4/90, 10/5/90, 9/7/91 & 1/8/91; Davis BDM 20/6/90; Riley BDP 25/4/90, 24/3/91, 14/4/91; Bond 15/9/91; Bromsgrove BDM 29/4/91; Bashford BDP 4/4/91; Berrow 31/10/92; Hockley 28/3/93; Bordesley 27/12/92; revolver BDM 5-7/5/92; Simpsons BDP 19&20/5/91, 27/6/93; Gilhooleys 21/4/91, 12/5/91; 9/2/92, 4/1/95; Farmer 23/6/90, 22&23/3/92, BDM17/5/97; Lupin BDP 2/11/92; Heneage BDM 26/6/93; Cleveland BDP 2/8/93; Surr 25/2/90, 30/5/93; death 4/3/92; police16/6/92, 25/2/92, 6/11/94.

Chapter 17: The Knife

Macilwee;
newspaper refs: chivier BDM 11/4/90, stabbings BDP 14/10/91, 2/12/92; Digbeth tragedy 4/2/90,26/1/94,17&19/3/94,3/4/94; 4/11/91, 20/1/94; Gallagher 22/10/89, 17/10/92, 12/4/93, 24/4/94; Giblin 14/2/82, 3/4/83, 15-17/4/95; Kelly 27/3/95, 3/4/95; Latham 30/9/95, 10&11/12/95; Gould 19/9/93, 1/11/93; William 4/9/94; 40 Thieves 23/3/92, 17/1/91, 25/12/94; Cook 5/9/93,2/1/94, Soho Villa18/9/94; Brampton 6/2/94; Hodgetts 17/1/95; Nyland, 11/4/94; Barn 17/4/95; Simpsons 3/12/95.

Chapter 18: Honours Even?

Barnsby, Bird, Reilly, Thrasher, A.Davies;
newspaper refs: Ansell BDP 18/1/95; Cheapside 18/4/95; Cuson

29/10/95; Lightfoot 3/12/95; flutes etc16/1/96; 6/3/96, 22/4/97; Wills 14/12/97, 25/2/98; Watch 1/4/96; noise 1/1/97; rules 8/5/96; Grosvenor 17/3/97; Ladywood 30/4/97; Heath Street 28/8/97; Green 24/8/97; Hooligan 24/8/94 ; Aston31/8/88; Glasby 3/6/95, BDP 24/12/95; Bayliss BDM 27/4/97; Thatched BDP 3/7/88, Welcome 26/3/95, 9/4/95; Kyrle BDM 10/7/89 ; Pinchard 17/11/96, 1/6/97, 19/11/96, Copestick 12/2/97; P.S.E.23/11/96; St Catherine's BDP 24/4/94 ; Vauxhall BDM 19/2/97; reputation 20/2/97; Snipe BDP 22 & 26-28/7/97; 4 & 12-14 & 19/8/97;14/10/97,17/12/97; 29/1/98, 10/2/98, BDM 17-19/3/98.

Chapter 19: Peace at Last?

Ward, Pearson, Reilly;

newspaper refs: BDP 16/2/93; BDM 20/7/97, meeting 27/7/97, void BDP 12/8/97, statistics 27/7/97; letter 5/8/97, Barford 30/6/1900; Cock BDM 4/8/97; Hagley 26/8/97; witness 2/8/97; revolvers 14/12/97,18/7/96; 6/1/98,12/1/98, BDG 17/8/99; Bebbington BDP 30/7/1900, 20/1/1900, Blakemore 1/5/1900; slums BDM 26/5/99, 4/8/99, 31/5/99, 17/9/99; Oldbury BDP 2/1/1900, Bordesley 7/3/1900; pantomime 27/12/95; bacillus Manchester Times 24/6/98, 5 years Newcastle Weekly Courant 20/8/98, BDP 2/7/1900; extension 4/1/88; Farndale BDM 30/5/99, BDP 29/5/00; Walker 9/9/98, Peck 15/6/98; pessimism 2& 14/7/1900, 5/10/97; War BDM 27/3/1900, Hocking BDP19/5/1900, Mafeking 21/5/1900, Aston BDM 19/5/1900, 3/7/1900; Curtin Times 21&24/12/1901; Garrison BDM 13 & 14/7/1900; Kenrick BDP 27/7/93, Tilton BDM 26/11/98; Victoria 7/11/90; Hooligan BDP 5/61900, Garrison BDM 10/7/1901, Germany BDP 11/5/91, Kyrle 3/8/00.

SOURCES

Newspapers: including
Birmingham Journal
Aris's Birmingham Daily Gazette (BDG)
Birmingham Daily Post (BDP)
Birmingham Daily Mail (BDM)
Birmingham and Aston Chronicle (BAC)

Aston Times (AT)
Others: The Times
Daily News
The New York Times

Birmingham City Archives: Watch Committee Minutes (quoted from news reports)
Census returns: 1861, 1871, 1881, 1891, 1901

Selected Bibliography

G.C.Allen, *The Industrial Development of Birmingham and the Black Country, 1860-1927*, London, 1929.

J.E.Archer, 'Men behaving badly? masculinity and the uses of violence, 1850-1900' in S.D'Cruz, *Everyday Violence in Britain, 1850-1950: Gender and Class*, Pearson Education Ltd, 2000.

ed. Peter Bailey, *Music Hall; the business of pleasure*, Open University Press, 1986.

George J.Barnsby, *Birmingham Working People: A History of the Labour Movement In Birmingham, 1650-1914*, Integrated Publishing Services, Wolverhampton, 1989.

C.Behagg, 'Secrecy, Ritual and Folk Violence: The Opacity of the Workplace in the First Half of the Century' in ed. R.D.Storch, *Popular Culture and Custom in Nineteenth-Century England*, 1982.

Vivian Bird, *Portrait of Birmingham*, Robert Hale, Ldn 2nd edn, 1974.

ed. David Bradby, Louis James and Bernard Sharratt, *Performance and Politics in Popular Drama*, Cambridge Uni Press 1980, inc. Douglas A.Reid, 'Popular theatre in Victorian Birmingham' pp 65 -89.

B.Bramwell, 'Public space and local communities: the example of Birmingham, 1840-80', in eds. G.Kearns and C.W.J.Withers, *Urbanising Britain: essays on class and community in the nineteenth century*, Cambridge University Press, 1991.

Asa Briggs and C.Gill, *History of Birmingham, Vol II Borough and City, 1860-1939*, Oxford, 1952.

A.Briggs, *Victorian Cities*, Odhams Press 1963, Pelican Books 1968; *Victorian Things*, B.T. Batsford 1988;

Danny Brown and Paul Brittle, *Villains: The Inside Story of Aston Villa's Hooligan Gangs*, Milo Books, 2006.

J.T.Bunce, *History of the Corporation of Birmingham*, Birmingham, 1885.

Gordon E.Cherry, *Birmingham: A Study in Geography, History and Planning*, John Wiley & Sons, Chichester, 1994.

C.Chinn, *They Worked All Their Lives: Women of the Urban Poor in England, 1880-1939*, Manchester, 1988; *Better Betting with a Decent Feller: bookmaking, betting and the British Working Class, 1750-1990*, Harvester Wheatsheaf, Hemel Hempstead, 1991; *Birmingham: The Great Working City*, University of Birmingham and Birmingham City Council, 1994; *Poverty amidst prosperity: the urban poor in England, 1834-1914*, Manchester UP, 1995; '"Sturdy Catholic emigrants": the Irish in early Victorian Birmingham' in eds R.Swift and S.Gilley, *The Irish in Victorian Britain: the Local Dimension*, Four Courts Press, Dublin, 1999; *Homes for People: Council Housing and Urban Renewal in Birmingham, 1849-1993*, Brewin, 1999; *Brum and Brummies*, Brewin, 2000; *Birmingham Irish. Making our Mark*, Birmingham Library Services, 2003; *The Streets of Birmingham*, 4 vols, Brewin Books, 2003, 2004, 2006, 2007.

Andrew Davies, *The Gangs of Manchester*, Milo Books, 2008; 'Youth, violence and courtship in late-Victorian Birmingham: The case of James Harper and Emily Pimm', *The History of the Family*, 11,2, 2006.

Patsy Davis, *Green Ribbons: the Irish in Birmingham in the 1860s*, University of Birmingham, 2003; 'Birmingham's Irish Community and the Murphy Riots of 1867', *Midland History*, XXXI, 2006.

R.K.Dent, *Old and New Birmingham*, Birmingham, 1880.

J.Denvir, *The Irish in Britain*, Kegan Paul, London, 1892.

Developing Birmingham 1889-1989: One Hundred Years of City Planning, Birmingham City Planning Department, 1989.

Richard Doty, *The Soho Mint and the Industrialisation of Money*, Smithsonian Institution, 1998.

E.Dunning, P.Murphy and J.M.Williams, *The Roots of Football Hooliganism*, Routledge Kegan Paul, 1988.

Andy Foster, *Birmingham*, Pevsner Architectural Guides, Yale University Press, New Haven & London, 2005.

S.Fielding, *Class and Ethnicity: Irish Catholics in England, 1880-1939*, Oxford University Press, 1993.

ed M.W.Flinn, *Edwin Chadwick's Report on the Sanitary Condition of the Labouring Population of Great Britain, 1842*, Edinburgh University Press, 1965.

J.R.Gillis, *Youth and History*, Academic Press, New York, 1974; 'Juvenile delinquency in England, 1890-1914', *Past and Present*, 67, 1975.

P.J.Gooderson, 'Terror on the streets of late Victorian Salford and Manchester: The Scuttling Menace', *Manchester Region History Review*, XI, 1997.

R.D.Holt, *Sport and the British: A Modern History*, Oxford University Press, 1989.

Eric Hopkins, *Birmingham, The Making of the Second City, 1850-1939*, Tempus Publishing Ltd, Stroud, Gloucs., 2001.

A.Lee, 'Aspects of the working class response to the Jews in Britain 1880-1914' in ed. K.Lunn, *Hosts, Immigrants and Minorities*, W.Dawson, Folkestone, 1980.

Michael Macilwee, *The Gangs of Liverpool*, Milo Books, 2006.

P&B.Mannion, *The Summer Lane and Newtown of the Years between the Wars, 1918-39*, Birmingham,1985.

T.Mason, *Association Football and English Society, 1863-1915*, Harvester, Brighton, 1980.

Sean McConville, *English local prisons, 1860-1900, next only to death*, Routledge, London & New York,1995; *Irish Political Prisoners, 1848-1922: Theatres of War*, Routledge, London & New York, 2003.

P Morris, *Aston Villa*, Naldrett, London, 1960.

John Muncie, *Youth and Crime*, second edition, Sage Publications Ltd, London, 2004.

G. Pearson, *Hooligan: A History of Respectable Fears*, Macmillan, London, 1983.

H.J.Perkin, *The Origins of Modern English Society, 1780-1880*, Routledge and Kegan Paul, 1969.

John Powell, 'The Birmingham Coiners, 1770-1816', *History Today*, July 1993, 49-55.

Philip Priestley, *Victorian Prison Lives: English Prison Biography, 1830-1914*, Methuen, London,1985.

D.A.Reid, 'The decline of Saint Monday, 1766- 1876', *Past and Present*, 1976.

John W. Reilly, *Policing Birmingham, An Account of 150 Years of Police in Birmingham, West Midlands Police*, Renault Printing Co Ltd, Birmingham 1989.

W. Showell, *Dictionary of Birmingham*, Birmingham 1885.

Victor Skipp, *The Making of Victorian Birmingham*, pub by author V.H.T.Skipp, Bmghm, 1983.

D.Smith, *Conflict and Compromise: Class Formation in English Society, 1830-1914*, Routledge Kegan Paul, 1982.

J.Springhall, *Youth, Popular Culture and Moral Panics: Penny Gaffs to Gangster Rap, 1830-1996*, Macmillan, London, 1998.

ed. R.D.Storch, *Popular Culture and Custom in Nineteenth Century England*, Croom Helm London 1982: P. Bailey, 'Custom, Capital and Culture in the Victorian Music Hall' pp180-208; also C.Behagg, article pp 154-179 and D.A.Reid, 'Interpreting the Festival Calendar: Wakes and Fairs as Carnivals' pp125-153.

Will Thorne, *My Life's Battles*, new edn, Lawrence and Wishart, 1989.

F.M.Thrasher, *The Gang*, Chicago, 1927.

ed. S.Timmins, *Birmingham and the Midlands Hardware District*, 1866, Frank Cass 1967.

Alex Tyrrell, *Joseph Sturge and the Moral Radical Party in Early Victorian Britain*, Christopher Helm, Bromley, 1987.

C.M.Wakefield, *The Life of Thomas Attwood*, London, 1885.

J.K.Walton, *Fish and Chips and the British Working Class*, Leicester University Press, 1992.

Roger Ward, *City-State and Nation, Birmingham's Political History c. 1830-1940*, Phillimore, Chichester, 2005.

Barbara Weinberger, 'The police and the public in mid-nineteenth century Warwickshire' in ed. V.Bailey, *Policing and Punishment in Nineteenth Century Britain* (London, 1982) p 65; also 'L'Anatomie de l'Antagonisme Racial de la Violence Urbaine: Les Bandes a Birmingham dans les Annees 1870', *Deviance et Societe*, 15, 4, 1991.

H.R.G. Whates, *The Birmingham Post 1857–1957, A Centenary Retrospect*, Birmingham 1957.

Index